LABOR MARKET
INSTITUTIONS
IN EUROPE

LABOR AND HUMAN RESOURCES SERIES

LABOR MARKET INSTITUTIONS IN EUROPE

A Socioeconomic Evaluation of Performance

Günther Schmid Editor

M.E. Sharpe
Armonk, New York
London, England

Library of Congress Cataloging-in-Publication Data

Labor market institutions in Europe : a socioeconomic evaluation of performance /
edited by Günther Schmid
p.   cm.—(Labor and human resources series)
Includes bibliographical references and index.
ISBN 1-56324-411-X.—ISBN 1-56324-412-8 (pbk.)
1. Full employment policies—Europe—Evaluation.
2. Labor policy—Europe—Evaluation.
I. Schmid, Günther, 1942–
II. Series.
HD5764.A6L27   1994
331.12′042′094—dc20
93–47020
CIP

Printed in the United States of America

The paper used in this publication meets the minimum requirements of
American National Standard for Information Sciences—
Permanence of Paper for Printed Library Materials,
ANSI Z 39.48-1984.

∞

BM (c)   10   9   8   7   6   5   4   3   2   1
BM (p)   10   9   8   7   6   5   4   3   2   1

Table of Contents

Tables and Figures

Figures

Preface

The contributions to this book are the harvest of three years work on the role of institutions in labor markets at the research unit "Labor Market Policy and Employment" of the Social Science Research Center Berlin (Wissenschaftszentrum Berlin). All contributions were presented at a conference in December 1992 before a distinguished group of experts in labor economics and policy evaluation. I want to express my special gratitude to the discussants whose constructive criticism considerably improved the final versions of the chapters:

- Lutz Bellmann, Institute for Labor Market Policy and Vocational Research (IAB), Nuremberg, Germany;
- Anders Björklund, Social Research Institute (SOFI) at the University of Stockholm Sweden;
- Dieter Bögenhold, University of Bielefeld, Germany;
- Louis Fina Sanglas, Commission of the European Communities, DG V, Brussels, Belgium;
- Bernard Gazier, University of Paris I, France;
- Anne Grey, PA Cambridge Economic Consultant, Great Britain;
- Kornelius Kraft, University of Essen, Germany;
- Robert Lindley, University of Warwick, Great Britain;
- Philip Méhaut, University of Nancy, France;
- Harald Niklasson, University of Växjö, Sweden;
- Inga Persson, University of Lund, Sweden;
- Sigrid Quack, Social Science Research Center Berlin (WZB);
- Jill Rubery, University of Manchester, Great Britain;
- Ronald Schettkat, Social Science Research Center Berlin (WZB);
- Jürgen Schupp, German Institute for Economic Research (DIW), Berlin;
- Marie-Claire Villeval, University of Lyon, France;
- Ulrich Walwei, Institute for Labor Market and Vocational Research (IAB), Nuremberg, Germany;

- Karin Wagner, Social Science Research Center Berlin (WZB);
- Jan van Wezel, University of Tilburg, Netherlands.

I would also like to thank the Commission of the European Communities, especially John Morley (General Directorate V), for advice, help, and financial assistance. The authors are also grateful to the Statistical Office of the European Commission in Luxembourg for providing unpublished information of the European Labor Force Survey. Many individuals assisted in the chores and art of statistics, graphs, and typing; thanks go especially to Christel Degen, Christel Hartmann, Gerold Kirchner, Thomas Kruppe, Lothar Linke, and Robyn Wiesener. Finally, I would like to express a special note of thanks to Karin Reinsch who coordinated the crucial final stage of the preparation of the manuscript for publication.

Günther Schmid

LABOR MARKET INSTITUTIONS IN EUROPE

Introduction

Institutions steer and regulate labor markets in a variety of ways: Codetermination and collective bargaining determine wages and working conditions. Statutory regulations, such as protection against dismissal and bans on night work, restrict employer and employee alike. Taxation and contributions reduce earned income, and the social security system guarantees a steady income stream against risks. Finally, the state itself acts as an employer and an entrepreneur. And behind the veil of these legal institutions a myriad of individual habits, values and preferences, group routines and norms have to be taken into account. Habitual, routine, and emulative behavior is the reason that even identical formal rules of the game might be played quite differently and different formal rules might end with the same results (Schmid and Schömann in this volume).

Remarkable changes have occurred in the pattern of these institutions of Western industrial and service societies. But labor markets in capitalist societies are not converging to a uniform pattern of formal organizations or cultural traditions. On the contrary. As the contributions collected in this volume show, it is these institutional differences that explain the disparity in the social and economic performances of national labor markets. However, these diverse national labor market institutions must enter into competition with one another not only as part of the process toward the completion of the European single market, but also as part of the globalization of the international economy.

The outcome of this contest remains uncertain. Will there be a slow, self-regulating process of institutional assimilation? Or is rapid harmonization—and hence substantial regulation at the European level—required? What do we know about the differential performance of varying labor market institutions? How can we improve this knowledge, both theoretically and methodologically? These are the fundamental questions underlying the evaluations of selected areas of labor market policy presented in this volume.

As theoretical "common ground" we share the opinion that labor market agents are embedded in institutions that are "socially constructed invariants" (Mirowski 1987, 1034). A socioeconomic evaluation of labor market performance, therefore, has to start not with autonomous individuals, but with individuals in their institutional context. Institutions, especially formal ones (like trade unions, labor and social security laws, labor market programs) can be taken as the units and entities of analysis. But because institutions are socially constructed, only in the short run is it justifiable to take institutions as given. And in contrast to mainstream evaluation research and its neoclassical background, we believe that institutions have not only constraining but also enabling qualities (Hodgson 1988; Matzner 1991).

The methodological common ground shared by all of these contributions is the persuasion that for understanding institutions a combination of qualitative and quantitative information is necessary. The collection of different elements of evidence and the composition of these puzzles to a reasonable configuration—micro and macro, *Verstehen* based on case studies, careful analysis of written documents, elasticity coefficients based on some kind of econometric models, and so on—make socioeconomic evaluation research more of an art than a routine technique. Finally, apart from expert interviews, official documents, and national statistics, the empirical common ground of almost all contributions lies in the recourse to previously unpublished data from the European Labor Force Survey.

In the first chapter, "Institutional Choice and Flexible Coordination: A Socioeconomic Evaluation of Labor Market Policy in Europe," Klaus Schömann and I present an overall perspective on the current state of comparative evaluation research. We outline an analytical framework for the socioeconomic evaluation of labor market institutions and illustrate our approach with a wealth of aggregate data from EC and OECD countries. Our critical review of the literature is supplemented by our own empirical applications, for instance by assessing the impact of active labor market policy on the Beveridge curve (the relationship of vacancies and unemployment).

In the methodological section we stress that only by perceiving the labor market as a "social institution" can one find a plausible explanation for the fact that permanent "equilibria" develop on entirely different levels of performance indicators such as unemployment, inflation, productivity, economic growth, and equality of opportunities. In addition, we demonstrate the law of "institutional equivalence": There are many paths to successfully managing or shaping structural change. Flexible coordination of wages and productivity can, for example, be achieved either by centralized or by decentralized wage negotiations. And when it comes to active labor market policy, quantity matters less than quality, such as the flexibility with which financial resources are employed.

At the beginning of the 1980s, "eurosclerosis" was a word on almost every economist's lips. This term referred to an increasingly restrictive web of constraints imposed on the labor market by regulations, in particular to restrictions on personnel policy in companies in the form of protection against dismissal, and the allegedly over-generous level of unemployment compensation, which, it was claimed, prevented occupational and regional mobility.

Deregulation, i.e., lifting such restrictions and cutting benefits, was the leitmotiv of this decade.

In the chapter "Employment Protection and Labor Force Adjustment in EC Countries," Hugh Mosley deals with the institutions of employment protection and their alleged or actual effects on employment in the EC member states. After describing the various regulation regimes in Europe and linking them with patterns of the termination of employment contracts, he selects four EC countries to demonstrate the functioning of the regimes. France has the highest (and still increasing) proportion of fixed-term contracts—a reflection of its policy of deregulation; Italy has the most stringent regulations on protection against dismissal and—apart from youth legislation—has changed almost nothing in recent years; in Great Britain, institutional restrictions on termination of employment contracts are traditionally almost unknown, which accounts for the extreme cyclical fluctuations in involuntary terminations; in Germany, the number of fixed-term contracts has increased dramatically (likewise as a result of deregulation measures), but in contrast to France, this has had little or no effect on rising figures for dismissals.

Apart from providing detailed information on diverse unemployment protection regulations, the originality of this chapter lies in its exploration of "institutional regimes" of employment protection. These include, in addition to regulations directly concerning contract termination, other institutions or specific employment policies, such as early retirement, further education, retraining and regulation of working hours (short-time and overtime), that provide institutional alternatives to compulsory redundancy. Under favorable conditions, e.g., supportive, active labor market policy alongside incentives for medium-term personnel planning in companies, employment protection can even have positive effects. This holds especially true for the preservation and creation as opposed to the allocation of innovative capacities. Individual employment security (not to be confused with individual job security) then becomes a prerequisite for a willingness to learn and internal flexibility.

The second part of the eurosclerosis argument, increasing and allegedly overgenerous unemployment compensation, is the subject of Bernd Reissert's and my chapter, "Unemployment Compensation and Active Labor Market Policy." Along with a synopsis of unemployment insurance systems, this study presents the first comprehensive details on central benefit indicators for all EC member states: the proportion of unemployed who actually receive benefits, classified according to sex, age, and duration of unemployment; the amount of unemployment benefit received (replacement rate) according to household status; the total social expenditure and benefit payments per percentage point of unemployment; the expenditure on active labor market policy and the proportion of this expenditure in relation to the entire national labor market budget (activity rate). When the impact of the relationship between the unemployment insurance system and the way labor markets operate is analyzed and systematically evaluated, the conclusion reached is (in contrast to popular opinion) that a well-organized and generous unemployment insurance system, in conjunction with an active labor market policy, can be seen as an investment in more flexible and more efficient labor markets.

Further vocational training is a fundamental part of active labor market policy, and one that is—as demonstrated—essential for the efficiency of the unemployment insurance system. What is important in this respect is to refocus on the original strategy of preventive labor market policy. With this in mind, Peter Auer's contribution, "Further Education and Training for the Employed: Systems and Outcomes," is dedicated to training and further education for the employed in five selected EC countries. In Denmark, government, employers, and workers have developed an attractive program offering unskilled or semiskilled wage earners a systematic post-school education; it is based on short-term modules, aiming at qualifications that are recognized nationwide, and could achieve model status for Europe; Great Britain has privatized the further education sector and is counting on decentralized joint initiatives by employers; in France, statutory and collectively negotiated regulations on funding ensure a minimum level of further vocational training; while in Italy, the business of further education is in the hands of regional development offices and the two sides of industry; in Germany, it is predominantly companies that provide further education independently, primarily, however, for those employees who already possess a qualification, and also at a relatively low level. The study endorses the view that national differences in further training reflect fundamental differences of initial vocational training systems more than industrial training policies, so that direct conjectures for competitiveness or indeed for a national rate of efficiency, such as productivity, are impossible.

Friederike Maier's contribution, "Institutional Regimes of Part-Time Working," explores the reasons for the increase in part-time employment. First of all, there are considerable national differences behind this general rising trend. In Belgium, France, and Germany, only 10 to 13 percent of the active labor force work part-time (though the figures are on the increase), while in Great Britain, Denmark, and the Netherlands, the proportion is 22 to 30 percent. In all countries women are most affected by part-time status, though in the Netherlands men account for 30 percent of all part-time workers. Here, too, the relatively stable quantitative and qualitative differences in part-time work are not the result of single institutional factors, such as regulation or taxation. Rather, it is institutional interrelatedness, i.e., the mutual reinforcement of individual factors (such as the combination of the breadwinner model as a sociopolitical guiding principle with the male-dominated organization of trade unions and employers' associations) that is responsible for such stable variances in employment structures.

Alongside part-time work, self-employment also became a predominant employment perspective in the 1980s and 1990s. Deregulation and the emergence of the small-business-based employment miracle nurtured this hope. Self-employment in the EC has expanded considerably, growing from 12.7 million in the nine member states of 1975, to 15.5 million in 1989, while the share of self-employment in total employment grew from 12.6 percent to 14.1 percent. The grand visions were soon blurred, however, by first studies, which saw in the new self-employed only the desperate unemployed. Nigel Meager ("Self-Employment Schemes for the Unemployed in the European Community: The Emergence of a New Institution, and Its Evaluation") looked into this question with great precision and with new methodological and empirical techniques. Although after a long historical decline the number of self-employed workers rose once again in most European countries, especially in Great Britain, in some countries, such as France and Germany, the level has stagnated, while in Denmark the decline has actually continued. At the same time, the existence of programs promoting self-employment for the unemployed is common to all countries.

Meager's comprehensive review, whose originality lies in the use of flow data as opposed to stock data, shows among other things that cautious selection and guidance, along with the subsidization of capital rather than income, may improve the chances of success of labor market policies aimed at creating good quality jobs in self-employment.

The concluding, theoretical chapter, "Equality and Efficiency in the Labor Market: Toward a Socioeconomic Theory of Cooperation," deals with the institutional factors that promote social as well as economic efficiency. Labor markets have been—since their historical differentiation—increasingly, and to a greater extent than other markets, subject to social control. Mainstream (neoclassical) economic theory maintains that this not only results in economic inefficiency, but also achieves just the opposite of well-meant social policy—when, for example, women are denied access to particular professions because of bans on night work. This chapter demonstrates not only that this view is undifferentiated, but also that it contains fundamental errors.

The core problem of advanced market economies, namely the coordination of capital and labor, can—in principle—be solved in various ways: via competition (markets), hierarchies (state, planning, firms), cooperative social relations (associations, networks, family), or legally guaranteed entitlements (status, civil rights). It is vital that these coordination mechanisms interact correctly and, moreover, that they be adaptable to new economic conditions and social values. If, for example, further qualifications, especially "extrafunctional" qualifications (such as communicative skills and willingness to learn and be innovative) become increasingly relevant to production, and such qualifications flourish in cooperative rather than in hierarchical social relations, then the organization of vocational training must be based on cooperative principles to a greater extent than before. To give a further example: competition can lead to the mobilization of tremendous vitality in the form of initiative, creativity, and immense effort. If, however, the winners and losers have been established at the outset, or no (distributable) additional profit is possible (as in the case of positional goods), then markets peter out or even develop self-destructive properties (ruinous competition). Social security, fair redistribution, codetermination rights, and a high "player competence" are prerequisites for well-functioning markets, prerequisites not created by the markets themselves.

All in all, the conclusion drawn from the chapters is that short-term institutional inflexibilities in labor markets—such as advanced notice of mass redundancies, generous unemployment compensation, further training obligations, the persistent linkage between wages and skill status—can in many cases serve as both a requirement and a stimulus for long-term adaptability. Not infrequently, supposed cases of eurosclerosis prove to be a specific "euro-efficiency," one that could be improved further along the lines proposed in the contributions of this volume.

References

Hodgson, Geoffrey M. 1988. *Economics and Institutions: A Manifesto for a Modern Institutional Economics*. Cambridge, U.K.: Polity Press.

Matzner, Egon. 1991. "Policies, Institutions and Employment Performance." In *Beyond Keynesianism*, eds., E. Matzner and W. Streeck, 231–60. Aldershot: Edward Elgar.

Mirowski, Philip. 1987. "The Philosophical Bases of Institutional Economics." *Journal of Economic Issues* 21, no. 3:1001–38.

1

Institutional Choice and Flexible Coordination

A Socioeconomic Evaluation of Labor Market Policy in Europe

Günther Schmid and Klaus Schömann

Introduction

"The End of Communism, the Beginning of What?" This was the question raised by the president of the Federal Republic of Germany, Richard von Weizsäcker, when he opened his speech on October 3, 1992, the second anniversary of the German unification. He didn't answer the question. He was, however, quite outspoken in his persuasion that the transformation of a bureaucratic and suppressive socialism could not be made simply by copying the Western style of capitalism.

In fact, there are different models of capitalism. For instance, the "free market" model represented by the Chicago School and most influential in the United States; the "social market" model of the "Ordo-Liberals" responsible for the German *Wirtschaftswunder;* the "welfare state" model of the Swedish School, shaping especially the societies in Scandinavia. Various subtypes exist even within these models. The process of European integration—now affected by the Eastern Europe developments and the prospective increase in members from the EFTA (European Free Trade Association) countries—will certainly further enrich and change the institutions in the present member states of the Economic Community. What is the task of evaluation research in times of such a great transformation?

Two visions affecting evaluation research explicitly or implicitly are influential in the debate on the future "model Europe." The first vision, the "institutional Darwinism," sees the market as a device for choosing between the most efficient institutions. The choice of each individual country then turns to the question of which country is the "best model" in order to adjust to the institutional regime of the best performer. Underlying this vision is the assumption that norms and rules have to be standardized, the standards being those provided by the model system and country. This vision amounts to nothing less than a frightening form of "neoimperialism, whereby one country and one system impose its own rules of labor-market organization and of social stratification on the rest of the world" (Edwards and Garonna 1991, 63).

In the second equally frightening vision, social engineers consider no country to be the ideal, but rather that a model Europe has to be constructed out of an eclectic combination of features borrowed from real cases, taken out of their historical and institutional context, and placed in some idealized design of optimal social structure and labor-market organization. Institutions, according to this technocratic vision, are taken like components of a menu that can be combined ad libitum. We could have "a combination of the German training system, the Swedish labor-market organization, the Japanese firm structure, the Anglo-American system of research and educational institutions, and finally (why not?) the Italian informal economy. It would take a hyper-rationalist faith and a Bolshevik-style intervention to expect that such a system, however carefully designed by intellectuals, rigorously modeled by social scientists, and diligently adapted by administrators, could work better than any individual real system. It is indeed doubtful that it would even 'work' at all" (Edwards and Garonna 1991, 63f).

Under the vision of "institutional darwinism," the role of evaluation research would be restricted to identifying the "best performer" and to leaving institutional adjustment to the anonymous historical process. Institutional analysis, if anything, would be narrative, and making sense out of it would tend to be functionalistic storytelling: Institutions would be rationalized as efficient, for they can only evolve and survive under such a premise if they are efficient; inefficient institutions could not persist. The pure fact of institutional persistence would be a proof for efficiency—a circular conclusion, which is common among functionalists although methodologically false (Langlois 1986, 251).

The vision of "institutional technocracy" would allocate to evaluation research the role of identifying the single best institutional components, of mixing them to an optimal "menu" (a horror vision even from a gourmet's point of view), and finally of following up the implementation by rigorous monitoring. Institutional arrangements would be regarded like the plans of an architect that leave no latitude for spontaneous actions of the constructors once society has decided to follow the plan.

In contrast to these visions, we consider the role of evaluation research as one of "social gardening." This role, to remain in the metaphor, consists of sowing, watering, and weeding. In other words: of generating, elaborating, testing institutional alternatives, and finally eliminating clearly identified failures. "Many roads lead to Rome." We assume "institutional equivalence," i.e., the possibility of choice between different labor market institutions leading to economic success. Institutional choices, however, are not optional ad libitum; they have to consider history, in other words: preceding institutional investments. We also believe that institutions are part of the preference structure of individuals. In addition, from the point of view of globalization and European integration, institutional variety is itself a guarantor of evolutionary efficiency. For such a diversity comes not by itself, it has to be an objective of policy action.

However, not each institutional choice or mix of regimes is efficient. Necessary conditions for efficiency are requisite variety of institutional response and institutional consistency, which means the necessity of coordinating flexibly the various factors that influence size and quality of employment. It is the task of evaluation to find out the necessary and sufficient conditions for a flexible coordination of the labor market.

The chapter starts with empirical evidence on the international diversity of institutional choice, and an analytical framework for socioeconomic evaluation and general principles of flexible coordination follows. The main part of the chapter is devoted to collecting evidence on the impact of labor market policy in various institutional frameworks by reviewing the literature of macro and micro evaluation; special emphasis is given to the role of active labor market policy and to public support of human capital formation aimed at improving matching processes and equal employment opportunities. The chapter ends with a summarizing discussion of the results and an outlook on the perspectives of comparative evaluation research.

Performance Diversity of Labor Market Policy

If we look at the most important and common indicators for successful labor market and employment policy, we observe that most Western industrialized countries reacted to the first oil price shock mainly by inflation, while they adjusted to the second oil price shock mainly by increasing unemployment. Only one country, Switzerland, succeeded in banishing both specters. Austria, the (old) Federal Republic of Germany, and Japan came near success. Some countries—especially Sweden and Norway—had to pay low unemployment with higher inflation, whereas other countries—especially the Netherlands—kept inflation low at the expense of increasing unemployment. Finally, there are countries that had to cope with increasing unemployment and inflation simultaneously—for example, the United Kingdom and Italy (Figures 1.1 and 1.2).

Unemployment and inflation, however, are not sufficient to describe efficient labor markets. At least two other dimensions have to be taken into account, one indicating growth performance (for instance, growth of employment and national product), the other representing social performance, for instance the qualificational potential of the labor force or the degree of gender equality. Figures 1.3 and 1.4 compare employment growth and economic growth in terms of gross

Figure 1.1 **Inflation and Unemployment in OECD Countries in the 1970s**

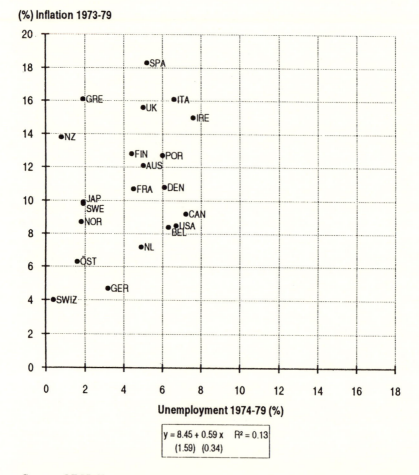

(%) Inflation 1973-79

$$y = 8.45 + 0.59 \, x \quad R^2 = 0.13$$
$$(1.59) \quad (0.34)$$

Source: OECD Historical Statistics 1991, tables 2.20, 2.15, 8.11; own calculations.

domestic product across OECD countries. There is a remarkable trend toward a closer link between employment and product growth than existed in the sixties and early seventies. We can only speculate about the reasons. It seems that successful stabilization policy, i.e., taming inflation, increased the pressure on employment flexibility as a functional equivalent to price flexibility. Deregulation and early retirement policies are other plausible candidates for increasing employment elasticity.

If we turn now to the individual countries, we see immediately that Switzerland, the champion in taming unemployment and inflation, is a flop with respect to employment and economic growth in the seventies, and only a mediocre

Figure 1.2 **Inflation and Unemployment in OECD Countries in the 1980s**

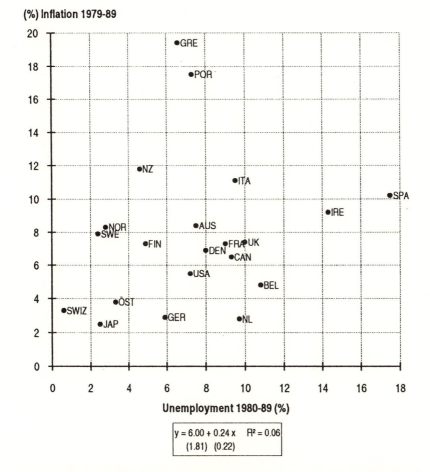

(%) Inflation 1979-89

$$y = 6.00 + 0.24\,x \quad R^2 = 0.06$$
$$(1.81) \quad (0.22)$$

Source: OECD Historical Statistics 1991, tables 2.20, 2.15, 8.11; own calculations.

performer in the eighties. The bad ranking in the seventies reflects the rigid Swiss policy of foreign and female labor force participation: The first oil price shock was solved mainly by exporting unemployment and displacing female labor from the labor market (Schmidt 1985). In the eighties, Switzerland seems to have adopted the capital-intensive productivity path of its neighbor states, reflected in a modest growth of employment and gross domestic product. Measured in terms of employment and economic growth, Japan remains successful in both periods, whereas the United States and Canada, weak and mediocre in terms of unemployment and inflation, become champions under these performance indicators.

Figure 1.3 **Change in Employment and Production in OECD Countries in the 1970s**

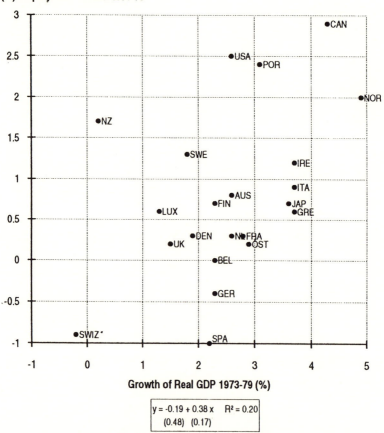

(%) Employment Growth 1973-79

Growth of Real GDP 1973-79 (%)

$$y = -0.19 + 0.38\,x \quad R^2 = 0.20$$
$$(0.48) \quad (0.17)$$

Source: OECD Employment Outlook 1991, tables 2.4 and 2.5; own calculations.

The rank order of the highly developed industrial countries changes again if we consider earnings and social performance indicators. In a nineteen-country study, Wilensky (1992) found a tradeoff between job creation and earnings growth. Similarly, in a comparative study of real wage growth and employment growth, Freeman (1988a, 298) concluded that "the United States paid for job creation with slow growth in real wages and productivity." We would also have to mention the increasing proportion of the "working poor" in the United States, i.e., the growing number of full-time working people under the poverty level (Appelbaum and Schettkat 1991; Levy 1988). Concerning Japan, we would probably have to put the traditional employment patterns on the negative side,

Figure 1.4 **Change in Employment and Production in OECD Countries in the 1980s**

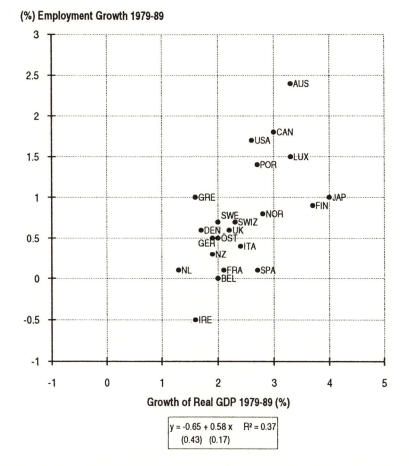

(%) Employment Growth 1979-89

$$y = -0.65 + 0.58 x \quad R^2 = 0.37$$
$$(0.43) \quad (0.17)$$

reflected in long working hours, the low and deeply segregated pattern of women's integration in the labor market, and the relatively low degree of part-time work, if we take this measure as an indicator of employment flexibility. Apart from Finland, the Scandinavian countries would get high scores for social integration and working time flexibility, whereas Austria, France, Germany, and the Netherlands would score low (see Figure 1.5).

We could add more indicators of labor market performance (e.g., various measures of productivity) to provide evidence for institutional diversity and equivalence. Yet the illustrations presented so far should suffice to turn now to the nagging questions: What are the reasons for these differences? Can we learn

Figure 1.5 **Female Labor Force Participation and Part-Time Work 1990**

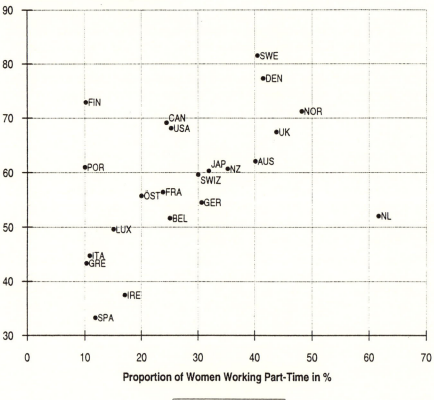

Female Labour Force Participation in %

Proportion of Women Working Part-Time in %

$$y = 47.48 + 0.40 \, x \quad R^2 = 0.21$$
$$(5.37) \quad (0.17)$$

from the successes and failures of other countries? Do globalization and eco-nomic integration lead to convergence of labor market institutions or is more harmonization required?

Our hypothetical conclusion stimulated by the evidence just given is the fol-lowing: First, different success stories can be told. Strictly speaking, there is no single performance indicator or a bundle of such indicators to compare objec-tively labor market efficiency. Even in a perfect competitive world, comparisons by income, productivity, unemployment, and so on would not be meaningful. Each country would have reached efficiency relative to its own preferences and resources. Each country would be superior to the others at its own preferences and inferior at the other countries' preferences (Hartog, Polachek, and Theeuwes 1992). Performance indicators are meaningful, however, if one agrees on preferences and if they are conditioned on available resources and institutional arrangements. Such relational studies are a necessary condition for "learning from traveling."

Second, even the successful countries across conventional performance indicators (such as a low unemployment-inflation equilibrium) are obviously quite different in their institutional frameworks. So, one single institutional model cannot be made responsible for success. The only obvious feature that good performers seem to have in common is the absence of spectacular single-policy interventions such as the freeze of wages by incomes policy, huge wage subsidy programs, and temporary public job creation. The secret of success seems to be an institutional framework that sets the right incentives to the various key actors in the labor market and employment system to cooperate in a competent way. What, then, are the conditions for such cooperation?

To answer this question we need to develop an analytical framework identifying the key actors, the coordinating institutions, and general principles of effective coordination. This will be the task of the following section.

Flexible Coordination in the Framework of Institutional Choice

The first step is to get to grips with the term *institution* and to set our own mark in contrast to the new neoclassical schools of public choice, rational choice, and institutional economics. The second step is to define the role of labor market policy in this institutional framework, and the third is to develop general criteria of institutional effectiveness.

Another Lesson from Ulysses and the Sirens

During his travels, as Ulysses anticipated coming into the vicinity of the sirens, he had himself bound to the mast of his ship in order to protect himself against this dangerous temptation. He thus resolved a decision-making problem prospectively in a rational way that would not have been possible if he had waited until the problem occurred (Elster 1979, 36).

This function of self-binding is performed in social life by institutions. Through norms, regulations, and the allocation of tasks and responsibilities, institutions determine how one is to behave in yet unknown decision-making situations or—if it is not possible to formulate a rule in advance—who decides what and when (Schmid, Reissert, and Bruche 1992, 21).

Institutions may be based on Ulysses's clever foresight that—because of weakness, confusion, or magical powers—one's own decisions in a critical moment can be ill-founded. "Fore-sight" thus becomes "pre-caution," the self-binding function of institutions. Precautionary measures can also be taken to protect oneself against the erroneous decisions of others, the other-binding function of institutions.

The tale of Ulysses and the sirens, however, also reveals immediately the ambivalent nature of institutions: If the foresight is wrong or something unexpected comes in between—for instance, a heavy storm that requires all hands at the helm of the ship—the supportive function of institutions turns into a perilous barrier. Thus, Ulysses's experience with the sirens teaches us a paradox: the requirement of establishing links that are stable and flexible at the same time—in other words, the requirement of "flexible coordination."

This paradox also holds true for the other common functions of institutions. Institutions may arise from the desire to reduce transaction costs (Coase 1992; North 1991) in similar and recurring decision-making situations, for instance in finding the prices of labor in exchange relationships of the labor market. Institutions are also created for specifying the locus of authority and responsibility. In both cases, institutions have the function of bringing about a behavior predictable for others, in other words, the function of stabilizing expectations and reducing uncertainty.

Finally, institutions may be established in order to regulate the settlement of future conflicts and cleavages that cannot be rationally resolved in advance. The necessary consensus for future decision-making situations under unknown circumstances and uncertain outcomes can be attained by establishing procedures and conditions that are perceived as being fair. In other words, institutions have also the function of fair bargaining and negotiation.

Whatever the form and combination of these institutions, they always act as a filter for information and interests, as incentives for individual or collective decision makers, or as norms for individual or collective behavior, so that they delimit the spectrum of possible decisions and actions and, as a consequence of their selective impact, favor certain solutions and impede or exclude others entirely. Relatively stable and nationally different collective behavior may go back to historical accidents such as traumatic strikes or inflation or (almost) revolutionary changes in the political systems (Flanagan, Hartog, and Theeuwes 1992). In other words, societies may also develop institutional idiosyncrasies.

Institutions are, therefore, not politically neutral: they reflect power relations, represent a congealed form of political will and collective behavior. As such, they are in principle changeable when political will changes. A seedbed for such changes is certainly a change in the competitive market forces; that is why these times are prone for institutional changes. Nevertheless, once established, institutions acquire their own dynamics and display unanticipated effects. Because of their steering function, which is in part indirect ("invisible hand"), and their own institutional momentum, they may come into conflict with new socioeconomic constellations and policy goals.

Institutional choice theory, thus, is fundamentally different from rational choice theory (Elster 1986; Esser 1990). Although, finally, an individual decision, institutional choice is at best a decision restricted by "intended and bounded rationality" (Simon 1976, xxviii). In many cases, however, institutional choice is an unconscious decision, a taking over of traditions that turns—if called into question—more often into a "rationalization" of choice than into a "rational" choice that calculates *sine ira et studio* cost-benefit ratios. This does not mean that institutional choices are irrational. But it is probably safe to say that most institutional choices are a-rational. Their rationality or irrationality has to be detected like a vein of gold in the mines. And this, not more and not less, is the task of a socioeconomic evaluation of labor market policy.

Labor Market Policy As an Institution

Labor market policy has not yet been clearly recognized as an institution of its own. The connotation of this term is either a kind of social policy, i.e., to alleviate the harmful consequences of unemployment, or very narrow supply-side measures (training, placement, counseling) to improve the situation of unemployed job seekers and other disadvantaged groups of the labor market.

From the institutional choice perspective, this is a much too narrow definition. It is too narrow because it excludes the interrelations of these measures with other determinants of labor market dynamics, and it does not properly account for the reasons of their evolution.

We therefore define labor market policy in a broader sense than usual and distinguish four basic forms:

(1) individual and collective agreements on wages, working time, and other working conditions; for any institutional analysis, it is important to distinguish between implicit and explicit contracts;

(2) regulation by laws setting standards, norms, and procedures for employment contracting; labor market policy examples are employment protection regulation, legal quality standards to enter a vocational profession, and collective bargaining laws;

(3) redistribution by taxing wage income or by compensating lack of wage income by transfer payments; most prominent example for this type of redistributive labor market policy is unemployment insurance; the impact of taxes and other forms of social security on demand and supply of labor, however, should not be neglected; wage subsidies belong also to this category;

(4) public services and public investment; in other words, the state can itself play the role as employer and entrepreneur in the areas of so-called "public goods," "merit goods," and "mixed goods"; most prominent public services for labor markets are placement services and labor market information or counseling; (temporary) public job creation, education, and training are typical forms of "public investments," which may be complementary or competitive to respective private investments; as far as these forms of public intervention are aimed at preventing or fighting unemployment, they are subsumed under the heading of "active labor market policy."

Flexible Coordination of Labor Markets

The four forms of labor market policy represent the "institutional menu" from which societies can choose. Apart from what has been said in the preceding paragraph—emphasizing the investment character of institutional choices, which makes choices hard to reverse once they have been made—institutional choices underlie some constraints to which we refer as necessary conditions for flexible coordination:[1]

First, from a systems theoretical point of view, institutional choice governed by the principle of flexible coordination has to follow the cybernetic principle of "requisite variety."[2] In other words, labor market institutions and respective policy interventions have to reflect the amount and nature of variety in their environments. For labor markets, the relevant environments are the product and capital markets and the social-cultural subsystems. This means, with respect to the latter, in liberal and social democracies, flexibility underlies "civilized constraints" such as free choice of profession, free spatial mobility, social security in terms of a continuous and decent income stream, and certain values and feelings about social justice. The importance of this principle of "bounded requisite variety" by civilized constraints has been brought to the point by the game theorist Oskar Morgenstern:

> The history of mankind manifests frequent changes in the means that society regards as being permissible for solving its problems. For example, one could eliminate unemployment very easily if enslavement of the unemployed, simply shooting them, confining them to a labor camp, or drafting them into military service were regarded as being suitable methods. On the other hand, in the present state of economic theory it is almost impossible to employ the unemployed if neither a temporary reduction in wages nor an allocation of workers to industries or to other geographic districts is permissible. There may possibly be solutions given these constraints, but clearly the situation is fundamentally more complicated and only distantly resembles the "purely theoretical" situation in which wage reductions and labor mobility are unrestrictedly permissible. (Morgenstern 1966, 18)

Second, institutional choice following the principle of flexible coordination requires institutional consistency and coherence, which means a complementary or at least a compatible combination of the various forms of labor market policy. One example for complementarity would be the autonomy of employers' and employees' associations in wage negotiations and the legal acknowledgment or even extension of collective agreements by the state. Another example: The social norm not to undercut the going wage as a strategy for unemployed workers to conquer a new job requires unemployment insurance and other public assistance and benefits as complementary institutions (Solow 1990, 39). An example of inconsistency would be the legal prohibition of dismissing certain target groups such as the disabled and the refusal of the state to support firms employing disabled persons by wage subsidies or by cost-sharing of workplace adjustment for the handicapped.

Whereas institutional consistency relates more to objective relationships, institutional coherence refers to subjective capabilities of using the regulatory framework of institutions. The development of such capabilities is a social learning process that entails a lot of "implicit knowledge." It is especially this condition of flexible coordination—together with the consistency principle—that prevents the easy transfer of institutions from one country to the other; it also destroys technocratic visions of designing and implementing an "optimal institutional mix" out of "best elements" from diverse countries.

Third, institutional consistency and coherence force the evaluation researcher, instead of succumbing to the temptation of technocratic design, to look at institutional equivalents that perform the same or a comparable role in the labor market. Labor market policy regimes work like communicating pipelines: If one policy form is underdeveloped, others very likely will enforce their activity. In the United States, for example, the state is restrained from regulating employment contracts by universal norms or standards. There is, for instance, little if any limitation on the termination of employment contracts, but on the other hand, management is quite restricted from changing internal worker assignment and allocation, especially in the unionized sector. In Japan and Germany the regulatory relationship tends to be the reverse: A substantial legal protection exists regarding dismissal of workers, but by and large, management is fairly free to organize work and allocate workers internally on the basis of skill and performance (Büchtemann 1991, 46; Sengenberger 1992, 156).

Another striking example for institutional equivalence is the small role of the state as employer compared to its important role as entrepreneur, i.e., as investor, moderator, or provider of public infrastructure, in Japan and Switzerland. In Japan, for example, the Ministry of International Trade and Industry (MITI) working with industry representatives presents "visions" as to where the economy should be going. These visions serve as guides to the allocation of scarce foreign exchange or capital floor and for public R&D funding at key industries. A small state in terms of employment must not be a weak state; conversely, a large state in terms of employment must not be a strong state.

Sweden and the Netherlands are good examples for the contrasting roles of the state as employer and redistributor: the Swedish welfare state developed mainly by extending public services and respective employment, whereas the Dutch welfare state was mainly realized by extending transfer payments (Rein and Freeman 1988).

Flexible coordination, thus, reminds us of the fact that labor markets can be appreciated and assessed in various ways, depending on cultural traditions and values. From an institutional point of view, the labor market can be in equilibrium with any one of a range of unemployment rates (Solow 1990, 59). Institutional choices and the corresponding policy strategies, thus, will vary from country to country, from time to time. Socioeconomic evaluation cannot make this choice, but it can make clearer the existence of such choices, show the implications, and detect inconsistencies between choices and policy strategies. Changing values and environments emphasize the dynamic aspects of institutions. Socioeconomic evaluation, therefore, is also interested in the adaptive capacity of institutions, especially in rapid transition processes.

We turn now to survey the recent literature on evaluating labor market institutions, especially labor market policies. The procedure is simply divided by approaches and evidence on the macro and micro levels.

Macrolevel Evaluation of Labor Market Policy

As institutional choice theory emphasizes institutional equivalents or alternatives to provide for the necessary "requisite variety," we look first at three indicators of how labor markets at the macro level adjust to fluctuations in demand in a cross-country perspective: flexibility in employment, weekly hours, and real hourly wages. The simple intention of this section is to see whether there are first-glance indications of labor market rigidity that would be reflected in an accumulation of low scores related to all three indicators. For many who still believe in eurosclerosis, the result of this exercise comes as a surprise: There is no general deficit of European countries with respect to combined adjustment flexibility compared to the United States or Japan.

Quantitative adjustment flexibility, however, is a necessary but not a sufficient condition for labor market efficiency. Qualitative criteria have to be taken into account, which will be exemplified by wage policy; here we will demonstrate that not flexibility as such but coordinated flexibility matters for labor market performance.

Only part of the differences in cross-country flexibility is explained by output changes; other forms of flexible coordination have to be checked. We choose as the main candidate active labor market policy and assess explicitly its impact on the Beveridge curve on a cross-section as well as on a time-series basis. In both cases, we are able to demonstrate positive effects of active labor market policy.[3] In the concluding section, the importance of implementation for effective labor market policy is demonstrated.

Patterns of Requisite Variety for Adjustment to Fluctuations in Demand

In the following paragraphs we summarize the interesting approach by Hashimoto and Raisian (1992) as a good starting point for developing a combined coefficient for quantitative adjustment flexibility of labor markets, and using changes of coefficients as measures to assess changes in labor market policies or institutions.

Table 1.1

International Comparison of Output-Normalized Variabilities in Labor Market Magnitudes for Manufacturing Industries: 1950–83

	Employment	1983–91	Weekly Hours	1983–91	Real Hourly Compensation	1983–91
United States	0.67	(0.18)	0.19	(0.07)	0.25	(0.26)
Japan	0.46	(0.23)	0.21	(0.09)	0.50	(0.37)
Germany	0.66	(0.36)	0.33	(0.13)	0.54	(0.73)
United Kingdom	0.71		0.30		0.54	
Canada	0.66		0.30		0.34	
Denmark	0.94		0.43		0.80	
France	0.59		0.40		0.79	
Italy	0.51		0.42		0.79	
Netherlands	0.63		0.29		0.82	
Norway	0.68		0.32		0.84	
Sweden	0.64		0.26		0.82	

Source: Hashimoto and Raisian 1992, table 3:85.
Note: Output-Normalized Variabilities = standard deviation of year-to-year changes in the logarithm of the variable in question (e.g., employment) divided by standard deviation of year-to-year changes in the logarithm of real output; own calculations for period 1983–91 on the basis of *OECD Main Economic Indicators*.

Table 1.1 presents output-normalized flexibilities for three labor market variables (employment, weekly hours, real hourly compensation) pertaining to manufacturing industries. These magnitudes are indices of the variability in the chosen variable (for instance, employment), standardized for influences of variability in output. Output-normalized flexibility gives us a first-glance impression of the relative importance of the three adjustment mechanisms, which reflect, by and large, different institutional choices of the countries.

Differences in these mechanisms also have a direct bearing on unemployment performance. For instance, the findings confirm a commonly held view that in the United States wages are relatively rigid over the business cycle with employment fluctuating a great deal, thus feeding unemployment, whereas in Japan employment tends to remain stable, while real wages are quite flexible, thus (*ceteris paribus*) holding unemployment down. This apparent trade-off between employment and wage flexibility in Japan and the United States is less apparent, however, when European countries are included in the comparison.

Denmark, for instance, is an interesting outlayer in terms of employment flexibility, which can only be explained by its almost nonexistent employment protection regulation (see Höcker 1992; Schettkat 1992; and chapter 2 by Hugh Mosley in this book) and by its particular unemployment insurance system which subsidizes extreme labor turnover (see chapter 3 by Reissert and Schmid in this book).

In Table 1.1 on the international comparison of output-normalized variabilities in labor market magnitudes for manufacturing industries, we added estimates for the time period 1983–91. During that period Japan witnessed the steepest increase in manufacturing output, followed by Germany and the United States. The OECD (Organization for Economic Cooperation and Development) index of manufacturing output rose from a value of 88 in 1983 to 128 in 1991 in Japan, from 93 to 122 in Germany, and from 88 to 117 in the United States.

This rise in manufacturing output has been accompanied by about a 10 percentage point increase in employment in Japan and in Germany during the same time period, but in the United States employment in manufacturing industries remained largely on the same level as in 1983. Actually, since 1989 employment in manufacturing industries in the United States has been declining. In 1991 the United States showed all signs of a recession with a reduction in manufacturing output and a further decline in real wages.

This brief sketch of economic indicators in U.S. manufacturing since 1983 should explain why output-normalized employment variability for the United States is lower than for Japan and Germany during the period 1983–91. While Japan and Germany were witnessing a strong recovery in manufacturing industries, the United States entered slowly into a recession.[4]

Due to the German reunification process, the "windfall" rise in manufacturing output has led to considerable increases in both nominal and real wages, which is reflected in the higher flexibility of real hourly compensation. Results presented by Hashimoto and Raisian in 1992 with data until 1983, therefore, have to be seen against the background of these more recent economic developments. The three countries for which we updated some of these results show an astonishing amount of convergence during the period of economic recovery 1983–91 (see Figures 1.6 and 1.7).

It is interesting to note the homogeneity of the United States and Canada in terms of real wage rigidity compared to Japan and most European countries. In addition, apart from the low employment flexibility in Italy (which may reflect the impact of Cassa Integrazione Guadagni), almost all European countries exhibit both or sometimes all three forms of variability: employment, weekly hours, and wage flexibility.

The picture does not change much if we use the relation between movements in labor market magnitudes and output (see Table 1.2). Although the statistical significance of some of the relevant coefficients is low, these findings confirm that the United States shows greater procyclical movements in employment and hours of work for a given percentage change in output than Japan, although West Germany and Canada are close behind, with Denmark again outperforming all other countries in employment flexibility. Japan exhibits greater procyclical movement in real compensation than the United States, but West Germany, the Netherlands, Norway, Sweden, and France exceed Japan in this respect. What are the reasons for the observed country differences? Do they matter in terms of labor market efficiency?

Figure 1.6 **Output-Normalized Variabilities** (country comparison 1950–83)

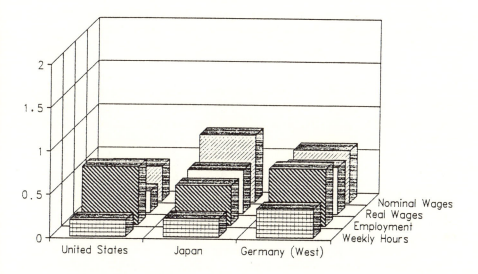

Source: Hashimoto and Raisian 1992.

Figure 1.7 **Output-Normalized Variabilities** (country comparison 1983–91)

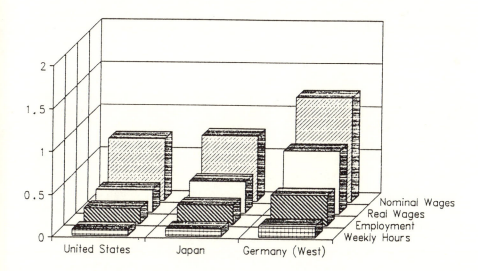

Source: OECD Main Economic Indicators, own calculations.

Table 1.2

Regressions of Percentage Changes in Labor Market Variables on Percentage Changes in Output by Country: Manufacturing, 1950–83

	Employment		Weekly Hours		Real Compensation	
United States	0.58	(9.6)	0.16	(9.1)	0.04	(0.8)
Japan	0.33	(5.7)	0.12	(4.0)	0.12	(1.4)
Germany	0.57	(9.5)	0.15	(2.8)	0.24	(2.7)
United Kingdom	0.47	(4.9)	0.18	(4.3)	-0.08	(0.9)
Canada	0.56	(9.1)	0.11	(2.1)	0.02	(0.3)
Denmark	0.71	(6.4)	-0.03	(0.3)	0.11	(0.8)
France	0.47	(7.4)	0.24	(4.2)	0.14	(1.0)
Italy	0.15	(1.7)	0.24	(3.9)	0.04	(0.3)
Netherlands	0.44	(5.3)	0.04	(0.8)	0.31	(2.2)
Norway	0.44	(4.7)	0.02	(0.3)	0.20	(1.4)
Sweden	0.44	(5.2)	0.01	(0.3)	0.24	(1.7)

Source: Hashimoto and Raisian 1992, table 4:86.

Note: Magnitudes in parentheses are absolute t-values; only output regression coefficients (= c) are printed; constants and R-square values have been suppressed; own calculations.

Relevant equations: (1) $\ln Y = a + b T + c \ln Z + e$; $\ln Y$ = log of chosen variable; T = time; $\ln Z$ = log of real output; a, b, c = regression coefficients; e = error term; (2) $d \ln Y = b + cd \ln Z + de$; output coefficient c indicates the percentage change in the chosen variable associated with a 1 percent change in output.

Are Real Wages Too High?

Mainstream neoclassical theory and common sense have three versions of referring to wage policy as the scapegoat of high persistent unemployment: too high real wages and downward wage rigidity, too narrow wage differentials, and too high nonwage labor costs. Trade unions are blamed for the first two "diseases," welfare-state–oriented governments for the third.

It would be hopeless to review the literature providing evidence for and against these stereotypes. Even if one could manage this gargantuan task, the result would probably be ambivalent and inconclusive. From the institutional choice perspective, however, another strategy of browsing through the literature seems to be more promising. We will concentrate on the question of whether there are plausible arguments for institutional equivalents of coordinating capitalist economies by flexible market wages: Which contrafactual evidence speaks against the neoclassical ideology of only "one best way"?

Since the rise of efficiency wage theory (see Akerloff and Yellen 1986 for an overview), we know of wages' incentive effects on individual performance and willingness to cooperate. Entrepreneurs have used this wisdom for a long time. Robert Bosch, the inventor of the "Boschzünder," who was one of the first to introduce the eight-hour day (1906) and the free Saturday (1910), expressed this knowledge in its briefest form: "I don't pay good wages because I have a lot of money, I have a lot of money because I pay good wages" (Heuss 1946, 456f). Henry Ford, who doubled the workers' wages to five dollars a day in 1914, added another reason. "Of course the higher wage drew a more productive worker. But that wasn't the real reason. The fact was, it was no good mass-producing a cheap automobile if there weren't masses of workers and farmers who could afford to buy it" (Newton 1987, 101).

The important consequence of efficiency wage theory is the indeterminateness of the relationship between wages and employment or unemployment. It depends on the institutional environment—in other words, on the coordination of wage policy with other policies—whether a strategy of high wages leads to high productivity and competitiveness or to the bankruptcy of firms unable to pay the high wages and engage in diversified quality production. The contributions in Matzner and Streeck (1991) and the work of Soskice (1990) and Soskice and Schettkat (1992) persuasively demonstrate the complementary institutional features to make a high wage strategy successful: continuing and high-quality training, long-term financing perspectives of firms, long-term career prospects of employees, and coordinated wage settlement.

Of special importance is Soskice's argument that it doesn't matter whether wages are centrally or decentrally bargained. What matters are wage settlements organized in such a way that they flexibly coordinate firms, sectors, and regions to avoid high transaction costs by permanent quarrels about wages at the firm level, wage-wage spirals by poaching skilled labor through high wage offers, and high volatility of wages by binding wage increases too closely to short-term profit gains (see also Bellmann and Emmerich 1992).

As regards the latter point, it is interesting to note that Japan's high wage flexibility is not so much related to the bonus system as is often maintained in the literature; it is the high elasticity of Japanese regular wages related to consumer prices and labor market conditions (Mizuno 1992), probably due to the yearly synchronized enterprise-wide collective bargaining in the so-called spring offensive (*Shunto*) and spillovers from the unionized large-enterprise negotiations to the nonunionized small and medium-sized firms (Koshiro 1992). Here we can add an explanation to the observation of relative wage rigidity in the United States and Canada: Both countries have no yearly but medium-term wage settlements, with three years as the normal length of contracts, compared to the yearly spring wage bargains in Japan and to the mostly one-year contracts in most of the European countries.

Another interesting case is Switzerland, as an example for institutionally decentralized wage bargaining but a high degree of flexible coordination by cooperative labor relations. Danthine and Lambelet (1987) explain this in the terminology of game theory and invite us to view the Swiss labor scene "as a set of numerous bilateral monopolies, generally at the firm level. Both sides basically find themselves in a bilateral prisoner's dilemma-game type of situation, the game being repeated, with no finite time horizon and with no possibility for players to 'kill' their opposite number. Therefore . . . cooperation as the dominant strategy under these circumstances would seem to apply nicely." In other words: If the "shadow of the future" is strong enough, players choose cooperation instead of defection. The evolution of such "bilateral monopolies," however, is not yet clearly understood and only poorly circumscribed by metaphors like "clans," "traditions," "ethnic homogeneity," etc.

If we now rank countries by their ability to coordinate wages in terms of functional flexibility—and not by conventional organizational characteristics like corporatism (centralization) or decentralization—a large part of the international variation in unemployment performance can be explained. Countries with completely different wage-setting institutions and low average unemployment rates (Switzerland, Sweden, Norway, Austria, and Japan) rank high in terms of their ability to coordinate and moderate wage changes, whereas the U.S.A., Canada, the U.K., France, and Italy, with high average unemployment, get low scores of flexible coordination (Soskice 1990).

Empirical evidence from the member states of the EC supports the view that low wages must not necessarily mean low wage costs. On the contrary: Low-wage countries have often lower productivity, so that unit labor costs do not differ very much between EC member states. The comparison of unit labor costs according to industries, however, is of greater importance. Here we find even cases where the unit wage costs of low-wage countries (e.g., United Kingdom) are higher than those of high-wage countries (e.g., Germany). There is also no clear relationship between low unit wage costs and improvement of competitiveness, as neoclassical textbooks would suggest. In the 1980s, Italy, Ireland, Spain, and West Germany had the highest increase of their export share in the EC; unit wage costs in Spain and Ireland remained almost constant during this period, whereas they soared in Italy and West Germany; Belgium, with the lowest increase of unit wage costs, even lost in its competitive position (EC-Commission 1990, 1991).

We end as we started with an example outside Europe: In spite of high wage flexibility, real wages at the aggregate level in Japan have exceeded the growth rate of national productivity since 1970 (Koshiro 1992, 69). This did not prevent Japan from becoming the competitive winner in the seventies and eighties and from keeping both inflation and unemployment low. Thus: Wages alone do not count; other factors—and probably noneconomic factors, too—have to be taken into account to evaluate labor market policy and related institutions. "The real problem for researchers is that we cannot be sure what constitutes a 'desirable' elasticity of bonus payments or basic wages that would be sufficient to solve the unemployment problem" (Koshiro 1992, 70).

The Role of Active Labor Market Policy

The empirical indeterminateness of the relationship between wages and (un)employment, which has been observed in the preceding paragraphs, does not mean a lack of any relationship in theory. *Ceteris paribus*, of course, real wages and employment are negatively correlated. But we are not living in a *ceteris paribus* world. Intervening variables do affect the wage-employment relationship. In reality and in a dynamic perspective, real wages and employment have often taken a parallel course. Active labor market policy (ALMP)—under which we subsume further training and retraining, wage subsidies, temporary public job creation, placement services, information, and counseling—is such an intervening factor.

In the last twenty years, and especially with the first oil price shock in 1974–75, ALMP has gained momentum; its importance further increased after the second recession in 1980–81—not to mention its tremendous role in East Germany after the fall of the Berlin wall.[5] Figure 1.8 shows the average unemployment rates and the average expenditure rates for ALMP in the OECD countries from 1985 to 1990; Figure 1.9 displays the average unemployment rate and the activity rate, which means the share of active labor market measures related to the overall labor market budget, i.e., including expenditures for unemployment benefits and unemployment assistance. Two interesting observations are worth mentioning:

Some countries, especially Japan and Switzerland, have kept unemployment low without high spending in ALMP; Belgium, Ireland, and Denmark are at the other end of the spectrum—with high spending and high unemployment rates. Sweden, Finland, and—to some extent—Germany are countries with high spending and relatively low unemployment. Altogether, taken at face value, there seems to be some correlation, which—at this stage—should not be interpreted causally.[6]

The second observation is more interesting: The higher unemployment, the lower the activity rate. If—following the plausible guideline—it makes more sense to finance employment or training instead of unemployment and idle capacities, then high and persistent unemployment creates its own barriers to implement ALMP. This observation supports the thesis that a proper global demand or supply management to prevent mass unemployment is a necessary condition for implementing micro-oriented ALMP.

Whereas the value of a moderate application of ALMP, especially measures related to training and placement services, is not any longer contested, the effectiveness of large-scale labor market programs (such as in Sweden or now in East Germany) is highly controversial. Only a few studies have attacked this question rigorously. Two opposing views and approaches will be discussed in the following pages, and then our own effort—closely following the Lund School—will be presented.

Figure 1.8 **Unemployment and Expenditure for Active Labor Market Policy in OECD Countries**

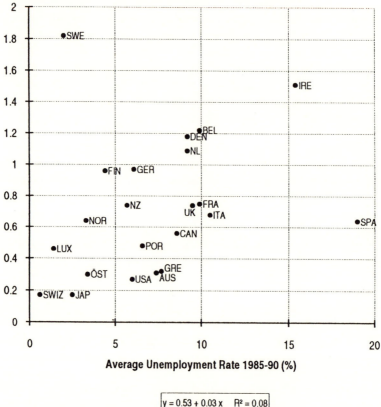

Average Expenditure for Active Labour Market Policy 1985-90 (%)

Average Unemployment Rate 1985-90 (%)

$$y = 0.53 + 0.03 \, x \quad R^2 = 0.08$$
$$(0.18) \quad (0.02)$$

Source: OECD Employment Outlook 1992; own calculations.

Because the evidence remains ambivalent at this level of aggregation, we suggest directing the evaluative eyes more on the quality dimension of specific labor market programs, especially on their implementation conditions including their institutional context. Given the present poor state of comparative qualitative evaluation research, only a few hints are possible to conclude this section.

Pros and Cons of ALMP at the Macro Level

In principle, ALMP can favorably affect the wage-employment relationship in two ways: By preserving, enhancing, or reestablishing the productivity capacity of the unemployed or employed, ALMP can shift the labor demand curve to the

Figure 1.9 **Unemployment and Activity Rate of Labor Market Policy in OECD Countries**

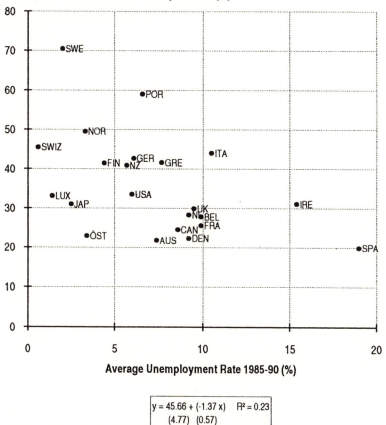

Activity Rate of Labour Market Policy 1985-90 (%)

Average Unemployment Rate 1985-90 (%)

$$y = 45.66 + (-1.37\,x) \quad R^2 = 0.23$$
$$(4.77) \quad (0.57)$$

Source: OECD Employment Outlook 1992; own calculations.

right and thus increase employment (or decrease unemployment) holding real wages constant; holding the labor demand curve constant, ALMP can reduce unemployment by employing "marginal" groups of the labor market (those who will not raise the average wage level, especially the hard-to-place people) in the public or semipublic sector or by inducing additional private employment by various forms of wage subsidies; such measures may even reduce real wages by increasing competition for jobs.

The counterargument is that participation in labor market programs removes incentives for wage restraint, which—in the theoretical imagination of neoclassical economists—is the only way to reduce unemployment. The main effect of labor market programs, so the argument goes, is to increase wages, because disemployed workers are presented with an attractive alternative to open unemployment. Hence, regular employment is reduced. If this reduction is big enough, labor market programs may even fail to reduce open unemployment.

This is what Calmfors and Forslund (1991) determined for the Swedish economy. In their model, ALMP enters the wage equation in two forms: Participation in all labor market programs in percent of labor force, and the "accommodation stance of labor market policies" as the ratio between the number of people in labor market programs and the total number of employees out of regular work.

For both measures, they found a surprisingly strong positive impact on their dependent variable, "product wages in the private sector." For example, a *ceteris paribus* increase of open unemployment from 2 to 3 percentage points reduces real wages by 4.5–7.3 percent. A *ceteris paribus* increase of labor market programs from 2 to 3 percentage points of the labor force raises wages by 2.0–5.3 percent.

Transferring the wage elasticity coefficient into a general equilibrium model, they came to the conclusion that an increase in the accommodation stance by 10 percentage points and in the share of the labor force participating in programs by 1 percentage point appear to raise open unemployment by 0.1 and 0.3 percentage points respectively. Despite some caveats raised by the authors themselves, they maintain that their "results strongly suggest that large-scale labour market programmes may not be an appropriate method of avoiding open unemployment" (Calmfors and Forslund 1991, 1147).

Such a strong conclusion, however, is far from justified. First, the specification of the model is problematic inasfar as the authors include in the right hand of the wage equation labor market policy indicators as well as unemployment, while unemployment is supposed to be affected directly or indirectly by ALMP. Second, the conclusion concerning the alleged increase of unemployment by ALMP is the result of the equilibrium model in which estimated coefficients are incorporated; the results depend thus on some stylized assumptions in the model, which are doubtful. Third, as the authors acknowledge, the labor market policy indicators may reflect other policies (for instance, aggregate demand policy or selective subsidies) causing a rise of real wages. Fourth, nothing is said about the quality of the different elements of their labor market policy indicator, which includes all kinds of active labor market policies, whether targeted to the long-term unemployed, to early retirement, or to unemployed with serious skill deficits.

The only conclusion, in our view, that may be justified from that study is that labor market programs probably have—as other programs—a declining marginal effectiveness. This would correspond to the results of other studies (e.g., Blau and Robins 1987; Johannesson and Schmid 1980, 403). But the range of this margin is variable according to the institutional framework in which labor market programs are working. Aggregate econometric studies are probably unable to contribute to a specification of such margins. Finally, a principal reservation against such equilibrium models remains, nourished by the authors themselves: "Established wage-unemployment relations have ever since the Phillips curve had an unfortunate habit of breaking down as new observations are added" (Calmfors and Forslund 1991, 1146).

Is this the end of the story on evaluating labor market policy at the macro level? Certainly not. The following example seems to be more promising.

Jackman et al. (1990) assess the impact of ALMP on the unemployment rate across fourteen OECD countries in the period of 1971–88. Size and duration of unemployment benefits and corporatism (as a proxy for unobserved features of labor market regimes) enter as additional policy variables on the right hand side of the equation. The analytical framework is the Beveridge curve, and the authors adopt a two-step procedure: In the first step, they regress all countries' unemployment and vacancies on nineteen zero-one dummy variables, for the nineteen years in their sample. As each dummy takes a value one in one year only and zero elsewhere, the estimated coefficients can be interpreted as estimates of the corresponding year's world shocks affecting unemployment and vacancies. Such shocks, it is assumed, may include some policy changes that are common to all countries but unimportant for unemployment differentials. The residuals, on the other hand, are interpreted as reflecting country-specific influences. In step two, therefore, they regress the unemployment residual on the vacancy residual and on a set of four other variables: the above-mentioned policy variables, country-fixed effects (that is, a different intercept for each country), one-year lag of the residual (the account for delayed responses), and country-specific time trends.

The results are straightforward. Labor market policies shift the Beveridge curve inward, and they also make it flatter. Thus, at given vacancies, countries that pursue these policies have less unemployment, and when they experience an increase in vacancies, unemployment falls by more (in proportional terms) than in other countries. Labor market policies also speed up the adjustment to equilibrium, by reducing the influence that past unemployment has on future unemployment—in other words, by reducing "hysteresis" (Jackman et al. 1990, 482).

Jackman et al. find also significant effects for the other policy variables. While a longer duration of unemployment benefits shifts the Beveridge curve outward, thus increasing unemployment, larger replacement rates do not clearly affect unemployment at given vacancies. Both results correspond with the majority of literature on this point (see among others Bourdet and Persson 1992; Florens et al. 1990; OECD 1991; Schmid, Reissert, and Bruche 1992; see also chapter 3 by Reissert and Schmid in this book). The strongest favorable effect to reduce unemployment, however, is corporatism, here supposed to measure—in our words—flexible coordination and not alleged centralized wage setting.[7] Flexible coordination not only fosters the fast reaction of real wages to demand or supply shocks, higher requisite variety in this respect also buffers "unemployment shocks," as the size of unemployment is one of the main causes for long-term unemployment. Thus concerning hysteresis, corporatism as an indicator for flexible coordination indirectly reduces unemployment. In addition, corporatist economies are more likely to be egalitarian, which means more likely to have narrower wage differentials than noncorporatist economies.

> Since the returns to search are less when wages are more uniform, unemployed workers in corporatist economies are not as likely to hold out for a good wage offer as in non-corporatist economies. With less search taking place, the Beveridge curve in corporatist economies is again likely to be closer to the origin. Finally, corporatism is as much a state of mind and an implicit commitment to help each other in the labour market as an explicit institutional arrangement for wage determination. Labour market policies are likely to be more frequently reviewed, better targeted and command more support from unions and employer groups than in non-corporatist economies. (Jackman et al. 1990, 475–76)

Although a seminal work, the study by Jackman et al. suffers from serious deficits that warn us not to take their results at face value. With respect to model specification, we see the use of residuals as the main problematic feature. The unemployment reaction of countries to "world shocks" is already filtered by country-specific institutional arrangements. There is, therefore, the danger that the authors measure and explain an artifact. We would prefer a model that assesses the impact of labor market policy on unemployment in a straightforward way, making allowance for an underspecification of all possible influences. Meanwhile, more data are available to allow for a differentiation of the labor market policy variable, which is rather crude in the model presented by Jackman et al. (see also Phelps 1992). The indicators for job openings (vacancy figures) also need improvement. The different legal framework with respect to employment protection would also have to be taken into account. All in all, the approach by Jackman et al. seems to us worthwhile to follow up.

Disaggregation of Comparative Macro Evaluation

As Bourdet and Persson (1992) have demonstrated in a comparison of France and Sweden, remarkable progress in comparative macro evaluation can be made by disaggregating ALMP in its components—size, composition, selectivity (or targeting)—and by analyzing the flexibility of these components. Using the framework of the Beveridge curve, they come to the conclusion that the deterioration of the UV curve of France compared to Sweden was mainly due to differences in the policy design for age groups. Whereas ALMP for young and elderly does not differ greatly, Sweden puts much more emphasis on labor market programs toward the prime-age group (25–54) and adjusts the size of programs flexibly to the variations of labor demand. These differences in design and timing, and not the sheer size, are the "secret" of the success of Swedish labor market policy (at least for the 1970s and 1980s): First, Sweden's ALMP was able to prevent an outward shift of the UV curve; second, the UV curve is flatter than in France, indicating a higher reduction of unemployment at given increases of vacancies; third, this success has not been achieved at the cost of increasing rates of labor market policy over time.

In Table 1.3, we have applied the same methodology for Germany.[8] Comparing the constant terms and coefficients at face value, the overall conclusion is that Germany lies in the middle between France and Sweden: First, the trend term in equations (1), (5), and (9) is significantly positive in France and Germany (and of the same size) but insignificant in Sweden; this confirms an outward shift of the UV curve in France and Germany but a stable curve in Sweden. Second, the same equations show that the coefficients of the vacancy variables (with a few exceptions mentioned later) are higher in Sweden than in France and Germany, and higher in Germany than in France, indicating flatter UV curves in Sweden and Germany.

If we break up unemployment into short-term unemployment (equations 2, 6, 10), we find lower but no significant trend coefficient in France and Sweden, and a lower but significant trend coefficient in Germany. This suggests that the outward shift of the UV curve in Germany, contrary to France, is a problem not only of long-term unemployment but also of short-term unemployment—in other words, the matching process in Germany has also deteriorated for short-term unemployed. The trend related to long-term unemployment (equations 3, 7, 11) mirrors the pattern of short-term unemployment: the coefficient is significant and very high in France, high also in Germany but lower than in France, higher even in Sweden compared to total unemployment but only near to statistical significance; thus, in Germany and especially in France, the deterioration of the UV curve is mainly due to the increase of long-term unemployment, indicating the occurrence of hysteresis.

In all three countries, long-term unemployment—in contrast to short-term unemployment—is more responsive to the lagged than to the nonlagged vacancy rate. This observation holds especially true for Germany and can easily be interpreted by the fact that the recovery makes inroads into long-term unemployment only after a time lag.

Does active labor market policy matter? Yes, as equations (4), (8), and (12) show. They report the results of estimating an "extended" Beveridge curve, with the rate of unemployment plus the rate of individuals in ALMP measures as the dependent variable. "Equation (8) indicates that Swedish labour market policy has achieved a remarkable record as a flexible policy instrument. There is no statistically significant time trend which means that the success in containing unemployment has not been achieved at the cost of increasing rates of labour market policy over time. The volume of labour market policy has been swiftly and massively adjusted both to downturns and to upturns in the economy so that the 'extended' Beveridge curve has remained stable over time" (Bourdet and Persson 1992, 27).

France (equation 4) shows a positive time trend, which means that the containment of unemployment by ALMP could not prevent an outward shift of the

Table 1.3

Estimates of the Beveridge Curves 1973–89 for France, Sweden, and Germany

	France				Sweden				Germany			
	(1) lnU	(2) lnSU	(3) lnLU	(4) lnULMP	(5) lnU	(6) lnSU	(7) lnLU	(8) lnULMP	(9) lnU	(10) lnSU	(11) lnLU	(12) lnULMP
C	1.73[a] (14.3)	1.58[a] (11.8)	0.25 (1.1)	1.92[a] (7.2)	0.94[a] (4.9)	0.75[a] (5.0)	0.84[a] (3.0)	1.65[a] (8.8)	1.08[a] (12.1)	0.63[a] (8.5)	-0.80[a] (2.7)	1.56[a] (13.8)
$\ln_v$	-0.29[a] (3.3)	-0.36[a] (4.5)	-0.13 (0.3)	-0.20[a] (2.9)	-0.40[a] (3.9)	-0.40[a] (4.00)	-0.44[a] (2.7)	-0.25[a] (2.3)	-0.36[a] (3.8)	-0.31[a] (3.7)	-0.26 (1.5)	-0.42[a] (3.2)
$\ln_{v-1}$	-0.21[a] (2.7)	-0.11[b] (1.9)	-0.64[a] (2.2)	-0.19[a] (3.8)	-0.30[a] (3.0)	-0.21[b] (2.1)	-0.68[a] (4.1)	-0.49[a] (4.5)	-0.18[b] (1.8)	-0.01 (0.1)	-0.80[a] (4.1)	-0.07[b] (1.8)
trend	0.04[a] (3.9)	0.01 (1.3)	0.08[a] (4.3)	0.04[a] (2.5)	0.01 (0.4)	0.00 (0.1)	0.02 (1.4)	0.00 (0.1)	0.04[a] (3.9)	0.01[a] (3.7)	0.05[a] (2.2)	0.02[b] (2.0)
R^2(adj)	0.98	0.96	0.96	0.99	0.89	0.85	0.91	0.87	0.87	0.81	0.73	0.73

Sources: Annual data; vacancies for Sweden and France in *OECD Main Economic Indicators*; for Sweden and France, Bourdet and Persson 1992, table 3; for Germany, Schmid 1991, table 4.

Notes: U=unemployment rate; SU=short-term unemployment rate (<12 months for France, and <6 months for Sweden and Germany); LU=long-term unemployment rate (>12 months for France and Germany, >6 months for Sweden); ULMP=unemployment plus labor market policy rate; v=vacancy rate; v−1=lagged vacancy rate.

[a] denotes statistical significance at the 5 percent level. All the equations are corrected for serial correlation with the Cochrane-Orcutt procedure.

[b] denotes statistical significance at the 10 percent level. All the equations are corrected for serial correlation with the Cochrane-Orcutt procedure.

Beveridge curve. The lower time trend coefficient in Germany compared to France indicates that German ALMP was able to dampen or retard the outward shift, but not as successfully as in Sweden. There is also a remarkable difference in the response of the German extended Beveridge curve to the lagged and nonlagged vacancy rate. Compared to Sweden, Germany shows a much stronger response of the extended Beveridge curve to the nonlagged vacancy rate and a much weaker response to the lagged vacancy rate. In other words, the German ALMP is more flexible and countercyclical in the short run and less flexible and countercyclical in the long run.

This result fits exactly with the outcome of our study on financing systems of labor market policy. In a six-country comparison (Austria, France, Germany, Sweden, United Kingdom, and the U.S.A.) we could show that Sweden turned out as the only country that has consistently varied expenditures for ALMP countercyclically[9] in order to smooth out the curve of the unemployment rate. Germany also manifested—at a lower average level of expenditures—an initially strong countercyclical pattern of expenditures, which, however, always culminated with a time lag in a clearly procyclical pattern. In Germany, it is particularly expenditures for short-time work and in part also for training and job creation that account for the observed quick short-term response of ALMP. Due to the particular German financing system, expenditures for training and job creation, however, were often restrained when long-term unemployment started to increase (Schmid, Reissert, and Bruche 1992, 210–20).

The Role of Flexibly Coordinated Policy Implementation

The Swedish example is a case for the conclusion that quality matters more than quantity. The right timing and targeting of policy measures is of crucial importance. So far, macro-level evaluations of ALMP have only indirectly hinted at the importance of policy implementation. How is the right timing and targeting brought about?

The Swedish success story would be incomplete without referring to the rich and decentralized policy network available for implementing ALMP. It is the close cooperation among local policy makers, trade unionists, employers, regional planners, and placement officers of local employment agencies that guarantees an effective implementation of ALMP measures and a coordination of ALMP with industrial policy (Delander 1991).

Studies in Germany confirm the Swedish experience. It has been shown in several implementation and evaluation studies conducted at the Wissenschaftszentrum Berlin, that regional employment agencies implemented rather differently the various measures of ALMP at their disposal, and that those differences did matter for their effectiveness (Maier 1988; Schmid 1979, 1980; Peters and Schmid 1982; Schmid and Peters 1982; Scharpf et al. 1982). Only around 50 percent of the variation in the take up of ALMP could be explained by the structure of the regional economy and the size of unemployment; the rest had to be referred to different implementation strategies and to the specific regional policy networks. Apart from different attitudes among the local employment officers—with a range from the typical bureaucrat to the entrepreneur type—it could be shown that cooperation between key actors at the local or regional level was decisive for an effective implementation of training and job creation policies.

These results correspond also to a recent study by Bellmann, who—on the basis of regressing the determinants of regional outflows of unemployment—had to speculate that the relative success of job creation schemes was "caused by the characteristics of the local employment office area in which these schemes operated" (Bellmann 1992, 171).

More in-depth studies of policy networks are necessary, especially in a comparative perspective. However, from what we know already, it is safe to speculate that the creation of incentives for the establishment of decentralized policy networks is a key for any improvement of ALMP. A survey by the OECD on various experimental programs and evaluations on ALMP hint in the same direction. The results of this survey suggest that in-kind transfers in the form of intensive counseling and placement services are very often more effective in reducing the duration of unemployment than cash transfers in the form of wage subsidies (OECD 1991, 216). This confirms the outcome of an evaluation study on labor market policy for the disabled, comparing Germany, Sweden, United Kingdom, and the U.S.A. (Semlinger and Schmid 1985; Semlinger 1988).

Microlevel Evaluation of Labor Market Policy

On the microlevel, labor market policy and specific labor programs aim at improving an individual's relative position in the labor market. This improvement can occur in multiple ways: enhancing reemployment possibilities of the unemployed, reintegration into the labor market of women who had left the labor force for some time, raising labor earnings through additional training, and other more general ways like developing more continuous patterns of employment. Microlevel evaluation of labor market policy and specific programs is a field of research best characterized by its multitude of approaches. This becomes most evident in the prevailing plurality of the choice of the dependent variable in the evaluation. There appears to be little consensus on such basic questions as what determines the success of a specific program. Program designers, administrators, and evaluators apparently choose different indicators to measure program effects and success. More traditional economic microlevel evaluation tends to favor short-term measures of program success such as individual labor earnings as the dependent variable. Broader socioeconomic evaluation stresses reintegration, employment duration, and long-term employment stability as appropriate indicators for program success.

In this section we will begin with reviewing the evidence on the earnings-enhancing aspect of training programs, since this issue has received the most attention in evaluations of labor market policies where overall the evidence indicates positive effects of various forms of training programs on post-program earnings. This part is followed by the review of an investigation of the demand for training of people who are unemployed and actively looking for a job. It is found that demand for training by the unemployed is highest at the beginning of unemployment. After nine months of unemployment, the probability of starting a training course is close to zero. We then review a study analyzing the reemployment possibilities of the unemployed after program participation. The results indicate that job search assistance does not enhance the chances of reemployment as much as basic skill, job skill, and on-the-job training does. More general socioeconomic evaluation is concerned with rates of job change, risk of job loss, and employment stability for people who participated in some form of training or other labor programs. Finally, we attempt a critical assessment of the state of the art of microlevel policy evaluation in the domain of labor market programs.

Earnings Effects of Training Programs

Microlevel evaluation of the earnings effects of personnel training programs intends to measure the increase in the program participants' labor earnings relative to those who had not participated in the program. Therefore, a choice needs to be made concerning the comparison group in order to indicate the size of the effect of a program. During the eighties there was an intense debate, mainly in the United States, whether experimental or nonexperimental control groups should be used for such comparisons (Lalonde 1986; Barnow 1987; Björklund 1988, 1989). In reviewing this literature we follow this separation of studies according to the kind of control group that is chosen.[10]

Shortly after the Comprehensive Employment and Training Act (CETA) became active law in the United States in 1973, data were collected to evaluate the effects of the program, which contained subprograms including direct work experience, public service employment, on-the-job training, and classroom training. Research dealing with this particular program is of interest, because a unique effort has been undertaken to evaluate the program. In a public-use data set, information from 6,700 program participants in 1975 and 13,300 participants in 1976 was collected and merged with data from both the Current Population Survey (CPS) and records from the Social Security Administration on incomes between 1951 and 1978 to cover pre- and post-program periods.

Among the efforts to review the literature on the evaluation of the CETA programs (Bassi and Ashenfelter 1986; Björklund 1989), Barnow concludes, after a careful discussion of econometric issues involved in control group selection, sources of selectivity bias, and issues of model specification, that an overall assessment of the impact of the CETA programs is that it had a "modest impact of several hundred dollars on earnings for men and a somewhat greater effect on women" (Barnow 1987, 189).

This overall statement of the positive effect of the program has to be considered against various sources of uncertainty, two of which are highlighted by Björklund (1989). Björklund demonstrates the error margins associated with every point estimate of regression coefficients. At a 95 percent confidence interval, an estimated effect needs to be complemented by plus or minus two standard deviations of the corresponding variable. Results taken from Bassi (1984) then show a positive program effect of $740 on post-program earnings for the first year for white women. Assuming a 95 percent confidence interval, the effect is in the range of $480 to $1,000. For women from minority groups, the point estimate is somewhat smaller, $426, and with a standard deviation of $235 the program effect is between $896 and -$44. In other words, the point estimates in this case do not allow us to conclude that there was a definite positive program effect. The error margins increase further in the analysis of men from minority groups.

A second source of differences in estimated effects is found in the kind of explanatory variables used in the estimation and the exact model specification. For example, some studies make use of the limited information on labor market experience and individual retrospective information on labor force participation contained in the data. In some studies general education is assumed to have linear effects on earnings (in this case education is entered directly in the model); others additionally test for nonlinear relationships (usually this is done by adding the square of the values for education to the model). These differences in model specification will cause other effects of explanatory variables common in all analyses to vary substantially due to the specification of the model applied in the estimation. Model specification itself depends on theoretical considerations of program evaluation in general[11] and labor market theories more specifically for evaluation of labor market programs.[12]

A major problem shared by all nonexperimental microlevel evaluation approaches is that the various stages of the selection of the control group and the program participants are hard to assess. The selection of program participants can be done in at least two ways: first, a self-selection of people who apply for participation in the program; second, selection by the program staff of eligible participants. Barnow (1987) mentions that results of the CETA evaluation are sensitive to control group members' commitment to the labor force. By including individuals in the control group who have not been members of the labor force immediately prior to the survey, the estimated program impact increases (Barnow 1987). This fact is interesting concerning the choice of target groups for possible future program participation by program administrators. It stresses the importance of having detailed knowledge of individual characteristics, labor force experience, and attachment to the labor force. Based on such knowledge, programs can be designed closer to the specific needs of possible participants. The more a program takes into account a person's specific labor force background, the more effective it probably is.

For evaluation research this means the sensitivity of estimated effects hinges to a large degree on the precise definition of who is eligible for the program by the legislator and the rigor of application of these rules by program staff. If program administrators had chosen only people with confirmed labor force attachment, program effects for those people might have been small, but in widening the group of eligible people to those who are not counted as members of the labor force, the positive effect of the program increases, in particular for women (Dickinson, Johnson, and West 1986). Hence, the original design of the program as well as design changes due to program implementation are important intervening processes that are part of the estimated effects but have largely been considered to be external to the microlevel evaluation of training programs.

There appears to be some kind of a trade-off between "good" program evaluation and "good" program implementation. For the purpose of program evaluation, it is desirable to have precise details of the program and the people eligible for participation. On the other hand, more scope for flexible implementation can increase positive program effects substantially.

With respect to so-called external effects, some results from policy evaluation making use of the experimental approach are of interest. Aiming at the same target group of welfare recipients as the CETA program, a two-week training course of how to seek employment was given to 916 participants in 1980 in Ohio (Burtless 1985). The experiment consisted of randomly selecting three groups. One group received a tax credit voucher that enabled employers of participants to obtain a tax reduction. Another group was endowed with a direct cash subsidy for the employer; and a third group, which constituted the control group, had no wage voucher at members' disposal. Surprisingly, the results revealed that those who approached their employers to make use of their wage vouchers fared worse than members of the control group with no wage voucher to offer. Twenty percent of the control group found employment within an eight-week period after the training, whereas only 13 percent of participants with tax credit vouchers and 13 percent with direct rebate subsidies found employment during the observed period.

In explaining these disappointing results of the wage voucher experiment, Burtless (1985) refers to the possibility that the wage voucher in this experiment could have operated as a warning signal to employers, since it revealed otherwise unknown information to the employer, i.e., that the applicant has been a welfare recipient for some time. If being a welfare recipient has a negative connotation to employers, a kind of stigmatization of job searchers with wage vouchers might have occurred that reduced their probability of finding a job. In this particular example, program participants had the possibility of correcting the random assignment of the "stigmatized" vouchers simply by not making use of them when applying for a job. However, in case of a positive association of program participation and employment opportunities, random selection of participants raises a basic ethical question of why some participants are denied access to beneficial training courses.[13]

In a similar experiment in Illinois that involved no training component, experimental subjects were offered a bonus if they became employed after no more than ten weeks of receiving unemployment benefits. The effect of this pecuniary incentive on the reduction of unemployment duration was significant but very small. The results of these experiments imply that employment, job search, and training choice of unemployed workers, as far as they have choices, "do not seem to be governed simply, or even predominantly, by any simple trade-off between income and the irksomeness of labor" (Solow 1990, 12).

The study by Groot, Hartog, and Oosterbeck (1990) takes a more general view of the decision-making process to participate in training. The decision of whether to participate in training consists of three options: on-the-job training, off-the-job training, or no training. They further distinguish whether the decision to take training and the decision of what type of training to choose are made at the same time or in a sequential manner. After the estimation of the probability of taking one or the other form of training, wage equations are estimated with the difference of the log hourly wage rate in 1986 less the log hourly wage rate in 1985 as the dependent variable separately by type of training.

Results suggest a positive effect of the number of years of general education on the probability to participate in on-the-job training but not for the participation in off-the-job training. Groot, Hartog, and Oosterbeck (1990) interpret this result as evidence for the complementarity of formal education and on-the-job training, which might be due to the fact that most on-the-job training is employer-initiated, while off-the-job training is more likely to be initiated by employees. However, estimates for the United States (Lynch 1990) show that the probability of participation in on-the-job training is not increased by a higher level of general education. This contrasts as well with findings for West Germany (Becker 1991; Becker and Schoemann 1992) that demonstrate that participation in training courses is higher for those who already hold higher education certificates. Additionally, results indicate that there are effects of birth cohorts, labor market segments, and the legislative framework on the probability of taking up further education and training. Country differences in the organization of the education and training and the employers' attitude to provide on-the-job training might explain these contrasting findings. In the Netherlands and West Germany firms seem to consider on-the-job training more as a complementary training effort, contrary to the practice in the United States.

The analysis for the United States by Lynch (1990) differentiates even further formal off-the-job training in for-profit educational institutions and training in public training institutes. Despite this interesting distinction, there remains the possible bias that consists of the differential impact of specific government assistance toward training programs. Such programs might take the form of on- or off-the-job training and might contain some form of financial incentives to either employers or employees, or both. Most estimates on program participation and subsequent earnings profiles with nonexperimental studies using survey data do not contain information on scholarships or any other form of assistance to finance training. This could yield biased results if different sources of financing training courses will influence motivation and likely successful completion of the course. So far, attempts to account for program costs are still very limited and largely restricted to experimental program evaluation (Burtless and Orr 1986).

There is considerable agreement in the literature on the increasing effects of training programs on earnings. Lynch (1990) finds that company-provided on-the-job training enhances wages in the current job but not in subsequent jobs, whereas off-the-job training has little effect on earnings in the current job but contributes to higher earnings in later jobs. Results by Groot, Hartog, and Oosterbeck (1990) confirm this pattern of the wage-increasing effects of training, although their analysis estimates such effects indirectly, making use of the tenure-wage relation. In fact, the inverse U-shaped form of the earnings profile is more adequate to describe earnings patterns for those who had no training or on-the-job training rather than those taking off-the-job training. A common result is that successful program completion is a precondition for any possible future wage gains, which emphasizes again the importance of program implementation.

Demand for Training Programs of the Unemployed

Successful program completion is closely related to the original motivation to take up some form of training. Higher motivation for training might itself have an effect on possible outcomes. A study that tries to address this kind of relation between program effects due to motivation or discouragement is the one by Allen, McCormick, and O'Brien (1991). They investigate the self-selection of training program participants from a slightly different perspective. Their analysis deals with the retraining policy in the United Kingdom aiming at reemployment of the unemployed. In particular, they focus on the question of who will seek to be retrained, which then constitutes the demand for retraining programs. Since they assume that for some workers brief spells of unemployment might be efficient, in their view not all of the unemployed need to be retrained. Findings concerning the structure of the demand for retraining should then yield insights into the need for future provision for retraining opportunities.

After construction of a model of a person's decision to go into retraining, the empirical analysis chooses as the dependent variable the probability of an individual to seek retraining. The data used in the analysis come from a random sample of persons leaving a job center in Sunderland, U.K. in the summer of 1985 who had been actively searching for at least four weeks. Results are based on a sample of 203 unemployed males of whom 133 had been made redundant. The statistical method applied is a hazard rate function where the "hazard" is the probability density of seeking retraining at a point in time t, conditional on not having done so before t.

Results indicate that the probability of applying for a retraining course declined after age twenty-seven for the whole sample. Men who worked in declining industries (engineering and shipbuilding) are more likely to seek retraining than those with traditional high labor turnover (services) and those with traditionally cyclical patterns of unemployment (construction). Formal education of primary and general secondary levels increases the probability of seeking retraining, whereas completed apprenticeships reduce this probability.

Their conclusion for the design of labor market programs is to take appropriate account of the fact that voluntary participation in retraining is a selective process. In particular, after about nine months of unemployment, people have either sought retraining, or they are very unlikely to seek it. Hence, the demand for retraining is likely to be high at the beginning of unemployment, and the number of places available to potential participants should take account of the timing of demand for retraining. For example, a suitable program design for training activities for the unemployed could make use of the self-motivated search for training programs by the short-term unemployed who have been unemployed for less than nine months. If search efforts for retraining have been frustrated over a one-year period, the motivation appears to have decreased to take part in any training course. This can then be expected to jeopardize even the generally positive impact of retraining for the unemployed.

So far we have reviewed studies that analyze earnings effects and the demand for training courses. We now turn to studies that take a broader socioeconomic approach rather than focusing on money wages or demand and supply considerations.

Job Training Programs and Reemployment Probability of the Unemployed

Ting's (1991) analysis takes a more socioeconomic approach. He looks into the impact of job training programs on the reemployment probability of displaced workers. Following a number of plant closings in many states in the United States at the beginning of the 1980s, Congress enacted the Job Training Partnership Act (JTPA), which was similar to the CETA program, but it differs from that program in that it allowed more local government influence, stronger private sector participation in program execution, and more state oversight of performance standards. Local government influence had an impact mainly on the mix of services offered, which included job counseling, job search assistance, classroom basic training, classroom skill training, and on-the-job training.

Data used in this study have been taken from the 1984 CPS Displaced Workers Survey, a supplement to the Current Population Survey. The sample in the analysis consists of people between twenty and sixty-five years of age who were displaced from nonagricultural jobs after 1979 due to plant closing or relocation. The sample size of people meeting these conditions was 2,394. The estimation method is a two-stage procedure that estimates in a first step the probability of workers being selected into job training programs and in a second step the probability of program participation as an independent variable in the estimation of the probability to be employed (unemployed) at the time of the survey in 1984.

The main result of Ting's study is that basic skill training, job skill training, and on-the-job training increase the probability of reemployment relative to those who received no training or only job search assistance. In order of size, it is basic skill training programs that appear to be most beneficial followed by on-the-job training programs and job skill training. As reported in this paper, the flexibility of the JPTA to target programs to state government needs has been concentrated too much on inexpensive job search assistance to produce high short-term placement rates. However, in respect of long-term awareness and concern for long-run reemployment probabilities labor market policies should not concentrate too much on just inexpensive job search assistance. There seems to be little way around the provision of more expensive job skill and basic skill training programs.

Ting (1991) mentions an intrinsic difficulty of the microlevel evaluation of training programs, which is due to the selection procedure by program administrators, since they might favor individuals who are most likely to succeed in the program with the least amount of assistance. In evaluation this phenomenon is called "creaming" and raises problems concerning the causality of training programs on reemployment chances. Creaming suggests that there is a simultaneous causality at work, since program participation of dislocated workers may already be predetermined by the higher reemployment probability of some of these dislocated workers. The sample selection procedure may capture some of these effects but cannot finally solve this difficulty.

Training Program Effects on Job Change, Job Loss, and Employment Stability

Next we review two studies that also focus more on the long-term labor market opportunities of program participants such as more general patterns of job mobility and employment stability but also on job loss. In a recent study on the high rates of job changing and unemployment of the youth labor market, Breen (1992) investigates the impact of state-run training programs on the probability of changing a job and the probability of losing a job after the person participated in a state-financed training course. He makes use of a follow-up study of primary school leavers in the Republic of Ireland who were interviewed when they left school in 1983 and reinterviewed in 1984 and 1988 in an attempt to collect complete labor market records for this time period. The sample used in the analysis consists of 1,116 individuals who had 1,824 jobs. Coverage is restricted to those who entered the labor market during the survey period excluding those who continued third-level education.

In estimating hazard rate models and carefully testing the implicit assumptions about the distribution of waiting times to the next event, either a job change or a job loss, the results indicate that the conditional probability for a job change increases rapidly at the beginning and then grows only very slowly. In the model estimated for the probability of a job loss, the time dependence shows support for a monotonically decreasing probability to lose a job with time spent in the job. On-the-job training had in both models the effect of increasing the "waiting time to the next event," which means if on-the-job training is provided, both the probability of choosing to change jobs and the probability of being dismissed are reduced. The effect of earnings in both models suggests, as was found for the provision of training, the presence of some form of labor market segmentation whereby jobs offering low wages reveal a higher risk of job loss and job change.

Variables measuring labor force status prior to the current job are of particular interest to us. They comprise five dummy variables indicating: (1) if the person was unemployed prior to the current job, (2) if the person held a job before, (3) if the person was on a state-run program of full-time training, (4) if the person was on a state-run temporary employment program, or (5) if the person was not in the labor force. The omitted category against which these effects are estimated is young people who were in full-time education prior to the current job. However, none of these "prior states" has a significant effect in the job change model. Having participated in a state-run program of either full-time training or temporary employment is not likely to enhance the probability of changing jobs compared to those who have been in full-time education prior to the current job.

In the job loss model there are significant effects of the prior state variables, but not in the usually expected direction. Individuals who enter a job directly from a state-run program or from unemployment spend a shorter time in that job before becoming unemployed again compared to those who lose their job having been in full-time education prior to the current job. This indicates that prior unemployment and having been in a state-run training program tend to stigmatize compared to entering the labor force directly from full-time education. Breen interprets the results such that these prior state variables might be proxies for other unmeasured features of jobs rather than characteristics of individuals.

An even more long-term evaluation attempt is undertaken by Korpi (1992). In an analysis of employment durations for a group of young unemployed who had participated in employment and training programs in Sweden, Korpi evaluates these programs focusing on the subsequent labor market careers of the unemployed. The data used for the analysis come from a longitudinal survey of 850 unemployed youth in Stockholm who were unemployed in 1981. The observed time period is between 1981 and 1985. The sample is constructed in a way that individuals included in the sample are those who held a job at time t, conditional on the fact that the previous job spell (j-1) was either a spell in unemployment or a spell in a relief job or labor market training if the preceding spell (j-2) was a spell in unemployment. A further distinction is made between temporary and more permanent kinds of jobs.

Based on descriptive statistics of these data Korpi finds that those in permanent jobs had already gained more employment experience and had spent less time in relief work and on training programs. Some indication of the enhancing effect of personnel programs on employment stability is reported in this analysis. Youth entering employment directly from unemployment have a median-concatenated employment duration across job spells of twenty-nine weeks, while those entering after program participation have a median duration of one year.

Similar to the analysis by Breen (1992), log logistic hazard rate models are estimated with the duration of concatenated employment, permanent and temporary employment respectively as the dependent variable. The duration of concatenated employment, Korpi's measure of employment stability, is positively related to having followed a personnel program. However, the length and number of such program spells have no significant effect on subsequent employment stability. In general terms program participation increases the duration of employment by a factor of two.

From an evaluation point of view, the result obtained for the ratio of the number of vacancies to the number of registered unemployed in the city of Stockholm at the beginning of a job spell is worthy of separate quotation. This indicator for the tightness of the labor market has the effect of shortening the duration of concatenated employment spells. A higher demand for labor does not contribute to enhancing the employment stability of the young. In this case, higher demand for labor will probably create more "good" job opportunities for the young with increased chances of upward mobility. In a transition model of the probability of becoming unemployed, the results show that when local labor demand is higher, the probability of losing one's job is reduced. Having followed a training program similarly reduces the risk of becoming unemployed.

These results fill to some extent the gap between a microlevel and a macrolevel evaluation of labor market policies. In Korpi's analysis an attempt is made to measure influences of the tightness of the local labor market on an individual's employment stability and unemployment risk, including a control variable of participation in a training program. Results seem to indicate the success of training programs on the micro level under varying macroeconomic labor market conditions. However, the results are not necessarily transferable to other countries because of the low overall unemployment levels in Sweden during the beginning of the 1980s.

Assessment of the Very "Diverse" Approaches of Microlevel Evaluation

Microlevel evaluation is also confronted with the issue of what extent specific program evaluation is transferable to work in the same way once applied on a larger scale. This touches to some extent on the problem of aggregation, i.e., how microlevel results can be aggregated to come to valid conclusions on the macro level. In what is usually summarized under the term *indirect effects* (Björklund 1989), it is possible that labor market programs lead to direct improvements of the labor market position of program participants, but it is hard to exclude the possibility that program participants, for example, obtained jobs at the expense of other members of the labor force. This might even lead to a certain kind of replacement or substitution effect in which companies, knowing of the existing commitment of retraining the unemployed, have an incentive to shed labor to benefit from public funds for retraining of the labor force. Although a microlevel evaluation could find positive effects of a specific public training program, the macrolevel evaluation might not be favorable, since within-company training has simply been transferred to the responsibility of the public domain.

In addition to this kind of "crowding out" effect, there is the possibility for a "queuing bias." Program participation could simply lead to the effect that participants are enabled to jump the queue in waiting for vacancies coming up after successful program termination. In this case, again a favorable microlevel evaluation of program participants finding a job faster than others could have a negligible effect in macrolevel evaluation of program effects, because for those of the unemployed remaining in the queue the duration of unemployment might be increased due to the effect that program participants have been preferred. The positive effects for the program participants could actually be gained at the expense of nonparticipants. In this case again a positive macrolevel effect is not to be found.

Lessons for Comparative Evaluation Research

To sum up, we return first to the fact of long-term multiple equilibrium of the labor market. This observation from cross-country comparisons finds plausible explanation by institutional choice theory. The labor market as a social institution is not like product markets. One important difference between the labor market and the market for bananas is that the performance of the worker depends on the price paid for his or her services.[14] Other important differences could be enumerated, such as fairness considerations in determining wage prices, mobility restrictions, asymmetric information, and strategic communication (negotiation).

If the wage rate enters the story in its double role, as productive factor as well as a simple cost, it is not any longer available "simply to balance supply and demand in the usual efficient way. It cannot perform both functions perfectly" (Solow 1990, 34). Institutions of wage formation, then, will determine the relationship between wage rate and employment. This nexus is further complicated by many forms of labor market policy, which is much neglected among mainstream labor economists, even among mainstreamers open to institutional questions like Robert Solow. We have them classified as regulating, redistributing, and job creating roles of the state. Active labor market policy, among others, emerged as an important "co-player" in the modern institutional arenas coordinating the labor market.

Thus, institutional choice is responsible for multiple labor market equilibrium in the sense that none of the participants is willing to choose, from among eligible strategies, something other than the strategy currently being pursued. If this were not the case, we could not explain the different labor market performances of European and OECD countries during the last decades, which we have demonstrated in the first section of our review. There is nothing like a "natural" rate of unemployment; the natural rate of unemployment can be almost anything the labor market has grown accustomed to (Solow 1990, 67).

What remains, then, for a socioeconomic evaluation of labor market institutions? We have identified two main contributions: First, to analyze patterns of institutional arrangements and labor market performance. There is not only an institutional choice that determines the range of possible equilibrium unemployment rates, but also an institutional choice with respect to attaining the same equilibrium level. In other words, there is institutional equivalence, which means, in principle at least, that there is always the possibility of substituting one institutional setting for another. Not any institutional setting, however, will be successful given the socioeconomic constraints. Detailed analysis of when and under what conditions such equivalences hold is the interesting and challenging endeavor of socioeconomic evaluation research.

If one prefers, as we do, low unemployment and inflation under the constraints of equality and efficiency (see chapter 7 on possible complementarities of these constraints), then the second possible contribution of evaluation research can be formulated: Identifying the characteristics of institutional choices that support a low unemployment equilibrium. This is an even more challenging task. Although the good news of "institutional choice" is the principal availability of options in choosing the range of "unemployment equilibrium" without affecting shared equity and efficiency principles, the corresponding bad news is that there seems to be an asymmetry in terms of political feasibility: It seems to be more difficult to shift the range of possible equilibrium unemployment rates downward than the other way round.

If this assumption is correct, it follows that institutions that resist high upward elasticity of unemployment and support high downward elasticity of unemployment related to demand fluctuations should be regarded as positive assets of a modern labor market. This is exactly the philosophy of active labor market policy: To prevent unemployment as far as possible and to respond as soon as possible with countermeasures (especially by training and temporary public job creation) in order to avoid "hysteresis effects" of unemployment. Also, on theoretical grounds, much speaks for active labor market policy. If, for instance, people care about status as much as about earnings (Frank 1985), the unemployed will decline job offers below their status and wait, even if this implies substantial loss of income. A policy of status rehabilitation by intensive training or temporary public job creation would reduce "wait unemployment" for status reasons (van de Klundert 1990).

To sum this up, we found more evidence for the validity of active labor market policy than against. However, one important qualification has to be made: Not the quantity but the quality of such an active labor market policy matters. Decisive for high-quality labor market policy is flexible coordination, for which we postulated four necessary conditions: bounded requisite variety, i.e., flexibility restricted by civilized constraints; institutional consistency; institutional coherence; and institutional equivalence.

In the search for sufficient requirements of good institutional choices, we screened some recent evaluation literature on the macro and micro levels. Instead of recalling single results from the previous sections, evidence for further successful conditions will be summarized in terms of general principles that we believe to have been detected. These principles are intended as guidelines both for decision makers to improve their policy design and for evaluation researchers to focus their analysis on the decisive issues. They can be summarized for convenience of memorizing as the three "C" conditions: compensation, competence, and cooperation. These conditions have to coexist if the labor market can be coordinated flexibly toward a low unemployment and inflation equilibrium.

(1) Mainstream economists still use the "Pareto Optimum" as the guiding principle for efficiency. According to this principle, a situation has to be evaluated as efficient if no further transaction can be thought of that improves the situation of one person without affecting another person negatively.[15] This is not only an unrealistic but also an unimaginative view. If societies had made their institutional choices dependent on this criteria, we probably would still live in the medieval age. We think that the "Kaldor Criterion" is much more realistic and imaginative: A situation is efficient if no further transaction can be thought of that improves the situation of one person without being able to compensate for negatively affected persons.

In most cases, structural change brings about winners and losers. Dynamic and open societies are characterized by their ability to create social innovations that institutionalize compensatory mechanisms[16] in two ways: to compensate immediate losses in the short term (income and so on), and to compensate status losses in the long run, which means the loss of positions in groups, organizations, and societies and the loss of the capacity to adjust to changing environments (skills and so on). Prominent examples of such innovations are the institutionalization of unemployment insurance systems, active labor market policy, guarantees of minimum income, entitlements to parental leaves, and training sabbaticals.

(2) Whereas compensation adds in a solidaric way something that individuals miss in concrete situations of need, competence means the individual's ability to solve problems. Problem-solving capacities, again, are combinations of routine skills and learning skills. Both types of skills and their parallel existence are import-

ant. Routine skills, an essential element of firm specific skills, without learning skills are risky if not disastrous in rapidly changing and uncertain environments. Learning skills, an essential element of general skills, without routine techniques lead to dilettantism, thus inefficient adjustment. The acquisition of both types of skills is a complex process, involving intellectual, emotional, and social elements.

Evidence of our survey suggests that the trend toward internal labor markets shifts the balance of both types of competence dangerously toward routine skills. The most important negative effect of this trend is the reduction of voluntary mobility, which produces, as far as we know, the most efficient adjustment to structural change in all respects: in terms of earnings, productivity, and equal opportunity. Micro studies on the impact of training confirm this impression: Although on-the-job training leads to higher short-term income effects, general training is superior in terms of long-term effects. Thus, labor market policy and corresponding evaluation research should focus on institutions strengthening the formation of learning skills and the complementarity of general and specific skills.

(3) Compensation and competence, finally, become effective only with cooperation at all levels of the labor market—at the firm level, the regional or sectoral level, the national, and, in the future more and more important, the supranational level. Cooperation seems to be the third key of any success story. Social institutions preventing opportunistic or free-rider behavior and ruinous competition (poaching) have been found in various forms.

The prevention of "leapfrogging" in wage formation, for example, can be brought about by centralized as well as by decentralized bargaining. Important is not the level of bargaining but the ability to institutionalize the "shadow of the future," which means long-term trust relationships and effective sanctions against defection in cooperation. Poaching and corresponding under investment in training can be prevented by collective funds and universal quality standards. In details, however, the knowledge of corresponding institutional equivalences is still poor. Apart from further evidence provided in the following chapters, we cannot abstain from the awkward conclusion that more research has to be done in this respect.

If the reader has arrived at this point, he or she may be disappointed by comparative evaluation research. Yet we hope that we are not blamed for having brought the message. Certainly, we could have told it better, but we are quite confident that this wouldn't have changed much of the content. On the other hand, there is no way out of comparative evaluation research. In a stimulating article on the comparative analytical power of case studies and comparative studies, Giovanni Sartori concluded:

> On balance, case studies sacrifice generality to depth and thickness of understanding, indeed to Verstehen; one knows more and better about less (less in extension). Conversely, comparative studies sacrifice understanding-in-context—and of context—to inclusiveness: one knows less about more. (Sartori 1991, 253)

Let us conclude with an analogy. We have to follow both routes, the macro as well as the micro approach of evaluation research in order to combine their respective strengths: Whereas macrolevel evaluation teaches us less about more, microlevel evaluation teaches us more about less.

Notes

1. The term is also used by Soskice, albeit in a narrower sense, replacing the term *corporatism* by referring to "relatively long-term and high-trust relations within and between institutions, and at micro as well as macro levels" (Soskice 1991, 5); Soskice restricts himself to "actor institutions" (firms, employers' and employees' associations, banks, governments), which we extend by "regulatory institutions" (civil rights, labor law, tax law, constitution of social insurance and of the political system). We argue that also "regulatory institutions" require coordination.

2. The "law of requisite variety" was originally formulated by W. Ross Ashby in his *Introduction to Cybernetics* and is expressed in the short version: "Only variety can destroy variety" (Ashby 1970 [1956], 207).

3. Impacts of other labor market policies such as negative or positive transfers and employment protection regulation will be mentioned in passing or dealt with in other chapters of this book.

4. At the beginning of 1993 the United States had already overcome its recession, whereas Japan, and even more so Germany, faced sharp reductions in manufacturing output employment throughout 1993.

5. In July 1992, without measures of active labor market policy (temporary public job creation, further training and retraining, short-time work, early retirement) unemployment in East Germany would have been 38.4 percent instead of the registered unemployment rate of 15.1 percent. *Employment Observatory*, no. 3/4 (1992): 14–15.

6. If any causal interpretation makes sense, then it is in the direction of high and persistent unemployment inducing increasing recourse of governments to ALMP.

7. To characterize, for instance, Sweden as a country with centralized wage setting (see, e.g., Freeman 1988b) is completely mistaken in view of the important local wage bargaining processes and the huge wage drift in Sweden (correctly stated, e.g., by Calmfors and Forslund 1991; Flanagan 1990).

8. The replication of their study by age groups is more difficult, since time series of labor market programs disaggregated by age groups and sex are not easily found.

9. With respect to the business cycle, i.e., the GDP growth rate.

10. In a similar review of microeconomic evaluations of labor market policies Gazier (1991) also refers mainly to results from the United States, apparently due to a lack of systematic evaluations for France. In West Germany there are a few attempts of microlevel evaluations (see Hofbauer and Dadzio 1987 and a summary of West German studies presented by Bellmann 1990). In general, results indicate positive effects of training programs on the probability of finding a job for the unemployed. However, Kasperek, Koop, and Koop (1991) criticized these results because of insufficient reliability of estimates and demonstrated a number of methodological deficiencies in the design of these evaluation attempts, notably the lack of adequate control groups and the risk of a serious selection bias in the estimated program effects.

11. General guidelines are outlined in Shadish, Cock, and Leviton (1991).

12. A recent overview of labor market theories and approaches to empirical tests of hypotheses derived from those theories is provided in Schoemann (1992).

13. A reason experiments are rare in Europe might be that program participation is

very much directed toward those who are most in need or who might benefit the most. Random selection of participants precludes such choices in the formulation of the program or of program administrators. The selection process involved in the discretionary power of program execution might itself become a subject for evaluation to test possible sources of discriminatory practices such as favoring male versus female participants or excluding ethnic minorities.

14. An influential economist in Germany has made this comparison explicitly to demonstrate the equivalence of labor markets and product markets: "At the core, unemployment is always a question of labor costs. For labor is like bananas, railway tickets or carpets: If the price increases, demand falls" (Engels 1985, 35; translation by the authors).

15. For a recent discussion about the usefulness and limits of P-efficiency see Hartog, Polachek, and Theeuwes 1992. We do not agree, however, with their conclusion that Pareto efficiency can be used to evaluate structural features such as rules, regulations, and institutions, except if one takes perfect competition as a reference point.

16. This concept is similar to "solidarity."

References

Akerloff, George A., and Yellen, Janet L., eds. 1986. *Efficiency Wage Models of the Labor Market.* Cambridge: Cambridge University Press.

Allen, H.L.; McCormick, B.; and O'Brien, R.J. 1991. "Unemployment and the Demand for Retraining: An Econometric Analysis." *Economic Journal* 101, no. 1: 190–201.

Appelbaum, Eileen, and Schettkat, Ronald. 1991. "Employment and Industrial Restructuring in the United States and West Germany." In *Beyond Keynesianism,* eds., E. Matzner and W. Streeck, 137–60. Aldershot: Edward Elgar.

Ashby, Ross W. 1970 [1956]. *An Introduction to Cybernetics.* London: Chapman & Hall University Paperbacks.

Barnow, Burt S. 1987. "The Impact of CETA Programmes on Earnings—A Review of the Literature." *Journal of Human Resources* 22, no. 2: 157–93.

Bassi, Laurie J. 1984. "Estimating the Effect of Training Programs with Non-Random Selection." In *The Review of Economics and Statistics,* 1984: 36–43.

Bassi, Laurie J. and Ashenfelter, Orley. 1986. "The Effect of Direct Job Creation and Training Programs on Low-Skilled Workers." In *Fighting Poverty,* ed., S. Danziger and D. Weinburg. Cambridge, Mass.: Harvard University Press.

Becker, Rolf. 1991. "Berufliche Weiterbildung und Berufsverlauf. Eine Längsschnittuntersuchung von drei Geburtskohorten." In *MittAB* 24: 351–64.

Becker, Rolf, and Schoemann, Klaus. 1992. *Zur Selektion beim Eintritt in die berufliche Weiterbildung.* Unpublished manuscript.

Bellmann, Lutz. 1990. "Labour Market Policies in Germany: An Evaluation of ABM and Training Measures." In *Labour Market Policies in the U.K and the F.R.G.: An Evaluation.* Report commissioned by the Anglo-German Foundation.

———. 1992. "Employment Measures in the Federal Republic of Germany: Their Effects on Duration Specific Outflow Rates from Unemployment." In *Labour Market Policies in the United Kingdom and the Federal Republic of Germany,* ed., R. Disney, 157–72. Mimeo.

Bellmann, Lutz, and Emmerich, Knut. 1992. "Union Bargaining, Wage Differentials and Employment." *Labour* 6, no. 2: 19–30.

Björklund, Anders. 1988. "What Experiments Are Needed for Manpower Policy?" *Journal of Human Resources* 23, no. 2 (Spring 1988): 267–77.

———. 1989. *Evaluations of Training Programmes: Experiences and Proposals for Future Research.* Discussion Paper FS I 89–13, Wissenschaftszentrum Berlin.

Blau, David, and Robins, Philip K. 1987. "Training Programs and Wages—A General Equilibrium Analysis of the Effects of Program Size." *Journal of Human Resources* 22: 113–25.

Bourdet, Yves, and Persson, Inga. 1992. *Does Labour Market Policy Matter? Long-Term Unemployment in France and Sweden.* Working Paper 6/1992 of the Department of Economics, University of Lund, Sweden.

Breen, Richard. 1992. "Job Changing and Job Loss in the Irish Youth Labour Market: A Test of a General Model." *European Sociological Review* 8, no. 2: 113–25.

Büchtemann, Christoph F. 1991. *Employment Security and Labour Markets: Assumptions, International Evidence, and Theoretical Implications.* Discussion Paper FS I 91–1, Wissenschaftszentrum Berlin.

Burtless, Gary. 1985. "Are Targeted Wage Subsidies Harmful? Evidence from a Wage Voucher Experiment." *Industrial and Labor Relations Review* 39, no. 1 (October 1985): 105–14.

Burtless, Gary, and Orr, Larry. 1986. "Are Classical Experiments Needed for Manpower Policy?" *Journal of Human Resources* 21, no. 4 (Fall 1986): 606–39.

Calmfors, Lars, and Forslund, Anders. 1991. "Real-Wage Determination and Labour Market Policies: The Swedish Experience." *Economic Journal* 101: 1130–48.

Coase, Roald H. 1992. "The Institutional Structure of Production." *American Economic Review* 82, no. 4: 713–19.

Danthine, Lennart, and Lambelet, Jean-Christian. 1987. "The Swiss Case." *European Policy* (October): 147–79.

Delander, Lennart. 1991. *Placement, Counselling, and Occupational Rehabilitation in Sweden.* Discussion Paper FS I 91–6, Wissenschaftszentrum Berlin.

Dickinson, Katherine P.; Johnson, Terry R.; and West, Richard W. 1986. "An Analysis of the Impact of CETA Programmes on Participants' Earnings." *Journal of Human Resources* 21, no. 1 (Winter 1986): 64–91.

Disney, Richard, ed. 1992. *Labour Market Policies in the United Kingdom and the Federal Republic of Germany.* Nürnberg/London: Report Commissioned for the Anglo-German Foundation, mimeo.

EC-Commission. 1990. *Employment in Europe 1990.* Luxembourg: Office for Official Publications for the European Communities.

———. 1991. *Employment in Europe 1991.* Luxembourg: Office for Official Publications for the European Communities.

Edwards, Richard, and Garonna, Paolo. 1991. *The Forgotten Link. Labor's Stake in International Economic Cooperation.* Savage, Maryland: Rowman & Littlefield.

Elster, Jon, ed. 1986. *Rational Choice.* Oxford: Basil Blackwell.

———. 1979. *Ulysses and the Sirens: Studies in Rationality and Irrationality.* Cambridge: Cambridge University Press.

Engels, Wolfram. 1985. *Über Freiheit, Gleichheit und Brüderlichkeit.* Frankfurt: Frankfurter Institut für wirtschaftspolitische Forschung.

Esser, Hartmut. 1990. "Habits, Frames and Rational Choice." Die Reichweite der Theorie der rationalen Wahl." *Zeitschrift für Soziologie* 19: 231–47.

Flanagan, Robert. 1990. "Centralized and Decentralized Pay Determination in Nordic Countries." In *Wage Formation and Macroeconomic Policy in the Nordic Countries,* ed., L. Calmfors, 395–416. Stockholm: SNS, Oxford: Oxford University Press.

Flanagan, Robert; Hartog, Joop; and Theeuwes, Jules. 1993. "Institutions and the Labour Market. Many Questions, Some Answers." In *Labour Markets and Institutions,* eds., J. Hartog and J. Theeuwes.

Florens, Jean-Pierre; Fougère, Denis; and Werquin, Patrick. 1990. "Durées de chômage et transitions sur le marché du travail." *Sociologie du travail* 32, no. 4: 439–68.

Frank, Robert H. 1985. *Choosing the Right Pond. Human Behaviour and the Quest for Status.* Oxford: Oxford University Press.

Freeman, Richard B. 1988a. "Evaluating the View That the United States Has No Unemployment Problems." *American Economic Review* 78: 294–99.

———. 1988b. "Labour Market Institutions and Economic Performance." *Economic Policy* (April): 64–80.

Gazier, Bernard. 1991. *Économie du Travail et de l'Emploi.* Paris, France: Éditions Dalloz.

Groot, Wim; Hartog, Joop; and Oosterbeck, Hessel. 1990. *Training Choice and Earnings.* Discussion Paper, Department of Economics, University of Amsterdam, no. 9027.

Hartog, Joop; Polachek, Solomon; and Theeuwes, Jules. 1993. "Evaluating Labour Market Performance." In *Labour Market Contracts and Institutions*, eds., J. Hartog and J. Theeuwes. Amsterdam: North-Holland, 415–46.

Hashimoto, Masanori, and Raisian, John. 1992. "Aspects of Labor Market Flexibility in Japan and the United States." In *Employment Security and Labor Market Flexibility*, ed., K. Koshiro, 78–101. Detroit: Wayne State University Press.

Heuss, Theodor. 1946. *Robert Bosch. Leben und Leistung.* Tübingen: Rainer Wunderlich Verlag.

Höcker, Herrad. 1992. *Berufliche Weiterbildung für Beschäftigung in Dänemark.* Discussion Paper FS I 92–8, Wissenschaftszentrum Berlin.

Hofbauer, H., and Dadzio, W. 1987. "Mittelfristige Wirkungen beruflicher Weiterbildung. Die berufliche Situation von Teilnehmern zwei Jahre nach Beendigung der Maßnahme." *Mitteilungen aus der Arbeitsmarkt- und Berufsforschung* 20, no. 2: 129–41.

Jackman, Richard; Pissarides, Christopher; and Savouri, Savva. 1990. "Labour Market Policies and Unemployment in the OECD." *Economic Policy* (October): 450–90.

Johannesson, Jan, and Schmid, Günther. 1980. "The Development of Labour Market Policy in Sweden and in Germany: Competing or Convergent Models to Combat Unemployment?" *European Journal of Political Research* 8: 387–406.

Kasperek, Peter, and Koop, Werner. 1991. "Zur Wirksamkeit von Fortbildungs- und Umschulungsmaßnahmen." *Mitteilungen aus der Arbeitsmarkt- und Berufsforschung* 24, no. 2: 317–32.

Koshiro, Kazutoshi. 1992. "Bonus Payments and Wage Flexibility in Japan." In *Employment Security and Labor Market Flexibility*, ed., K. Koshiro, 45–77. Detroit: Wayne State University Press.

Korpi, Tomas. 1992. *Employment Stability Following Unemployment: Manpower Programmes, Turnover and Recurrent Unemployment.* Paper presented at the Conference of the European Association of Labour Economists, Coventry, 1992.

Klundert, van de Th. 1990. "On Socioeconomic Causes of Wait Unemployment." *European Economic Review* 34: 1011–22.

Lalonde, Robert J. 1986. "Evaluating the Econometric Evaluations of Training Programs with Experimental Data." *American Economic Review* 76, no. 4 (September 1986): 604–20.

Langlois, Richard N., ed. 1986. *Economics As a Process. Essays in the New Institutional Economics.* Cambridge: Cambridge University Press.

Levy, Frank. 1988. *Dollars and Dreams. The Changing American Income Distribution.* New York and London: W.W. Norton.

Lynch, Lisa M. 1990. *Private Sector Training and the Earnings of Young Workers.* Revised NBER Working Paper no. 2060–88, June 1990.

Maier, Friederike. 1988. *Beschäftigungspolitik vor Ort.* Berlin: Edition sigma.

Matzner, Egon, and Streeck, Wolfgang, eds. 1991. *Beyond Keynesianism. The Socioeconomics of Production and Full Employment*. Aldershot/Brookfield: Edward Elgar.

Mizuno, Asao. 1992. "Japanese Wage Flexibility: An International Perspective." In *Employment Security and Labor Market Flexibility*, ed., K. Koshiro, 102–26. Detroit: Wayne State University Press.

Morgenstern, Oskar. 1966. *Spieltheorie und Wirtschaftswissenschaft*. Vienna-Munich: Verlag Oldenbourg.

Newton, James D. 1987. *Uncommon Friends. Life with Thomas Edison, Henry Ford, Harvey Firestone, Alexis Carrel, and Charles Lindbergh*. San Diego/New York/London: HBI Book.

North, Douglas C. 1991. "Institutions." *Journal of Economic Perspectives* 5, no. 1: 97–112.

OECD. 1991. *Employment Outlook*. Paris: Organisation for Economic Co-Operation and Development.

Peters, Aribert, and Schmid, Günther. 1982. *Aggregierte Wirkungsanalyse des arbeitsmarktpolitischen Programms der Bundesregierung für Regionen mit besonderen Beschäftigungsproblemen: Analyse der Beschäftigungswirkungen*. Discussion Paper IIM/LMP 82–32, Wissenschaftszentrum Berlin.

Phelps, Edmund, S. 1992. "A Review of Unemployment." *Journal of Economic Literature* 30: 1476–90.

Rein, Martin, and Freeman, Richard. 1988. The Dutch Choice. A Plea for Social Policy Complementarity to Work, 's-Gravenhage.

Sartori, Giovanni. 1991. "Comparing and Miscomparing." *Journal of Theoretical Politics* 3, no. 3: 243–57.

Scharpf, Fritz W. et al. 1982. *Implementationsprobleme offensiver Arbeitsmarktpolitik*. Frankfurt a.M.:Campus.

Schettkat, Ronald 1993. *Beschäftigungsstabilität in den Ländern der Europäischen Gemeinschaft*. Discussion Paper FS I 93–301, Wissenschaftszentrum Berlin.

Schmid, Günther. 1979. "The Impact of Selective Employment Policy: The Case of a Wage-Cost Subsidy Scheme in Germany 1974–75." *Journal of Industrial Economics* 27, no. 4: 339–58.

———. 1980. *Strukturierte Arbeitslosigkeit und Arbeitsmarktpolitik*. Königstein i.Ts.:Athenäum.

———. 1991. *Flexible Koordination: Instrumentarium erfolgreicher Beschäftigungspolitik aus internationaler Perspektive*. Discussion Paper FS I 91–8, Wissenschaftszentrum Berlin.

Schmid, Günther, and Peters, Aribert. 1982. "The German Federal Employment Program for Regions with Special Employment Problems: An Evaluation." *Regional Science and Urban Economics* 12: 99–119.

Schmid, Günther; Reissert, Bernd; and Bruche, Gert. 1992. *Unemployment Insurance and Active Labor Market Policy. An International Comparison of Financing Systems*. Detroit: Wayne State University Press.

Schmidt, Manfred. 1985. *Der Schweizerische Weg zur Vollbeschäftigung*. Frankfurt: Campus.

Schoemann, Klaus. 1992. *Country, Sex and Sector Differences in the Dynamics of Education and Wage Growth*. Ph.D. thesis submitted to the Free University of Berlin.

Semlinger, Klaus. 1988. *Staatliche Intervention durch Dienstleistungen*. Berlin: Edition sigma.

Semlinger, Klaus, and Schmid, Günther. 1985. *Arbeitsmarktpolitik für Behinderte*. Basel: Birkhäuser.

Sengenberger, Werner. 1992. "Revisiting the Legal and Institutional Framework for Employment Security: An International Comparative Perspective." In *Employment Security and Labor Market Flexibility: An International Perspective*, ed., Kazutoshi Koshiro, 150–82. Detroit, Wayne State University Press.

Shadish, William R.; Cook, Thomas D.; and Leviton, Laura C. 1991. *Foundations of Program Evaluation—Theories of Practice*. Newbury Park: Sage Publications.

Simon, Herbert A. 1976 [1945]. *Administrative Behavior. A Study of Decision-Making Processes in Administrative Organization*. New York/London: Free Press/Collier Macmillan, 3rd ed.

Solow, Robert M. 1990. *The Labor Market As a Social Institution*. Oxford: Basil Blackwell.

Soskice, David. 1990. "Wage Determination. The Changing Role of Institutions in Advanced Industrialized Countries." *Oxford Review of Economic Policy* 6, no. 4: 36–61.

———. 1992. "The Institutional Infrastructure for International Competitiveness: A Comparative Analysis of the UK and Germany." In *The Economics of the New Europa* (International Economics Association Conference Volume), eds., Anthony B. Atkinson and Renato Brunetta, forthcoming. London: Macmillan.

Soskice, David, and Schettkat, Ronald. 1993. "West German Labor Market Institutions and East German Transformation." In *Labor and an Integrated Europe*, eds., Lloyd Ulman, Barry Eichengreen, and William T. Dickens. Washington: Brookings Institution, 102: 127.

Streeck, Wolfgang. 1991. "On the Institutional Conditions of Diversified Quality Production." In *Beyond Keynesianism*, eds., Egon Matzner and Wolfgang Streeck, 21–61.

Ting, Yuan. 1991. "The Impact of Job Training Programmes on the Reemployment Probability of Dislocated Workers." *Policy Studies Review* 10, nos. 2/3: 31–44.

Wilensky, Harold L. 1992. "The Great American Job Creation Machine in Comparative Perspective." *Industrial Relations* 31, no. 3: 473–88.

2

Employment Protection and Labor Force Adjustment In EC Countries

Hugh G. Mosley

Introduction

Although employment protection policies have been controversial—and are likely to be increasingly so as the current recession persists—relatively little is known in practice about the importance and impact of these regulations across the European Community as a whole. This chapter surveys differences and similarities in regulations and attempts to assess their impact. It examines, in particular, how these policies have been modified in the face of the widespread deregulation trends of the 1980s and, using data from the European Labor Force Survey (ELFS), attempts to assess the impact of national regulatory frameworks. It also considers the impact of employment protection regulations in relationship to active labor market policies, which may promote softer forms of external adjustment (e.g., early retirement) or alternative forms of internal adjustment (e.g., short-time work).

Employment protection regulations consist of both individual protection against unfair dismissal and special procedures relating to collective or mass redundancies—whether based on law or collective agreement—that limit the discretion of firms in terminating an employment relationship. They include, for example, prior consultation with trade unions or works councils, notification of

The author would like to thank Marie-Claude Villeval and Ulrich Walwei for their comments and suggestions on an earlier version. The present version has also benefited greatly from Terry Ward's expert editorial queries and suggestions in preparing a revised version, which was published in part as chapter 7, "Employment Protection and Labor Force Adjustment in the Member States," in the European Commission's 1993 *Employment in Europe* report. The author is indebted in particular to Günther Schmid for his careful reading and perceptive comments on both previous versions. The research on which this chapter is based was done in collaboration with Thomas Kruppe.

dismissals to public authorities, the right of appeal against unfair dismissal, and special protection for certain groups (such as pregnant women and the disabled). They also include provisions specifying notice requirements and severance pay arrangements.

Although not a component of dismissal regulations, regulations pertaining to fixed-term, temporary, and other atypical forms of employment are an essential element of the broader employment security regime in that they determine the scope for alternative "flexible" forms of employment and have been a primary focus of deregulation. These various aspects are discussed in turn below. Although occupational health and safety, child labor, and minimum wage legislation complement employment protection in a broad sense and should also be considered in any full assessment of the regulatory framework, they are outside the scope of this chapter.

While the explicit goal of employment protection regulations is to protect against unfair dismissal and, increasingly, to promote alternatives to redundancy, by constraining the freedom of firms to reduce their work forces, they may also entail considerable costs for enterprises, especially under adverse economic conditions (Giersch 1985).[1] Much debate about employment protection regulations has, therefore, focused on allegedly negative effects on the hiring behavior of firms and on the efficient functioning of the labor market. Because of the regulations, it is argued, firms are likely to be discouraged from taking on new employees and encouraged to make more use of contingent workers as well as to discriminate against female, handicapped, or older workers, who might enjoy special protection against dismissal. It is also argued that regulations might reduce labor mobility, increasing labor market segmentation between those covered by regulation and those not (i.e., "insiders and outsiders") and thus prolonging the average duration of unemployment.

Persuasive arguments are also made for the beneficial effects of employment protection. Apart from its principal historical rationale based on equity considerations, economic arguments based on market failure have also been advanced: For example, it is argued that there is a power asymmetry in the labor market in the absence of intervention and that, by reestablishing the balance, labor legislation creates the preconditions for efficient market transactions (Buttler et al. 1992; Büchtemann 1991). Similarly, it is argued, free contracting between labor market parties does not adequately take into consideration the full costs of lay-offs to individuals and to communities, and to some extent dismissal regulations compel firms to take more account of these when making employment decisions (Hamermesh 1987; Addison 1989).

At the same time, regulations can impose significant nonwage labor costs on firms and national economies, causing concern—as the recent controversy over the closing of Hoover's plant in Dijon and transfer of its operations to Scotland illustrates—that countries with more stringent employment protection regimes may be put at a competitive disadvantage.[2]

Dismissal Regulations

The following section presents an overview of dismissal procedures in the EC states applicable to individual contract terminations and to collective redundancies. The relative levels and group incidence of national notice and severance pay requirements are compared, and collateral regulations on fixed-term employment, which have been a focus of deregulation, are surveyed.

Unfair Dismissal Procedures

Although the stringency of unfair dismissal regulations and applicable sanctions differs, sometimes markedly, all EC states, except Denmark, provide some form of statutory right against unfair dismissal. Most countries require that employees be given a written statement of the reasons (which can serve as the basis for a subsequent unfair dismissal claim) or that employers consult in advance with employee representatives. Four—Luxembourg, Portugal, Spain, and the United Kingdom—require both. Only one country—the Netherlands—still requires prior administrative authorization even in cases of individual dismissal.

In all other countries some form of monetary compensation is usual, though there are large differences in the maximum statutory amounts—which vary from a low maximum of six months' pay in Belgium to more than three years' in Spain. In seven countries, severance payments are mandatory either for all except summary dismissals (Denmark, France, Greece, Italy, and Spain) or for those made redundant (Ireland and the United Kingdom).[3]

In general, the extent of protection depends on the length of service. In a number of countries workers have to serve a probationary or qualifying period before being eligible for dismissal protection (e.g., six months in Germany and two years in the United Kingdom). Moreover, monetary compensation for unfair dismissal varies with length of service (and even explicitly with age) even for protected workers. In a number of countries unfairly dismissed employees may also in principle be able to claim reinstatement, although this is rarely achieved in practice, except apparently in Italy.

Collective Redundancy Procedures

There is a great deal more convergence within the EC with regard to procedures applicable to collective redundancies. Special procedures on this exist in all countries. All require prior consultation with employee representatives and advance notice of mass dismissals to labor market authorities. This uniformity is primarily a reflection of the impact of the EC Council Directive on collective redundancies (75/129 of 17 February 1975).[4]

Under this directive, EC countries are required to establish a statutory consultation procedure for the purpose of avoiding proposed redundancies or alleviating their impact. The employer is required not only to notify and consult with employee representatives but also to provide them with all necessary information (in written form) on the number of dismissals, the reasons for them, the time-table, and so on, and to communicate the same information to the national labor market authorities. The directive also requires a delay of at least thirty days before the redundancies are implemented.[5]

Although not required by the EC directive, all member states, apart from Germany, provide some form of statutory redundancy payments, and in Germany obligatory "social plans," in which severance payments are a key feature, are a partial equivalent. EC states differ primarily in the way in which they define mass dismissals, to which the special regulations apply. In France, Portugal, and Spain the definition is stricter than the EC minimum specified in the directive.[6] Moreover, four countries—the Netherlands, Greece, Portugal, and Spain—go significantly beyond the relevant EC directive in requiring not only prior notification but also prior authorization of mass dismissals by national labor authorities.

Although this is also a policy area in which EC-level regulations have already established meaningful international standards, major differences in the stringency of the applicable procedures still exist.

Notice and Severance Requirements

Mandatory periods of notice and severance payments are an important constraint on labor force adjustment, due to the firing costs they impose on firms. Indeed, they probably represent the largest component of firing costs, since they are a normal cost of dismissals, in contrast to relatively infrequent unfair dismissal claims.[7] Unlike unfair dismissal procedures, their costs can be readily compared in terms of entitlements to weeks of pay due certain hypothetical types of em-ployees under the respective national regulations (Figure 2.1). The (unweighted) European average cost for all subgroups amounted to 22 weeks' pay c. 1989–90. Since only statutory regulations and those based on nationally applicable collective agreements are considered (information on sectoral agreements or company practices is not available), the reported entitlements represent national floors rather than actual levels of protection. Nevertheless, it seems plausible to assume that the index reflects broad national differences in levels of protection.[8]

There are, however, striking differences across subgroups. Whereas for white-collar employees the EC average was 27.6 weeks of pay, it was only 16.7 weeks for blue-collar workers. This difference is entirely attributable to five of the ten EC countries surveyed in which white-collar employees enjoy markedly higher levels of statutory protection—Belgium, Denmark, Germany, Greece, and Italy.[9] In four of the other countries—Ireland, the Netherlands, Spain, and the United Kingdom—the two groups are treated equally. Only France provides somewhat better protection for blue-collar employees.

Figure 2.1 **National Notice and Severance Pay Entitlements by Status and Age Groups**

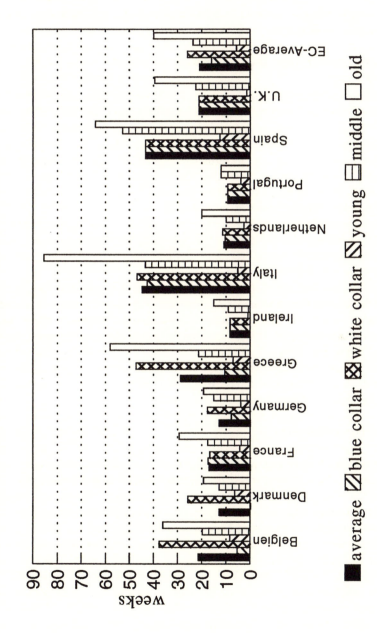

weeks

■ average ▨ blue collar ▨ white collar ▨ young ▦ middle □ old

Sources: Based on European Commission 1991, European Industrial Relations Review 1989, and national sources.
Note: Includes changes up to 1990. See explanation in footnote 8.

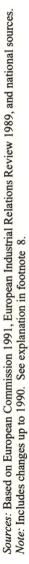

The second and most universal feature is the greater protection provided to more senior workers in all national employment protection regimes, this being especially so in Italy and Greece. In the former, someone aged fifty-five with more than twenty years service is entitled to 85 weeks' pay if made redundant. For young employees under twenty-five years of age, the average entitlement was less than 5 weeks' pay in six EC states, though over 12 weeks in Spain.[10]

Fixed-Term and Temporary Employment

Fixed-term contracts and other temporary arrangements give enterprises the possibility of engaging workers for a limited period and, therefore, of bypassing normal dismissal procedures and notice and severance requirements. While there are often good reasons for the choice of fixed-term rather than permanent employment contracts, they are, nevertheless, potentially open to abuse precisely because they enable employers to avoid the restrictions and costs attached to the latter. Restrictive dismissal regulations thus usually require collateral regulation of fixed-term contracts to prevent such abuse.

Since Denmark, Ireland, and the United Kingdom have relatively weak employment protection regulations, it is not surprising that they also do not regulate fixed-term contracts (Figure 2.2). All other countries with moderately strong or strong dismissal protection, except Belgium and the Netherlands, restrict the circumstances under which fixed-term contracts may be used. In Belgium and the Netherlands it is probable that the "missing" regulation is based on collective bargaining—which is strong at a sectoral level in both countries—rather than on legislation. Moreover, in both countries, unlike in Denmark, Ireland, and the United Kingdom, there are limits on the renewal of fixed-term contracts. In Belgium no renewal is allowed except under special circumstances, while in the Netherlands, a contract can be renewed only once (and then can only be terminated by authorization of the regional labor office).

Recent National Trends

The impact of deregulation trends on employment protection has differed significantly in EC states over the past decade (see below). In brief, there have been substantial changes in six states, the five largest plus Portugal. No uniform pattern of liberalization is, however, evident. In only three countries have employment protection regulations been weakened by eliminating the requirement of official authorization of redundancies (France), by formally permitting dismissals for economic reasons (Portugal), by directly limiting unfair dismissal coverage (the United Kingdom). In two countries employment protection was actually strengthened by extending coverage to smaller enterprises (Italy) or by increasing sanctions (Spain).

Perhaps the most significant common pattern is not the weakening of employ-

Figure 2.2 **Regulations Applicable to Fixed-Term Contracts in EC Member States**

COUNTRY	Special Cir- cumstances	Max. Duration (including renewals)	Limitations on Renewals
Belgium	no restrictions	no limit	not permitted[1]
Denmark	no restrictions[2]	no limit	no limit
France	restricted	18 months	once
Germany	restricted[3]	no limit[4]	no limit[5]
Greece	restricted	no limit	two
Ireland	no restrictions	no limit	no limit
Italy	restricted[6]	6 to 12 months	once[7]
Luxembourg	restricted	24 months	twice
Netherlands	no restrictions	no limit	once[8]
Portugal	restricted	three years	twice
Spain	restricted	three years	no limit
U.K.	no restrictions	no limit	no limit

Notes:

1   Except under exceptional circumstances.
2   Trade union consent required.
3   Fixed-term contracts under the Employment Promotion Act (EPA) require no particular justification.
4   18 to 24 months for contract under the EPA.
5   Fixed-term contracts concluded under the EPA may not be renewed.
6   Fixed-term contracts may also be concluded in derogation of these regulations when based on a collective agreement.
7   Under exceptional circumstances.
8   If renewed, contract can only be terminated with authorization of director of regional labor office.

Sources: ''The Regulation of Working Conditions in Member States of the European Community,'' *Social Europe Supplement* (April 1992) and national sources. Statutory regulations as of January 1992.

ment protection regulations per se but the recurrent pattern of liberalization of regulations governing the use of temporary employment as a means of achieving work force flexibility. This has been the case in five of the six countries where significant changes occurred, the United Kingdom being the exception, though here the extension of the qualifying period for unfair dismissal protection to two years had the same effect by excluding short-term employment relations from coverage.

Deregulation Trends in EC States

France shows the most erratic pattern of development, due largely to major shifts in the composition of government during the 1980s. The focus of deregulation—and after 1989, "reregulation"—has been on redundancies and fixed-term contracts. The requirement for prior official authorization of all dismissals for economic reasons (redundancy) was abolished after the change of government in 1986. Obligations were also placed on firms with fifty or more employees to formulate a "social plan" whenever ten or more employees were made redundant, and a general requirement was introduced that all employees dismissed for economic reasons be offered an opportunity to undergo training (*contrat de conversion*). After another change in government in 1989, there was some reversal of policy, the timetable for redundancy procedures being extended and the role of public authorities strengthened. This trend toward reregulation continued in January 1993, in response to the current recession, with the introduction of a requirement for prior official approval of obligatory social plans in the event of collective redundancies. Regulations pertaining to unfair dismissal for disciplinary reasons were largely unaffected by these shifts.

Regulation of temporary work in France has fluctuated in a similar way. After initially attempting to reverse the trend toward temporary employment, the socialist government itself changed course in 1985. New legislation extended the maximum duration of temporary employment and expanded the catalog of reasons justifying exceptions to permanent employment contracts. In 1986, the new center-right government further liberalized temporary employment by eliminating any requirement for such contracts to be justified in terms of specified circumstances as well as extending their maximum duration to two years. In 1990, after another change of government, fixed-term contracts had once more to be justified in terms of a limited number of special circumstances.

By contrast, in Germany deregulation tendencies have been weak and largely confined to a limited liberalization of fixed-term employment contracts. Whereas before labor fixed-term contracts were restricted to certain well-defined situations such as seasonal work, temporary replacement of an absent employee, and temporary peaks in demand, the 1985 Employment Promotion Act permits the use of such contracts without reference to special justifying circumstances.[11] Originally enacted as a time-limited measure, the legislation was extended in 1990 for an additional six years, until the end of 1995. Although the 1985 act was controversial, its impact appears to have been less than was anticipated. On the other hand, a social plan is still enforceable in cases of partial or total plant closures. Unfair dismissal regulations themselves remained substantially unchanged.

Italy, which has the most highly regulated labor market in the EC, is the only country to have actually strengthened employment protection. In particular, in 1990, unfair dismissal regulations dating from the late 1960s were extended to previously exempt small firms. Deregulation in Italy has been mainly confined to liberalizing fixed-term contracts for youth fifteen to twenty-nine years of age, under the guise of training contracts.

The United Kingdom shows the most consistent trend toward liberalization of unfair dismissal regulations largely in the form of an extension of the qualifying period for unfair dismissal coverage from 26 to 105 weeks of continuous employment. There have also been a number of technical changes in procedures designed to discourage frivolous claims. Regulations pertaining to collective redundancies have been unaffected, while fixed-term and other atypical forms of employment have never been subject to regulatory restraint in the United Kingdom.

Spain and Portugal, with relatively strong protection against dismissal for permanent employees, have liberalized the use of fixed-term contracts. In Spain, beginning in 1980, the circumstances in which fixed-term contracts are permissible were progressively expanded, and by the late 1980s Spain had by far the highest percentage of employees on such atypical contracts (c. 25 percent) of any EC country (Amoros and Rojo 1991). Spain still requires prior administrative approval of collective redundancies, and in 1990 the already relatively high maximum on monetary compensation for unfair dismissal was increased from forty-two to fifty-four months of pay.

In Portugal dismissal without "just cause" is prohibited by the constitution and until recently limited to cases of personal misconduct. In practice, employers made liberal use of fixed-term contracts to circumvent those restrictions, and Portugal is second only to Spain in the use of such contracts. In 1989 reformers finally succeeded in securing a statutory basis for dismissal for economic reasons, while at the same time imposing new limitations on the use of fixed-term contracts (maximum duration of three years including at most two renewals).

Employment Protection and Labor Force Adjustment

This section investigates the impact of employment protection regulations on national adjustment patterns. First, the stringency of employment protection regulations is compared based on results of ad hoc employer surveys. Then national patterns of the incidence of involuntary outflows from employment are described based on results from the ELFS. Finally, evidence for the impact of the regulatory framework on national patterns is assessed.

Employers' Perceptions

Dismissal procedures cannot be assessed simply by comparing the regulations themselves. Despite differences in detail described above, regulations on unfair dismissal or collective redundancies are broadly similar in EC states, especially in comparison with laissez-faire regimes such as found in the United States. This formal similarity is, however, misleading, since judicial interpretation as well as industrial relations practice may differ markedly. Moreover, statutory provisions

Figure 2.3 **Reputational Employment Protection, 1985 and 1989**

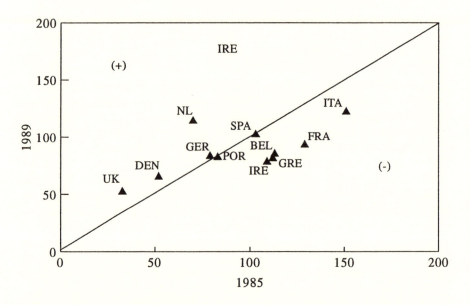

Sources: Indices calculated on basis of survey results reported in *European Economy* no. 27 (March 1986) and no. 47 (March 1991).

Note: Spain and Portugal did not participate in 1985 (1989 values imputed). Denmark values interpolated for both years as described in text. See footnote 12 for explanation of Index.

are supplemented in all countries by collective agreements, which can also vary among sectors. Statutory regulations are, however, a useful indicator of national differences in minimum standards.

Employer surveys provide a more direct basis for comparing the perceived impact of employment protection regulations. Ad hoc employer surveys sponsored by the European Commission in 1985 and 1989 included questions on the importance of regulatory restraints on hiring and firing of workers, which we have used to compute an index of the stringency of employment protection in EC states.[12] The results show that employers' perceptions of the severity of constraints tended either to remain largely unchanged or to diminish between these two years, though the rank order of countries remained much the same (Figure 2.3). The Netherlands is the principal exception, with restrictions becoming much more stringent in the eyes of employers, even though there were no substantial changes in regulations.[13] While the perceived stringency of regulations also increased in the United Kingdom, it remained significantly lower than in any other EC country. The rank order of employers' perceptions largely confirms the conventional wisdom, in that restrictions are regarded as most severe in Italy and least severe in the United Kingdom, with France and then Germany in between.

The liberalization of French employment protection policies, in the later half of the 1980s, seems to be reflected in the lower relative ranking of France in the 1989 survey compared with 1985 (fourth instead of second); Germany ranked sixth in both surveys.

Involuntary Termination in EC States

The impact of national differences in employment protection on employers and on the functioning of the labor market can be assessed only by examining the adjustment behavior of firms. Unfortunately, only limited comparative data are available on flows into employment and on the composition of outflows—and certainly not for all EC countries. Due to these data limitations most comparative research on adjustment has focused on changes in employment levels. There is no alternative, therefore, but to resort to indirect evidence.

One source of relevant data is the European Labor Force Survey (ELFS) coordinated by the Statistical Office of the European Communities (EU-ROSTAT) in Luxembourg. The data reported below on outflows from employment are drawn in particular from the ELFS's question "Main Reasons for Leaving Last Job," which gives details on the number of people who have lost their jobs during the preceding six months and their reasons for leaving. Relating these figures to the number of people in dependent employment gives some indication of the rate of involuntary job loss in EC countries.

The results, however, need to be interpreted with caution. The principal shortcoming of the data is that the ELFS survey design reports only on those job losers who are without employment (unemployed or inactive) at the time of the survey. Those job losers who have already reentered employment are not included. In periods of employment growth, the latter group may even outnumber the former.[14] This means that the data underestimate the actual level of involuntary separations and are primarily useful as a comparative indicator of national differences in the relative level of involuntary terminations. For this reason the ELFS data on involuntary outflows are reported here in the form of indices based on the unweighted average for all EC countries.[15]

Second, the scale of job losses will clearly be affected by the rate of economic growth, which may vary significantly across EC countries. In order to compare rates of involuntary job loss, the ELFS results ideally should be corrected for this influence. This is not easy to do, but to reduce its importance, the results discussed here are for 1989, a year of good economic growth near the peak of the last business cycle in most EC countries except Denmark, where GDP growth was only just over 1 percent.

The ELFS data show a significant variation in the rate of involuntary job loss among EC countries, whether due to dismissal or at the end of a fixed-term contract.[16] Rates of involuntary job loss were highest in Spain and Denmark, whereas Germany together with Belgium had the lowest overall reported rates of involuntary separations during the period surveyed, followed by the Netherlands and the United Kingdom.[17] Italy has an intermediate rate of involuntary separations, and France is above average, ranking third behind Denmark and Spain. At the extremes, the risk of involuntary job loss in Spain was more than five times as great as in the two low-risk countries (Figure 2.4).

There was also significant variation among EC states in the relative importance of dismissals as opposed to terminations at the end of fixed-term contracts in national patterns. Whereas Denmark ranked relatively high in both, Germany, Belgium, Italy, and the Netherlands were low in both categories. Spain and Portugal combine high reliance on fixed-term terminations with relatively low dismissal rates. By contrast, Ireland shows a pattern of high reliance on dismissals with below-average adjustment via fixed-term terminations.

These results generally correspond with what would be expected given the differences in institutional regimes. The principal exceptions are Belgium and the Netherlands, where there is little statutory regulation of fixed-term contracts, but where this form of employment adjustment is relatively little used (possibly because it is constrained by collective bargaining, as noted above).

The other exception is the United Kingdom, where, despite the laxity of regulations, the dismissal rate was relatively low. There appear to be two possible explanations for this. The most plausible is that the spring of 1989, when the ELFS was conducted, was near the peak of the business cycle, which would naturally depress the rate of job loss, especially since the elasticity of the British dismissal rate over the economic cycle is unusually high. In all other years between 1983 and 1991 the rate of involuntary job loss in the United Kingdom was higher. A second possible reason is that a relatively high proportion of job losses in the United Kingdom may have taken the form of voluntary redundancies, which may not be reported as dismissals in the ELFS.

We can examine the impact of regulatory regimes on adjustment patterns more systematically by juxtaposing our index of the severity of employment protection in 1989 (see Figure 2.3 above) with observed patterns of relative risk of involuntary job loss as reflected in the ELFS (see Figure 2.4). Although countries with more stringent employment protection regimes, as perceived by employers, might be expected to have lower rates of involuntary job loss, this is *not* reflected in the ELFS data. A different picture emerges, however, if we distinguish between dismissals and terminations at the end of fixed-term contracts. While there is no association between employment protection and fixed-term separation rates—and hence total involuntary job loss—there is a fairly strong negative relationship between our index of the strength of employment protection and dismissal rates (Figure 2.5). This relationship is even stronger if the dismissal rates for males are examined separately.

Apparently, our index of employment protection based on employers' perceptions is a good predictor only of protection against dismissal. These results are plausible in light of the frequent coincidence of liberalization of temporary employment with stringent regulation of dismissals.

Figure 2.4 **EC Relative Risk of Involuntary Termination, 1989**

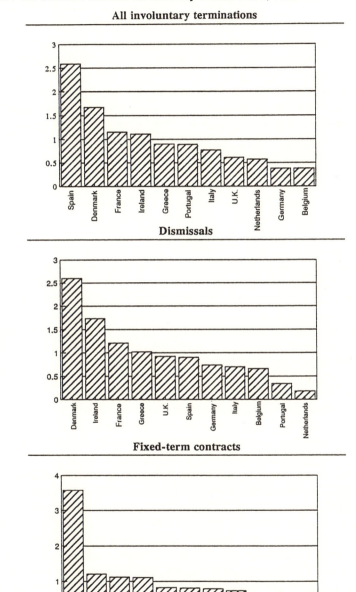

Source: Eurostat, Labor Force Survey 1989 and own calculations.

Figure 2.5 **Employment Protection and Dismissals, 1989**

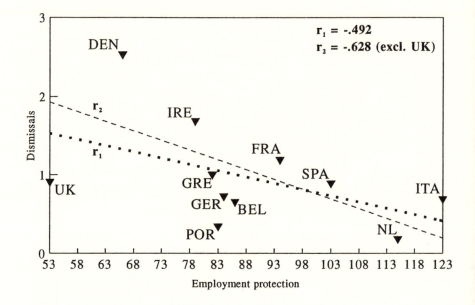

Source: See Figures 2.3 and 2.4.

Trends in Temporary Employment

As noted, those countries that have liberalized the use of temporary work, especially fixed-term contracts, in the 1980s showed a correspondingly high rate of job loss at the end of fixed-term contracts in 1989. The impact of deregulation is also reflected in changes in the importance of temporary employment in EC states.

In several countries in which restrictions on fixed-term contracts were relaxed, their importance increased significantly during the 1980s. This is especially the case in Spain, where the share of employees in temporary jobs increased from 16 percent in 1987 to over 32 percent in 1991, and in France, where the rise was from 3 percent in 1983 to over 10 percent in 1991 (Figure 2.6). It also seems to be true of Portugal until 1988, although no ELFS data are available for the years prior to 1986. The share of temporary jobs rose from 13 percent in 1986 to over 16 percent in 1991—and according to national accounts there was a substantial increase during the early 1980s. Only cyclical fluctuations but no secular changes in the level of temporary employment are discernible in other EC countries.

Although, with the exception of Spain and to a lesser extent Greece and Portugal (where they represent 14–15 percent of the total), temporary jobs still

Figure 2.6 **Temporary Employment in EC States**

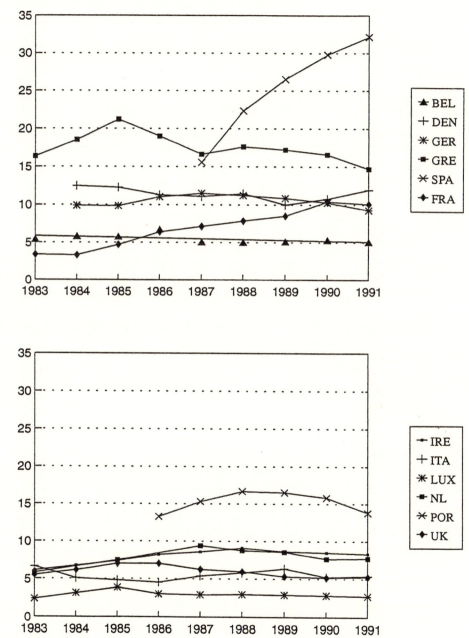

Source: Eurostat, Labor Force Survey 1983–1991 as reported in Eurostat 1993, Table 30.

account for a relatively small proportion of total employment, in a number of states—France, for example—they have come to be a significant form of entry into employment. (For firms with fifty or more employees in France, most new recruits start on fixed-term contracts).

Another factor that may have considerable influence on adjustment patterns is the linkage between active labor market policies and labor force adjustment, which is discussed in the following section.

Employment Protection and Active Labor Market Policies

This section discusses the impact of labor market policy measures on adjustment patterns. Drawing on data from the ELFS, particular attention is given to the incidence of short-time working and early retirement for labor market reasons in EC countries and to national patterns of labor market policy expenditure for employment adjustment.

In our view, employment protection regulations are best understood as one component of a broader set of policies for dealing with redundancy situations, in which labor market policies also play an important role. Active policies may promote either more benign forms of external adjustment for redundant employees (e.g., early retirement) or alternative forms of internal workforce adjustment such as retraining or short-time work. From this point of view, labor market policies not only impose constraints on firms in the form of dismissal regulations but also positively facilitate employment security in enterprises through "public risk sharing" (Osterman 1993).

Short-Time Work

Most EC countries have schemes to promote temporary reductions in working time during periods of slack demand, whether achieved through short-time work or temporary layoff. ELFS data on reduced working time for economic reasons provide some indication of the relative frequency and scale of variation in working hours as a mechanism for adjusting employment.

In 1989, when economic activity was near its peak in most countries, only a small proportion of employees worked fewer than normal hours for economic reasons, as might be expected. Nevertheless, the numbers were significant in relation to the number of dismissals—in the EC as a whole about one-third as high and in Italy almost the same (Figure 2.7). Although not all short-time work would have otherwise resulted in redundancies, the data suggest that it certainly had a significant impact on national dismissal rates even during a period of economic expansion (Italy being the most outstanding example).

Early Retirement

Since employment protection in many countries is especially strong for older workers, early retirement programs might be expected to be an important strategy for firms in those countries to shed labor. ELFS data for 1989 on those

Figure 2.7 **Dismissals and Short-Time Work, 1989**

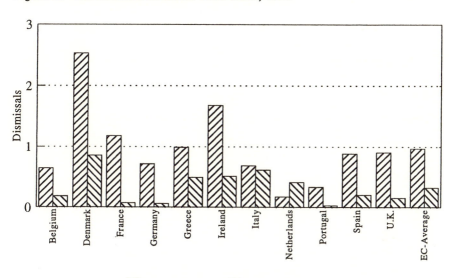

☑ Dismissal rate ◨ Short-time work rate*

Source: Short-time estimated on basis of 1989 Eurostat Labor Force Survey results. Dismissals as in Figure 2.4 (EC average = 1).
* Full-time equivalents.

retiring early indicate some relationship between the frequency of early retirement and the perceived severity of employment protection, though this association seems to be confined to northern European countries. In the Netherlands, Belgium, France, and Germany, where employment protection is relatively stringent, the proportion of workers taking early retirement was well above that in other countries (Figure 2.8). In Spain and Italy, however, where employment protection is also regarded as relatively stringent, there was a low incidence of early retirement. If early retirement for health reasons is included, which may, in many countries, be a functional equivalent for early retirement for economic reasons, we find a much stronger relationship, although Spain in particular is still an extreme outlier.[18]

Expenditures for Employment Adjustment Measures in Public Labor Market Policy

Examination of patterns of labor market policy expenditure in the four largest European states indicates that the constraints imposed on enterprises by employment protection regulations are significantly offset by public spending on employment adjustment measures.

Figure 2.8 **Employment Protection and Early Retirement, 1989**

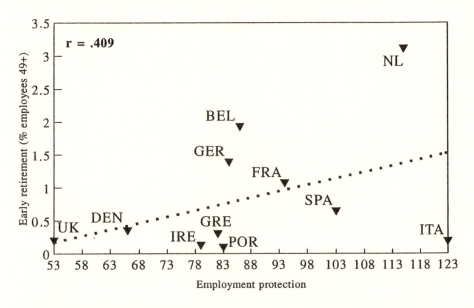

Sources: Early retirement estimates from Eurostat, Labor Force Survey 1989. Employment protection as in Figure 2.3.

This is particularly true of France, where such expenditure over the period 1985–88 was higher than in the other three countries, at over 2 percent of GDP, and accounted for a much larger share (74 percent) of total labor market spending (Table 2.1). Support for firms and industries undergoing restructuring was especially important, exceeding expenditure on other active measures by more than five to one, and taking predominantly the form of early retirement. French labor market policy also offers a full range of regular active labor market programs as well as relatively generous unemployment benefits. Although France also has a major short-time work program, this form of internal adjustment was less important than in Germany or Italy.

While labor market policy expenditure in Italy was below average at c. 1.5 percent of GDP, a relatively high proportion was directed at employment adjustment and, in particular, at firms and industries in economic difficulty. This took the form largely of short-time work. By contrast, expenditures for regular programs for active workers and even unemployment benefits were negligible in Italy during the 1985–88 period examined.

The United Kingdom had the lowest level of expenditure on adjustment measures, both as a percentage of GDP (0.5 percent) and as a percentage of all labor market expenditure (20.4 percent), with correspondingly higher levels of expenditure on problem groups. There is, therefore, in the United Kingdom a lack of

Table 2.1

Adjustment-Oriented Measures for Employees at Risk and Displaced Workers (% GDP)
(average 1985–1988)

	France		Germany		Italy		U.K.	
	% GDP	% Total	% GDP	% Total	% GDP	% Total	% GDP	% Total
Accompanying measures	2.19	73.9%	1.20	52.3%	0.89	57.9%	0.52	20.4%
Special programs[a]	0.99	33.6%	0.16	6.9%	0.83	54.0%	0.08	3.0%
Internal adjustment	0.03	1.0%	0.12	5.1%	0.37	24.0%	—	0.0%
External adjustment	0.97	32.6%	0.04	1.7%	0.46	29.9%	0.08	3.0%
Regular active programs[b]	0.19	6.5%	0.27	11.7%	0.01	0.4%	0.07	2.7%
Unemployment compensation[c]	1.00	33.8%	0.77	33.7%	0.06	3.6%	0.37	14.7%
Placement service and administration	0.13	4.3%	0.21	9.3%	0.08	5.4%	0.14	5.7%
Measures for problem groups[d]	0.65	21.8%	0.88	38.5%	0.56	36.7%	1.87	73.9%
Total labor market expenditure	2.96	100%	2.30	100%	1.54	100%	2.54	100%

Source: Adapted from OECD labor market policy expenditure data (OECD 1990), Eurostat and national sources.

[a] This category includes programs directed largely or exclusively at adjustment situations in enterprises in economic difficulty or displaced workers.

[b] Programs primarily for individuals with a continuous work history and strong labor force attachment but not targeted on employees in enterprises in difficulty or displaced workers.

[c] Excluding special programs for displaced workers included above.

[d] Programs predominantly for labor market problem groups. Criteria are long-term unemployment, ineligibility for unemployment insurance benefits. Includes unemployment assistance.

both regular active programs—almost all resources being concentrated on problem groups—and special adjustment-oriented programs. Moreover, the United Kingdom is the only country of the four without a short-time work scheme to help firms avoid redundancies during cyclical downturns or when undergoing restructuring.

In Germany the ratio expenditure on employment adjustment to problem groups was lower than in France or Italy. Moreover, unlike the other three countries, expenditure on regular active programs exceeds that on support for special programs for firms and industries undergoing restructuring (by more than 2 : 1). The large German short-time work scheme has been the principal special program directed at adjustment situations, whereas other active programs, especially training programs, are administered as individual entitlements.

In the four countries, therefore, there is a strong correspondence between the stringency of employment protection and public expenditure for special programs providing alternative forms of internal and external adjustment. Thus, the United Kingdom, the country with the weakest employment protection regulations, also has the lowest level of expenditure on GDP (0.1 percent) and the lowest concentration of national expenditures (c. 3.0 percent) in the area of special measures. By contrast, Italy, which has the strongest tradition of employment protection, also shows the highest concentration of expenditures on special programs (54 percent) and ranks (at 0.8 percent) only slightly below France (1.0 percent) in expenditures on GDP in this category, although labor market policy expenditure on GDP is otherwise lowest in Italy. Germany ranks behind France and ahead of the United Kingdom in both categories, which is plausible in terms of the relative stringency of employment protection in these countries during the 1985–88 period.

General Conclusions

Although regulations differ in detail, there is a broad similarity in systems of employment protection in Europe. All EC states, except Denmark, provide statutory protection against unfair dismissal, and there is an even higher degree of convergence in procedures for collective redundancies, due in part to EC directives.

In practice, EC states can be divided into three groups in terms of restriction on firing workers, with Denmark, Ireland, and the United Kingdom having the least restrictive dismissal regulations, especially for terminations for economic reasons, and Greece, the Netherlands, Portugal, Spain, and Italy forming another group with very significant restraints even on terminations for economic reasons.[19] Belgium, France, and Germany would then form a middle group between these two extremes. This categorization of regulatory regimes is also consistent with independent evidence from ad hoc employers' surveys on the stringency of employment protection conducted for the European Commission.

It is noteworthy that the group with the most restrictive regulations consists almost exclusively of Mediterranean countries, which in large measure have the lowest labor costs. Moreover, in three of those countries, Italy, Spain, and Greece, the costs imposed on firms by statutory periods of notice and severance pay requirements are also relatively high.

Regulations on unfair dismissal and collective redundancy have survived the deregulation tides of the 1980s relatively unscathed. The limitation of coverage against unfair dismissal to employees with at least two years of continuous service in the United Kingdom is the clearest case of deregulation, whereas the substitution of mandatory social plans and other accompanying measures for prior official authorization of redundancies in France and the abandonment of the pro forma prohibition of ordinary dismissals for economic reasons in Portugal represent examples of sensible reregulation. On the other hand, the extension of unfair dismissal coverage in Italy to include smaller enterprises represented a significant extension of a traditional regulatory style. In five countries—France, Germany, Italy, Spain, and Portugal—there was an indirect form of liberalization of employment protection in that it was made easier for firms to employ workers on a temporary basis.

Regulatory regimes matter for adjustment practice. We found major national differences in both the levels of involuntary terminations as a whole and the extent to which countries rely on dismissal or fixed-term separations in national adjustment patterns. These differences largely reflect variation in the stringency of dismissal protection found in our survey of regulatory regimes or in European employers' own perceptions as well as the extent to which national regulatory frameworks permit the use of temporary employment as an alternative to permanent contracts. ELFS data on the trends in temporary employment also corroborate these results.

Finally, employment protection policies tend to be complemented by active labor market policies, which support, through public expenditure, employment adjustment and restructuring. This is an important role of active measures in most countries and, in some countries, their primary role.

Notes

1. See also Blanchard and Summers 1987.

2. Employment protection regulations are, of course, only one component of nonwage labor costs and, insofar as they have an impact, presumably discourage entry rather than easing exit for international firms. See Mosley 1990 for a discussion of diversity in social regulation and the potential for social competition in the EC.

3. Only white-collar workers have statutory claim to severance payments in Denmark.

4. The International Labor Organization's (ILO) guidelines have certainly also been influential; nevertheless, the EC directive is the proximate cause.

5. Independent of national notice provisions for individual dismissal. In June 1992, the 1975 directive was amended to make it applicable to situations in which the redundancies are decided by another undertaking that controls the employer. Moreover, the information rights of workers' representatives were strengthened, and the previous exclusion

of workers affected by the closure of an establishment as a consequence of a court decision (e.g., bankruptcy) was rescinded.

6. The minimum definition as specified in the directive is: Dismissal of at least 10 persons in establishments with from 20 to 99 employees, or 10 percent in firms with 100 to 299, or at least 30 in larger firms, and any case of the dismissal of at least 20 employees within 90 days.

7. See Büchtemann 1991 for an overview of the evidence on the incidence of unfair dismissal claims.

8. The index is based on the sum of weeks' pay due in the form of severance pay or notice in the respective national employment protection regimes. Since notice and severance pay requirements vary with age, tenure, and employment status, there are actually quite different levels of protection for different categories of employees. Hence, the national data on weeks' pay reported in the index represent averages of three component subtypes (young, midage, and older employees); separate indices for white- and blue-collar employees were computed.

9. Since 1993, a four-week minimum notice period is required for both blue- and white-collar workers in Germany.

10. Young employees = twenty-five with less than two years of service; midage employees = forty-five years of age with more than ten years' service; older employees = fifty-five with more than twenty years' service.

11. As noted in Figure 2.2, fixed-term contracts under the EPA are limited in duration to eighteen months (under certain circumstances twenty-four) and may not be renewed.

12. The index is derived from the results of the two ad hoc surveys of employers conducted in 1985 and 1989. Companies were asked to assess the importance of "insufficient flexibility in hiring and shedding labor (i.e., necessary redundancies/dismissals and new recruitment may be difficult and costly)" as a reason for "not being able to employ more people." The possible responses were "very important," "important," "not (so) important." The index for each year was computed by assigning one point for the percentage of all employers in industry responding "important" and two points for the percentage of employers responding "very important." Since Denmark did not participate in the EC surveys, Danish values were imputed based on evidence from another employer survey (a 1985 study by the International Organization of Employers reported in Emerson 1988) according to which Denmark ranks lower than all EC countries except the United Kingdom in the stringency of employment protection. Accordingly, Denmark was assigned an index value for each year equidistant between the United Kingdom and the EC country with the next lowest rank (in 1989 Ireland). On the other hand, Luxembourg, which participated in the survey, had to be excluded because the number of persons reported leaving employment within the last six months was too low for statistical significance.

13. Although there was no change in regulations in the Netherlands during this period, employment protection did become a public issue, which may explain employers' increased sensitivity.

14. Results from the 1989 British national labor force survey, which is in some respects more differentiated than the composite results reported in the Eurostat standardized version of the same survey, indicate that about one-third of those made "redundant" in the last three months had already found new employment by the time of the survey (Bird 1990).

15. An unweighted average is appropriate, since it is national employment systems that we wish to compare.

16. The survey results on which the data are based do not include all exits at the end of fixed-term contracts (many of which are voluntary) but only involuntary ones in which the expiration of a fixed-term contract was the "main reason" for leaving the last job. Personal reasons for leaving are captured in other possible responses.

17. The case of Denmark reflects not only the low level of employment protection but also slower growth in 1989.

18. Both Italy and, to a lesser extent, Portugal have high separation rates based on retirement of older employees for reasons of health. See Mosley and Kruppe 1993, 59ff.

19. In Greece, the Netherlands, Portugal, and Spain prior official authorization of collective redundancies is still required; in Italy industrial relations practice places severe constraints on mass dismissals.

References

Addison, J.T. 1989. "Job Rights and Economic Dislocation." In *Microeconomic Issues in Labor Economics: New Approaches*, eds., R. Drago and R. Perlman. New York: Harvester-Wheatsheaf.

Amoros, F.P., and Rojo, Eduardo. 1991. "Implications of the Single European Market for Labour and Social Policy in Spain." *International Labour Review* 130: 359–72.

Bird, D. 1990. "Redundancies in Great Britain: A Review of Statistical Sources and Preliminary Results from the 1989 Labour Force Survey." *Employment Gazette* (September 1990): 450–54.

Blanchard, O.J., and Summers, L.H. 1987. "Hysteresis in Unemployment." *European Economic Review* 31: 288–95.

Büchtemann, C.F. 1991. *Employment Security and Labor Markets: Assumptions, International Evidence, and Theoretical Implications*. Discussion Paper FS I 91–1, Wissenschaftszentrum Berlin für Sozialforschung.

Buttler, F., et al. 1992. "Flexibility and Job Security in the Federal Republic of Germany." *SAMF Arbeitspapier* 1992–1. Gelsenkirchen: SAMF.

Emerson, Michael. 1988. "Regulation or Deregulation of the Labour Market." *European Economic Review* 32: 775–81.

European Commission. 1992. "The Regulation of Working Conditions in Member States of the European Community." *Social Europe Supplement* (April).

―――. 1993. *Employment in Europe*. Luxembourg: Office for Official Publications.

European Industrial Relations Review (EIRR). 1989. *Termination of Contract in Europe. Dismissal and Redundancy in 15 European Countries*. London: Eclipse Publications.

Giersch, H. 1985. *Eurosclerosis*. Kiel discussion papers, no. 112. Kiel: Institut für Weltwirtschaft. Mimeo.

Hamermesh, D.S. 1987. "The Costs of Worker Displacement." *Quarterly Journal of Economics* 102: 51–75.

Mosley, Hugh. 1990. "The Social Dimension of European Integration." *International Labour Review* 129: 147–64.

Mosley, Hugh, and Kruppe, Thomas. 1993. "Employment Protection and Labor Force Adjustment: A Comparative Evaluation." Discussion Paper FS I 92–9, Wissenschaftszentrum für Sozialforschung Berlin.

Osterman, P. 1993. "Pressures and Prospects for Employment Security in the U.S." *In Employment Security and Labor Market Behavior*, ed., C.F. Buechtemann. Ithaca, N.Y.: ILR Press.

3

Unemployment Compensation and Active Labor Market Policy

The Impact of Unemployment Benefits on Income Security, Work Incentives, and Public Policy

Bernd Reissert and Günther Schmid

Introduction

This chapter identifies the basic types of unemployment compensation schemes that are in operation across the European Community and examines their features in terms of the scale of payments relative to earnings and their budgetary cost. It also considers their possible effects on the incentives for the unemployed to seek work and on labor market flexibility, as well as the interdependencies between "passive" measures of income support and "active" labor market policies. It finally considers the problems that arise, or might arise, from the juxtaposition of different national systems of social security within a single labor market and economic area.

The difficulties of comparing unemployment compensation schemes need to be emphasized at the outset. The rules and regulations governing their operation are often complex. To understand how they work in practice, it is not sufficient to read the social security manuals; it also requires a knowledge of the institutional environment and of the general financial conditions that exist. Policy alternatives to merely providing income support for the unemployed, such as

The authors would like to thank Lutz Bellmann (Institute for Labour Market and Vocational Research, Nuremberg), Anders Björklund (Swedish Institute for Social Research, Stockholm), and Anne Gray (PA Cambridge Economic Consultants, Cambridge) for their comments and suggestions to an earlier version of this paper.

alternatives to merely providing income support for the unemployed, such as subsidizing short-time work, temporary jobs in the public sector, and training or early retirement schemes, also need to be taken into account. In addition, a proper evaluation of unemployment compensation schemes on the dynamics of unemployment and labor supply requires information, on flows into and out of work in particular, that cannot usually be obtained from official national statistics.

Despite the voluminous literature on this topic,[1] there is, in fact, relatively little evidence on the effects of unemployment benefits on labor market behavior, especially for the European Community. The following is a first step toward a more comprehensive evaluation of the institutions regulating unemployment compensation systems.[2]

Insurance Versus Assistance Schemes

There are two basic principles governing how unemployment compensation is determined: one relates payments to the previous wage (unemployment insurance); the other guarantees a minimum level of income (unemployment assistance). A common requirement for receiving either type of income compensation is that of being available for work. Unemployment insurance typically depends on previous contributions, with benefits being set in proportion to income when employed, independent of need, for a specific period of time. Eligibility for unemployment assistance, on the other hand, is (largely) unrelated to previous contributions, and payments are not related to previous income but are typically means-tested and usually apply for an unlimited period of time. In practice, however, compensation schemes can involve both principles. The German unemployment assistance (*Arbeitslosenhilfe*), for instance, is wage related, whereas the unemployment benefit system in the United Kingdom has not been related to wages since 1982. At the same time, ceilings imposed on benefits can substantially reduce the proportion of previous income received, as in Belgium, Denmark, and Spain. Moreover, in a number of countries, general assistance is paid to all persons in need, including the unemployed, irrespective of whether they are available for work. In terms of the above principles, the Community countries can be divided into three groups:

- *unemployment insurance (UI) only*: Italy.
- *unemployment insurance and unemployment assistance (UA)*: Germany, Greece, Spain, France, Ireland, and Portugal.
- *unemployment insurance and guaranteed minimum income (GI)*: Belgium, Denmark, Luxembourg, the Netherlands, and the United Kingdom. In addition, some of the countries with a UI and a UA scheme—Germany, in particular—provide a guaranteed minimum income to people in need who are not, or not sufficiently, covered by any of the other two schemes.

From a theoretical point of view, the features of an insurance-based scheme can be clearly formulated:

- the bulk of finance comes from wage-related contributions (paid by employers and/or employees);
- entitlement to benefits requires a minimum period of previous employment (which excludes new entrants to the labor market and those, mostly women, who reenter after a long break);
- abuse of the system is controlled by requiring that unemployment be involuntary or that a waiting period elapse before benefits can be received;
- the rate of benefit is a significant proportion of the previous wage and related to the length of insured employment; and
- the period over which benefits are paid is strictly limited and also related to the period of insured employment.

In practice, however, it is difficult to rank the systems in Community countries according to these criteria. The regulation of unemployment insurance and assistance is very complicated and often inconsistent (see Table 3.1). The schemes in Germany, Spain, and France seem most to reflect the insurance principle in terms of their financing. The relative scale of employers' and employees' contributions, however, varies widely among these countries as among other member states. Nevertheless, because of the possibility of forward or backward shifting of nonwage costs, such differences are likely to be relatively unimportant so far as the functioning of labor markets is concerned. Three major types of divergence from the insurance principle are apparent on the financing side:

- high state subsidies to the benefit fund in Denmark, Italy, and the Netherlands;
- the submergence of unemployment insurance in the social security system in Ireland, Portugal, and the United Kingdom; and
- flat-rate instead of wage-related contributions in Denmark.

All member states require a minimum period of insured employment as a qualifying condition for the receipt of unemployment compensation. This ranges from 360 days in Germany to 78 days for workers under the age of eighteen in Belgium. Since the mid-1970s, in response to high and prolonged unemployment and to escalating budget deficits, countries with strong insurance principles (Germany, France, and Spain, in particular) have increased the qualifying period and/or linked the duration of benefits more closely to the length of insured employment.

Typically, countries with relatively low or short-term benefits (Greece, Italy, Ireland, and the United Kingdom) impose a waiting period of several days before benefits can be claimed, whereas in countries with relatively high rates of benefits (Denmark, Germany, Spain, France, and the Netherlands) there is no waiting period at all.

Table 3.1

The Regulation of Unemployment Insurance and Assistance, January 1992

	Belgium	Denmark	Germany	Greece	Spain	France
Unemployment Insurance (UI)						
Title of Benefit	Allocation de chômage	Arbejdsløsheds-forsikring	Agrbeitslosengeld	Ordinary unemployment benefit	Prestacion por desempleo, nivel contributivo	Allocation de base (AB); Allocation de fin de droits (AFD)
Financing	Contributions by employers (1.35%) and employees (0.87%), state subsidies	Fixed membership contributions to recognized UI Funds, employers' contributions, state subsidies covering about 70% of expenditure	Employers' (3.15%) and employees' (3.15%) contributions, state subsidies to cover deficit	Employers' (2.35%) and employees' (1%) contributions; state subsidies	Employers' (5.2% + 0.4% for Wage Guarantee Fund), and employees' (1.1%) contributions	Employers' (4.51%), employees (2.33% + 0.50%) contributions
Qualifying Conditions	Varies according to age from 78 days in the past 10 months to 624 days in the past 36 months	Membership contributions of at least 12 months and employment of at least 26 weeks within the past 3 years	At least 360 days contributory employment during the last 3 years	At least 125 days contributory employment in the 14 months before unemployment	6 months contributory employment in last 4 years	Depending on age and length of insured employment; minimum for AFD at least 6 months insured employment
Waiting Period	None	None	None, except if job voluntarily quit (8–12 weeks)	6 days	None except if job voluntarily quit (6 months)	Depends on the number of holidays not yet taken

Rates of Benefits (Initial)	60% of gross wage (55% for cohabitants without dependents), taxable	90% of gross wage; ceiling of DKR 2,502 per week, taxable	68 (63%) of net wage; ceiling 6,800 DM per month (West), 4,800 DM (East)	40% of daily wage for manual workers, 50% of monthly wage for employees, non-taxable	80%; ceiling 170% (220%) of statutory minimum wage, nontaxable	AB: 40% + lump sum; AFD: flat rate (81.30 FF/day), taxable
Duration and Dynamics of Benefits	Indefinite but degressive; benefit can be suspended if unemployment duration doubles the regional average	2.5 years; with extension up to 7 years if using the right to job offers	156 to 832 days depending on insured employment and age (6 days per week)	5 to 10 months depending on insured employment and age	3 to 24 months depending on insured employment; degressive (60% in second year)	AB: 3 to 45 months degressive; AFD: 6 to 27 months, both depending on age and insured employment
Alternatives to Regular Unemployment Compensation	Short-time working compensation; temporary unemployment allowance	Compensation for involuntary part-time unemployment and layoff periods	Short-time allowance; promotion of winter production; bad weather allowance		Short-time working; early retirement with replacement conditions	Short-time working; early retirement

continued

Table 3.1 continued

	Belgium	Denmark	Germany	Greece	Spain	France
Unemployment Assistance (UA)						
Title of Benefit	No separate UA; Bestaansminimum (BM)	No separate UA; Social Bistand	Arbeitslosenhilfe (AH); Sozialhilfe (SH)	Extraordinary Benefit; no scheme guaranteeing a national minimum income	Subsidio por disempleo (SD); various social assistance schemes	Allocation de Solidarité Spécifique (ASS); Allocation d'Insertion (AI); Revenu Minimum d'Insertion (RMI)
Qualifying Conditions for UA			Registered as unemployed but not qualifying for AG or having exhausted AG, and in need; at least 150 days insured employment in preceding year	Unemployed having exhausted ordinary benefits, and in need	Registered as unemployed but not qualifying for insurance benefits, or exhausted those benefits, and in need; at least 3 months insured employment	ASS: unemployed but not qualified or have exhausted AB/AFD, and in need; AI is for young people looking for first job, single women with children, ex-prisoners, etc.
Size and Duration of Assistance			AH: 58% of net earnings and 56% for recipients without children; unlimited, as long as no suitable job available	Same rate as ordinary benefit; for 45 days	75% of current minimum wage; 3 to 18 months; (for unemployment 55 until retirement age)	ASS/AI/RMI in 1988: FF 2,000 per month for wage earner (+ conditional supplements); ASS/RMI unlimited; AI one year max.

	Ireland	Italy	Luxembourg	Netherlands	Portugal	United Kingdom
Unemployment Insurance (UI)						
Title of Benefit	Unemployment Benefit (UB) and Pay-Related Benefit (PRB)	Trattamento ordinario di disoccupazione	Indemnité de chômage complet	Werkloosheids Uitkering (WW)	Subsidio de desemprego (SD)	Unemployment Benefit (UB)
Financing	Employers' and employees' contributions included in overall social insurance contributions (PRSI)	Employers' contributions (4.11% industry, 1.61% commerce); state subsidies	Contributions to employment Fund by employers, communes, and income tax	Employers' (1.44%) and employees' (1.04%) contributions; variation according to industry; ceiling	Contributions included in health insurance	Progressive employers' and employees' contributions to National Insurance Fund
Qualifying Conditions	At least 39 weeks PRSI-contributions	Insured employment of at least 2 years, 1 year in 2 years preceding unemployment	At least 26 weeks employed during 12 months preceding unemployment	At least 26 weeks employed during 12 months preceding unemployment	540 days of contributory employment during 2 years preceding unemployment	Within the last 2 years contributions for at least 50 times the lower weekly earning limit
Waiting Period	UB: 3 days; PRB: 3 weeks: 6 weeks if unemployment voluntary or through misconduct	7 days; 30 days if unemployment voluntary or through misconduct	None, except young entrants (39 weeks)	None	None	3 days; up to 6 months if unemployment voluntary or through misconduct
Rates of Benefits (Initial)	Flat rate (UB) + 12% (PRB) of weekly earnings over IR£ 72 and below IR£ 220, nontaxable	20% of last salary	Up to 80% of gross earnings depending on partner's income; ceiling 2.5 times statutory minimum wage	Up to 70%, taxable	Up to 65%; ceiling 3 times the guaranteed minimum wage, taxable	Flat rate + adult dependents addition, taxable

continued

table 3.1 continued

	Ireland	Italy	Luxembourg	Netherlands	Portugal	United Kingdom
Duration and Dynamics of Benefits	UB: up to 390 days; PRB: up to 375 days (6 days per week)	Up to 180 days (extension to 360 days in the building sector possible)	365 days; extension up to 12 months possible, then partially degressive	6 months to 5 years depending on length of service and age; 70% of minimum wage for another year	10 to 30 months; extension for aged over 55 possible up to early retirement at 60	1 year
Alternatives to Regular Unemployment Compensation		Special unemployment benefit for redundant workers (66% up to 180 days); Wage Compensation Fund (CIG) for short-time work		Disability pensions and early retirement regulated by collective agreement	Early retirement	Redundancy payments; occupational pensions
Unemployment Assistance (UA)						
Title of Benefit	Unemployment Assistance (UA)	No general UA; Sussidio straordinario (SS) in some regions	No separate UA; Revenu Minimum Garanti (RMG)	Bijstandsmitkering (ABW, RWW)	Subsidio social de desemprego (SSD)	Income Support (IS)

Qualifying Conditions for UA	Unemployed who do not qualify or have exhausted their right to UB; and in need	Registered unemployed who do not qualify or have exhausted their right to WW, and are in need; scheme open to other persons in need	Unemployed who do not qualify or have exhausted their right to SD, and are in need; at least 180 days insured employment in preceding year	Registered unemployed who do not qualify or have exhausted their right to UB; scheme open to other persons in need
Size and Duration of Assistance	Up to IR£ 52 per week depending on needs, duration of unemployment etc.; unlimited	Flat rates depending on age and status, e.g., HFL 1,148 per month for singles living alone; unlimited	70% of the minimum wage + supplements depending on children; half the period for which SD has been granted or SD-period if no SD has been granted	Flat rate depending on age and status, e.g., UK£ 39.65 per week for singles 25 years and over; unlimited

Source: Derived from Mutual Information System on Employment Policies in Europe (MISEP) and own compilation of national sources.

Where unemployment benefits are wage related, the initial rate of benefit ranges from 20 to 50 percent of previous gross earnings (Italy, Ireland, Greece) to 90 percent (Denmark). Only in Germany is the benefit rate related to net rather than gross earnings, and only in the United Kingdom are benefits flat-rate rather than being related to wages. As long-term unemployment has increased, there has been a growing tendency for the period over which benefits are payable to be linked to the length of insured employment. In some countries—such as Belgium and France—this tendency has been combined with reducing the rate of benefit over the payment period.

In a number of countries, there are important alternatives to unemployment compensation in operation. This is especially the case in Italy, where the general unemployment insurance scheme covers only a small proportion of the unemployed who have previously worked. In 1990, only an estimated 56,000 of the 468,000 unemployed with work experience received unemployment benefits, most of the remainder receiving payments from various special schemes. More important, the wage compensation fund (Cassa Integrazione Guadagni) guarantees a certain level of income to redundant workers who, however, remain formally employed.

In Germany (and to a lesser extent in Belgium, France, and Spain) compensation for short-time working is a practical alternative to unemployment compensation, which has most extensively been used in the first phase of transforming the East German labor market after unification. Early retirement schemes (in France and the Netherlands, especially), disability pensions (particularly in the Netherlands), and redundancy payments (in the United Kingdom, for example) are other alternatives.

Six countries—Germany, Greece, France, Spain, Ireland, and Portugal—have specific means-tested assistance schemes for the unemployed. In other countries, general social assistance schemes are the only means to provide a minimum level of income to those who do not qualify for, or have exhausted their rights to, unemployment benefits. With the exception of Greece, Spain, and Portugal, means-tested unemployment assistance is payable for as long as the person concerned has no other source of income and is available for work. Assistance payments are usually flat-rate, though they vary with age, marital status, and number of children, and in three of the six countries operating such schemes (Germany, Spain, and Portugal) eligibility requires a minimum period of insured employment. Germany and Greece are alone in relating the assistance payable to previous earnings, though the level is lower than for unemployment benefits.

Taking all aspects together, Germany, France, and Spain appear to be the countries where the insurance principle applies most strongly, in that unemployment compensation is most closely linked to previous employment and the financial contributions made. The United Kingdom and, to a lesser extent, Ireland are at the opposite extreme. In the United Kingdom, social welfare principles prevail in that the emphasis is on guaranteeing a minimum level of income; welfare rather than insurance principles are reflected in the financing of payments from progressive rather than proportional contributions, the payment of flat-rate rather than wage-related benefits, and the differentiation of all benefits according to marital status and number of children.

The history of regulations governing unemployment compensation schemes since the mid-1970s shows that there has been no convergence between systems based on insurance principles and those based on welfare principles. Instead, the particular characteristics of each type of system seem to have become more pronounced.[3] In insurance schemes, like those in Germany, France, and Spain, benefits have become more closely linked with previous employment. By contrast, in the welfare-oriented U.K. system, this link has been weakened by abolishing earnings-related benefits in 1981, introducing progressive insurance contributions in 1985, and gradually shifting from unemployment benefits to general social assistance ("income support").

Beneficiary Rates

Differences in unemployment compensation systems are reflected in national patterns and trends in beneficiary rates—i.e., in the proportion of the unemployed actually receiving benefits or assistance—as well as in variations and changes in rates relative to wages—i.e., the so-called replacement rate. If unemployment insurance funds go into deficit, and if there are economic and political difficulties in increasing contributions or subsidies from the state budget, the policy response will be to reduce benefits in relation to wages, or to reduce the beneficiary rate, through imposing stricter qualification conditions. Apart from changes in regulations a reduction in the beneficiary rate can also result from changing labor market conditions, such as an increase in the number of long-term unemployed who have exhausted their benefit entitlements.

In practice, the total beneficiary rate varies markedly between the member states of the European Community. According to the European Labour Force Survey (ELFS), the proportion of people claiming benefits among all those without work for at least one hour a week, who are also seeking work and available for work, ranges from 6 percent in Greece in 1990 to 86 percent in Denmark (Figure 3.1). These figures, however, need to be interpreted with caution, since the sample of households covered by the survey may not necessarily be representative in this respect, and the likelihood of a positive response to the question on benefits may depend both on the amount received and on whether the respondent is registered at an employment office. In both Greece and Portugal, registration rates are low compared with most other member states. Moreover, in both countries official figures of beneficiary rates, which are partly based on other definitions—from the Ministry of Labor or the social security administration—are two to six times higher than those reported by the ELFS. In countries where unemployment insurance contributions are integrated into the social security system

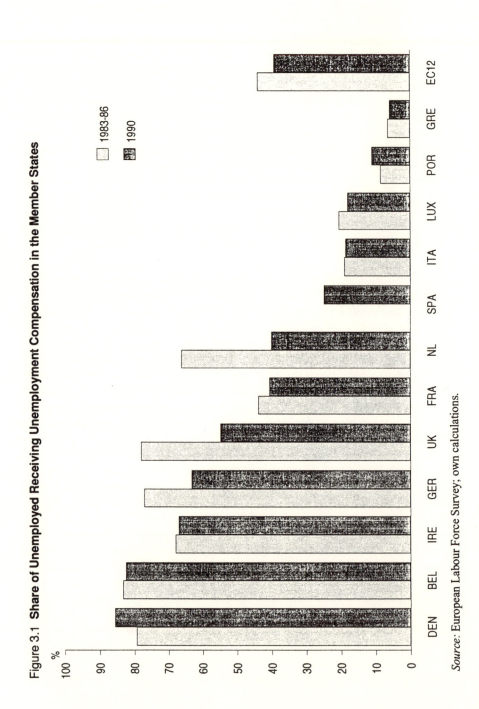

Figure 3.1 **Share of Unemployed Receiving Unemployment Compensation in the Member States**

Source: European Labour Force Survey; own calculations.

(as in Portugal and the United Kingdom), or where employees do not, or hardly, pay contributions into a separate fund (as in Greece, Italy, Luxembourg, and Spain), individuals may not be aware of receiving unemployment benefits or assistance. Despite these and other caveats concerning the reliability and validity of the data, however, differences in beneficiary rates among member states remain substantial and require explanation.

In particular, at 41 percent in 1990, the beneficiary rate in France is surprisingly low. This may reflect the fact that the French unemployment insurance scheme is barely subsidized at all by the state budget and so is more insurance oriented than, for example, in Denmark and Belgium, where the rates are around twice as high. Qualification requirements for receiving benefits in those two countries are much less strict than in France, and the period for which benefits are payable is much longer (unlimited in the case of Belgium).

With the exception of Denmark, Germany, the Netherlands, and the United Kingdom, beneficiary rates changed little between 1983 and 1990. Apart from Portugal (where the validity of the data is uncertain), Denmark is the only country in which the beneficiary rate rose (by 6 percentage points) over this period. This reflects Denmark's success in reducing the relative numbers of long-term unemployed—who are likely to have exhausted their benefit entitlement—through active labor market measures. Denmark, for example, is the only member state that has established a right for the long-term unemployed to a temporary job in a private or public enterprise or to training.

In contrast, significant reductions in beneficiary rates occurred between 1983–84 and 1990 in Germany (from 77 percent to 63 percent), the United Kingdom (from 78 percent to 55 percent), and the Netherlands (from 66 percent to 40 percent). In the United Kingdom and in Germany, the reduction was similar for men and women; in the Netherlands, it was much larger for women than for men. In Germany, the fall in the beneficiary rate was especially marked for the young and the long-term unemployed, reflecting both a tightening in eligibility criteria and an increase in the relative numbers of long-term unemployed—women being especially affected, often receiving no unemployment assistance after exhausting their benefits if their husband is working.

In the United Kingdom, the fall seems to have been caused by changes in the qualifying conditions, the decline in the beneficiary rate being greatest among short-term unemployed and young unemployed women. (A major reform in 1987 reduced benefits to young unemployed if they refused an offer from the Youth Training Scheme or dropped out of the program, while those quitting jobs voluntarily had to wait longer before being eligible for benefits.) Similarly, in the Netherlands, it is young unemployed who have experienced the biggest fall in the beneficiary rate (from 72 percent to 32 percent), also as a result of a major change in qualifying conditions. (In 1987, the qualification period for continuing to receive benefits after the first six months of unemployment was extended to at least three years of insured employment within a period of five years—a requirement that rules out many young people.)

Except in Belgium, Denmark, and Italy, women are less likely to receive benefits than men (Figure 3.2). This is particularly the case in Ireland, the United Kingdom, and the Netherlands, where beneficiary rates of women are less than half of those of men, but it is only slightly less true in Spain, Greece, Luxembourg, and Germany. The two main reasons for such a difference are, first, that the relatively strict qualifying conditions exclude more women—who are more likely to be reentering the labor market—than men, and, second, that means-tested unemployment assistance schemes tend—according to the traditional breadwinner model—to apply to men rather than to women.·

The strength of insurance principles in the unemployment compensation schemes of many member states is also reflected in the age breakdown of beneficiaries (Figure 3.3). In principle, the relationship between unemployment protection and age is influenced by two offsetting factors. On the one hand, the older the person, the more likely he or she is to satisfy eligibility criteria; on the other hand, the probability of being unemployed for a long period and so exhausting entitlements to benefits tends also to increase with age. In some countries—Germany, France, and Spain, where the insurance principle is especially marked—protection for older people was strengthened over the 1980s in response to persistent high unemployment by making the duration of benefits more dependent on age or on the length of employment. In those countries, older people are now much better protected than younger people.

In other countries, where the compensation scheme is also based on insurance principles, though less strongly—Denmark, Greece, the Netherlands, and Portugal—the same kind of relationship between age and unemployment protection is apparent. In welfare-oriented systems—as in the United Kingdom and Ireland—where unemployment protection is largely designed to provide a minimum level of income independent of previous earnings, there is no rationale for a policy of linking the duration of benefits to age or the length of previous employment, and, therefore, beneficiary rates do not increase with age (Figure 3.3).

Just as older people tend to be better protected under insurance-based systems, so the young are less well protected. In France, for example, whereas 47 percent of the unemployed were below thirty in 1990, only 32 percent of beneficiaries of unemployment compensation were also below thirty. On the other hand, 12 percent of the unemployed who were over fifty accounted for 19 percent of beneficiaries. Insurance-based systems are, therefore, biased toward protecting core workers (mostly male and elderly) over marginal workers (mostly young, female, and casual), whereas people tend to be more equally treated—though not women who are not the main wage earners—under welfare systems.

The variation in beneficiary rates with the duration of unemployment reveals another interesting difference between insurance-based and welfare-oriented sys-

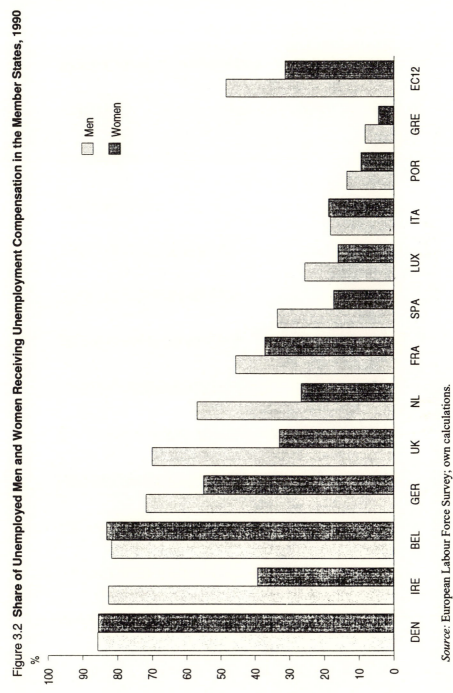

Figure 3.2 Share of Unemployed Men and Women Receiving Unemployment Compensation in the Member States, 1990

Source: European Labour Force Survey; own calculations.

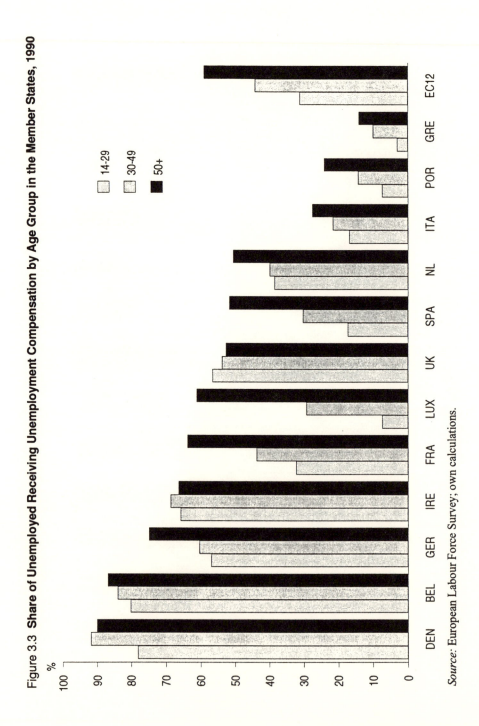

Figure 3.3 Share of Unemployed Receiving Unemployment Compensation by Age Group in the Member States, 1990

Source: European Labour Force Survey; own calculations.

tems (Figure 3.4). In Germany, France, and Spain—where the systems are most strongly insurance based—beneficiary rates of the long-term unemployed are lower than for those who have been out of work for three to twelve months. In the United Kingdom and Ireland, on the other hand—where the systems are largely welfare based—beneficiary rates are consistently higher for the long-term unemployed than for those unemployed for less than a year. This reflects the fact that insurance-based systems tend to exclude "poor risks" (i.e., the long-term unemployed) from the receipt of benefits, whereas welfare systems tend to treat most of the unemployed equally, though only in the sense of guaranteeing a minimum level of income.

Wage-Replacement Rates

The scale of benefits that the unemployed are entitled to receive differs considerably among member states. This variation can be illustrated by taking someone of prime age who becomes unemployed after being in a full-time job for the previous ten years and seeing how the proportion of the previous wage that person receives over time differs among countries.

It is assumed that the person concerned is forty years old, either single or married but without children, and was previously receiving the average earnings of a production worker in the country concerned. Although such a hypothetical person is not necessarily representative of the unemployed, given their wide variety of personal characteristics, details for others, such as young people, older workers, those with no insurance, part-timers, and so on, are much more difficult to compile. For the hypothetical person, in each country, gross wage-replacement rates—i.e., the ratio of (pretax) benefits to average gross earnings—are calculated on the assumptions that the person is, first, single; second, married with a spouse who is employed full-time; and, third, married with a spouse who is unemployed and dependent. In each case, benefits comprise all forms of compensation applying—unemployment insurance benefits, unemployment assistance payments, and guaranteed minimum income transfers—at the rates and rules prevailing in 1989. (In the case of Germany, where benefits are officially calculated in relation to net rather than gross earnings, estimates have been made at their ratio to gross earnings in order to ensure comparability with other countries.)

The estimates for each country (excluding Italy, for which there are no comparable details) show that the degree of income protection does not vary widely across the Community for those in short-term unemployment (Figure 3.5).

When a person first becomes unemployed, the wage-replacement rate is similar in most member states (ranging from 50 to 70 percent) and in most cases invariant to marital circumstances. This reflects the fact that unemployment insurance schemes in most countries provide a wage-related income, without differentiating according to need, for at least an initial period of unemployment. It is worth noting that the actual wage-replacement rates in a number of member

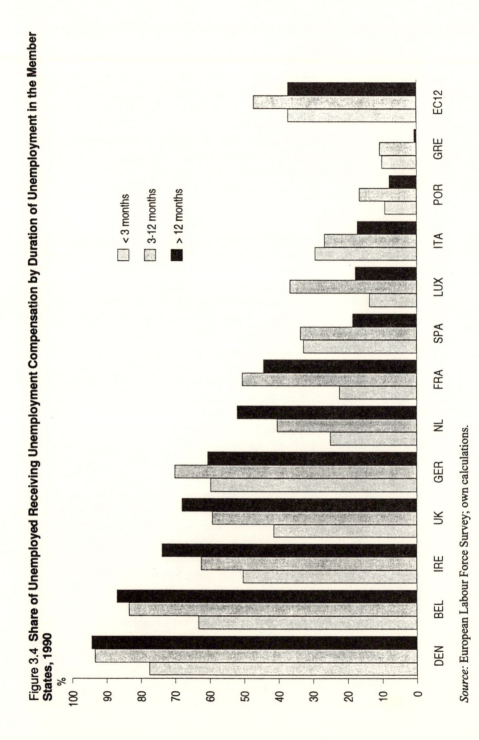

Figure 3.4 Share of Unemployed Receiving Unemployment Compensation by Duration of Unemployment in the Member States, 1990

Source: European Labour Force Survey; own calculations.

Figure 3.5 **Unemployment Compensation in Relation to Previous Wage**

Unemployment Compensation in Relation to Previous Wage

———— All prime-age recipients

· · · · · · Single recipients

— · — · Married with working spouse

———— Married with dependent spouse

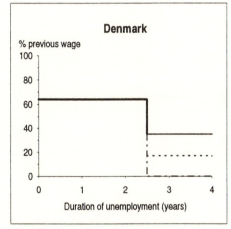

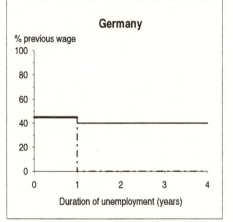

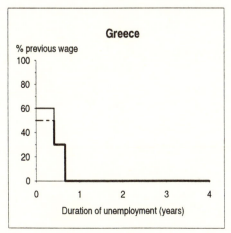

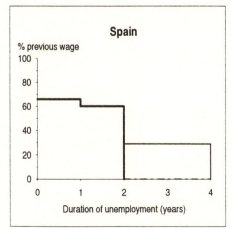

Figure 3.5 *(continued)*

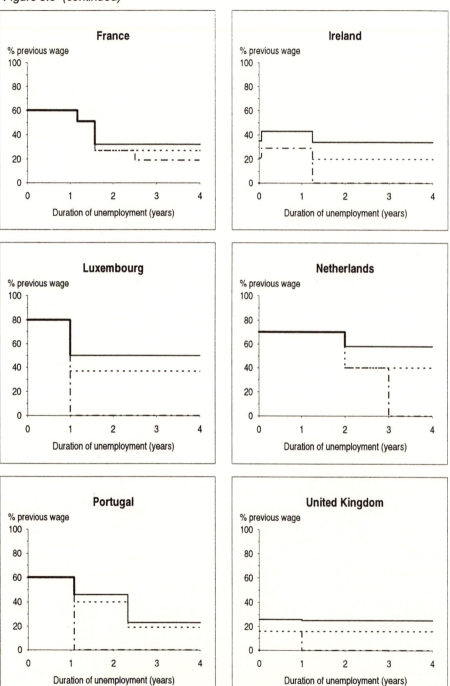

Source: Employment in Europe 1992: 165–66, Commission of the European Communities.

states (Belgium, Denmark, Spain) are significantly below the statutory rates implied by unemployment insurance regulations (see Table 3.1). This is because of ceilings that set an absolute limit to benefit payments.

In the United Kingdom and Ireland, in contrast to other countries, initial replacement rates are well below the Community average, and benefits are differentiated according to marital circumstances from the very beginning of a spell of unemployment. This reflects the fact that insurance principles play only a minor role in unemployment protection in these two countries, and that, therefore, even initial benefits are designed to provide a minimum level of income according to need rather than being related to previous wages.

As the spell of unemployment increases, so wage-replacement rates become increasingly dependent on marital and family circumstances in most member states. This is largely because entitlement to unemployment insurance benefits becomes exhausted as the duration of unemployment increases, and the unemployed then have to rely on unemployment assistance or guaranteed minimum income if they lack other means of support. In this situation, a married person with a working spouse usually cannot claim any further compensation, because household income is above the minimum level. A single person or a married person with a dependent spouse, on the other hand, usually continues to be eligible for compensation for an indefinite period of time. Their wage-replacement rates are, however, lower than when they first became unemployed; rates also are usually lower for single than married people with dependents.

Some member states, however, diverge from this general pattern so far as long-term unemployment is concerned. In Belgium and France, for example, a married person with a working spouse is also eligible for compensation for an indefinite period, though at a low level. In Spain, entitlement to means-tested benefits is limited to a four-year spell of unemployment and is usually restricted to married people with dependents. In Germany, the same level of means-tested benefits applies to both single and married people with dependents. In Greece, on the other hand, no further compensation is available when initial insurance benefits, applying for a period of eight months, and unemployment assistance, applying for a period of forty-five days, have been exhausted.

Except for Greece, the most obvious case of divergence from the general pattern of protection in respect to long-term unemployment is the United Kingdom, where single and married people with dependents continue to receive compensation indefinitely at the same low level as the initial insurance benefit, reflecting the emphasis on providing a minimum level of income according to need irrespective of how long a person has been unemployed.

Denmark, the Netherlands, Spain, and France have the longest periods of wage-related unemployment compensation, and the Netherlands, Germany, Luxembourg, and Belgium, the highest replacement rates for single or married people with dependents in long-term unemployment. In these two groups of countries, most of which follow strict insurance principles, the income of a

Figure 3.6 **Unemployment Benefits in Relation to GDP and Unemployment Rate in the Member States, 1991**

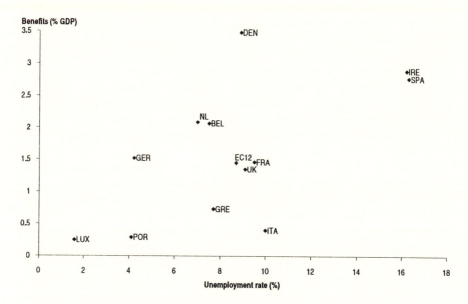

Source: European Labour Force Survey, National Statistics; own calculations.

prime-age worker, after a long period of employment, is most protected in the event of long-term unemployment.

The Costs of Benefit Systems

The intercountry differences in beneficiary and wage-replacement rates described above are reflected in the levels of public expenditure on unemployment compensation in member states. Although the total amount spent on compensation in relation to GDP tends to vary with the rate of unemployment—with countries like Spain and Ireland with high rates spending around 2.5 percent of GDP on unemployment payments in 1990, as against a Community average of 1.25 percent—some countries spend significantly more than others on each unemployed person.

Denmark, the Netherlands, and Belgium spend roughly two to three times as much on unemployment protection as countries with similar unemployment rates like France, Germany, and the United Kingdom, while Greece and Italy spend considerably less (Figure 3.6). These differences are only to be expected in light of the above description of system characteristics: Belgium pays unemployment benefits to an exceptionally high proportion of the unemployed for an indefinite period of time; Denmark has an equally high beneficiary rate because of a low number of long-term unemployed; and in the Netherlands wage-replacement rates are exceptionally high for the initial period of unemployment. In Greece

Figure 3.7 **Unemployment Benefits per 1 Percent Unemployment in the Member States, 1985 and 1991**

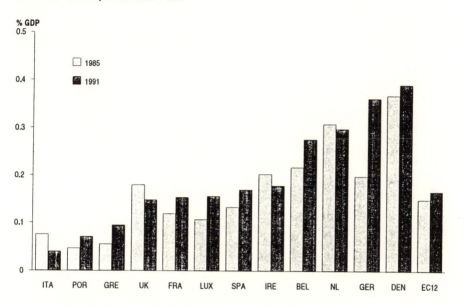

Source: European Labour Force Survey; own calculations.

and Italy, on the other hand, unemployment compensation schemes, as such, protect only a small proportion of the unemployed, and, hence, their cost is low (though in Italy at least, the burden of supporting the incomes of the unemployed falls on other items of the public budget).

The level of expenditure on unemployment compensation does not appear to be related to whether systems are based on insurance or welfare principles. Expenditure per person unemployed in the United Kingdom, with its welfare-oriented system, is similar to that in France and Germany, where the systems are insurance based, while expenditure in Ireland, where the system is similar to the United Kingdom's, is almost the same as in Spain. This finding reflects the main trade-off between welfare-oriented and insurance-based systems: the former tend to provide low benefits for almost all claimants, the latter high benefits for a limited number of core workers. They seem to result in similar levels of public expenditure.

Another interesting difference between insurance-based and welfare-oriented systems emerges when the changes in unemployment rates and expenditure on compensation that occurred in member states between 1985 and 1990 are compared. In most countries, expenditure on compensation in relation to GDP declined roughly in line with the fall in unemployment that most of them experienced during that period. In the majority of cases, however, expenditure on each unemployed person increased relative to GDP (Figure 3.7). The exceptions are Denmark, Italy, Ireland, and, most markedly, the United Kingdom, where payments to the unemployed, adjusted for the fall in unemployment, declined significantly.

Since the United Kingdom and Ireland are the two countries where the compensation system is most strongly based on welfare principles, the evidence of this recent period suggests that such systems are more prone to reductions in assistance as compared with insurance-based systems, under which benefits are explicitly related to previous earnings. As real incomes increase, the support given to the unemployed will also tend to increase under the latter kind of system. Under welfare-based systems, on the other hand, the tendency may be merely to raise assistance levels in line with inflation, to preserve their real value, but not necessarily to maintain their relationship to average earnings.

Effects of Unemployment Benefits on the Labor Market

The potential effects of unemployment insurance schemes (UI) on the functioning of the labor market can best be examined in terms of a transition model of labor market flows. Flows in nine possible directions can be distinguished:

To From	Employment	Unemployment	Inactivity
Employment	1	2	3
Unemployment	4	5	6
Inactivity	7	8	9

Although UI mainly affects flows 2 and 4—i.e., of people moving from employment to unemployment and out of unemployment into a job—policy on compensation may also indirectly affect the other possible flows. These potential effects are considered in turn below. These are stylized effects, however, that will differ in detail according to the institutional arrangements in force in the different member states.[4]

(1) Moves from one employment status to another, i.e., labor mobility, may be encouraged by UI insofar as they involve a greater risk of unemployment. This might apply, in particular, to moves from large to small firms, from permanent to fixed-term contracts of employment, and from the public to the private sector (the latter being relevant to recent suggestions that civil servants should contribute to funding UI schemes). Unfortunately, there is no empirical evidence on how important this effect is in practice.

(2) Because UI subsidizes the costs of searching for employment, it makes it easier for people to quit their jobs and spend time finding alternative, possibly more suitable, work. The evidence suggests that voluntary quits increase at times of economic growth—when there are more jobs available—and decline during

recession (Rothschild 1988, 33). One reason for this is that voluntary quitting entails the risk of being disqualified from unemployment benefits (see Table 3.1). There is little, however, to suggest that a waiting period (in which no benefits are paid) is an effective means of preventing abuse of the UI system.

At the same time, employers are likely to find it easier to dismiss workers under a UI regime; those affected will tend to demand less compensation for losing jobs, while employers will tend to have less feeling of responsibility for depriving them of their livelihood. Other things being equal, employers may, therefore, be more inclined to adopt methods of production that entail a higher risk of redundancy. The evidence, however, does not suggest that UI has a major impact on the dismissal policy of employers, except in the case of seasonal work (in the construction industry, hotels, and catering) where the existence of unemployment compensation effectively subsidizes such jobs. Abuse of such systems, however, can easily be counteracted by administrative rules, such as an extension of the period to qualify for benefits. Apart from temporary layoffs, which are fairly widespread in the United States but not in Europe, there is no strong evidence that benefits have much effect on inflows (Atkinson and Micklewright 1991, 1715).

Insurance-based schemes have also been used to support early retirement, which is a means employed to tackle the unemployment problem in several member states. In Germany, France, and the Netherlands, especially, unemployment has become an intermediate stage between working and retirement, which is reflected in an increased flow from employment into unemployment (Casey and Bruche 1983; Kohli et al. 1991).

(3) In cases where elderly people out of work are no longer required to register as unemployed, they are no longer included in the unemployment count and, in the case of the European Labour Force Survey, no longer considered to be unemployed, even though they might receive insurance benefits. In such cases, the flow from employment into inactivity will tend to be increased by UI. On the other hand, the so called "entitlement effect" (Hamermesh 1977, 1979)—the incentive for employees to remain in the labor force in order to become entitled to benefits—will tend to reduce the movement from employment into inactivity. Which of these two opposing effects is stronger remains an empirical question.

(4) According to conventional economic theory, generous wage-replacement benefits increase the "reservation wage" and thereby reduce the probability of someone moving from unemployment into employment (Johnson and Layard 1986). This effect becomes stronger the longer the unemployed are entitled to claim benefits. It becomes weaker, however, as the end of the benefit period approaches or as the rate of benefits declines. For people who are uninsured and out of work, and even for unemployed near the end of benefit entitlement, the opposite effect is likely: the existence of insurance schemes increases the incentive for them to find employment as quickly as possible in order to become (again) eligible for benefits (Mortensen 1977). To some degree, the insured and uninsured may be in competition for jobs, such competition tending to increase

as vacancies become scarcer and expected benefits become more generous. In addition, assuming that an active job search requires financial resources, generous unemployment compensation would increase the resources devoted to systematic search and hence increase the probability of return to work (Atkinson and Micklewright 1991, 1700). These effects potentially offset the negative effects of generous benefits on the incentive of the insured to look for work.

It seems, therefore, plausible that a great deal of empirical research into this issue has either produced contradictory results or found only a weak relationship between unemployment benefits and the duration of individual spells of unemployment. And even where robust results are claimed, the effects are rather small.[5] Most studies do not qualify the status of employment after a spell of unemployment. Evidence, however, suggests that unemployment compensation affects the transition to precarious jobs more negatively than the transition to regular jobs; also, the willingness to participate in training programs (thereby increasing the outflow from unemployment) is likely to decline if unemployment benefits fall relative to payments made to trainees on government schemes (Atkinson and Micklewright 1991, 1714).

Finally, the transition from unemployment to employment might be speeded up by designing unemployment compensation as an incentive system. Australia and the United States have experimented with financial bonuses rewarding active individual job search. The reported positive results of these experiments, however, have to be qualified if one considers moral hazard problems and possible disincentives and if such experiments become more widespread and institutionalized (Atkinson and Micklewright 1991, 1719).

From a European perspective—where such schemes are not yet established on a larger scale—the Japanese Reemployment Bonus seems the most promising one. This bonus is paid when beneficiaries start a new job within the first half of their benefit entitlement period. Depending on the original benefit entitlement and the timing of the start in the new job, the bonus is equivalent to between one-third and two-thirds of the capitalized value of the remaining benefit entitlement. For example, when the original entitlement to benefit is ninety days, as long as fewer than forty-five days have actually been paid, a bonus equivalent to thirty days of benefit can be paid as a lump sum upon finding work. Because only jobs found through the Public Employment Service (PES) qualify, one side effect of the Reemployment Bonus may be to create an indirect incentive for employers to register their vacancies. An employer who does not notify jobs to the PES may occasionally learn that the worker hired has lost a large sum of money because the hiring was not through the PES; conversely, an employer who notifies vacancies to the PES may find some applicants from the PES particularly enthusiastic to start. The Japanese Reemployment Bonus, however, so enthusiastically praised by the OECD (1992, 143), constitutes only 7 percent of all unemployment compensation expenditure (OECD 1992, 129).

(5) The probability of someone out of work remaining unemployed will

clearly tend to increase if insurance benefits are available, most empirical studies finding that the duration of benefits is more important than their level (Atkinson and Micklewright 1991, 1716–17; Florens et al. 1990, 455–63). More time spent looking for a job, however, is not necessarily detrimental to allocative efficiency (Rothschild 1988, 31). Indeed, an extended period of job search is probably necessary in the case of specialized occupations, so that in these cases at least, making it easier for people to remain unemployed for longer is a desirable effect of UI (Franz 1982, 47). Moreover, improved matching of people to jobs might also reduce the likelihood of future spells of unemployment and so the scale of movement out of employment into unemployment over the longer term (Burtless 1987).

(6) UI reduces the probability of people who are unemployed moving into inactivity, even if they are effectively no longer available for work. Empirical evidence suggests, however, that abuse of the system in this way is not a significant explanation of persistently high unemployment. Active labor market programs, coupled with the need for the unemployed to prove periodically that they are actually available for work, also tend to limit the scale of abuse, as do early retirement schemes that enable someone out of work to become legitimately inactive.

(7) The "entitlement effect" of UI increases the probability of those who are not part of the labor force joining it. Moreover, when one member of a household becomes unemployed and is not insured, or is underinsured, other members not in the labor force may be impelled to seek employment in order to supplement household income. On the other hand, since UI has to be financed, the wage-related contributions that employees are required to pay reduce their take-home pay and their incentive to seek employment. Insofar as employers find it difficult to pass on the contributions that they are required to pay, their incentive to hire workers may be reduced, and so the scale of movement from inactivity, or unemployment, into employment. Which of these effects predominates is an empirical question, to which as yet there is no clear answer.

(8) The "entitlement effect" of UI may also induce inactive people to register as unemployed even if they receive no cash benefit. There are often nonmonetary benefits attached to registration, such as participation in special employment measures, use of placement and counseling services, and reduced charges for private or public services, as well as credits for periods of unemployment in respect to other social benefits such as health care and pensions.

(9) The entitlement effects outlined above seem to reduce the probability of someone remaining inactive. UI, in effect, subsidizes formal labor force participation and may, therefore, reduce the incidence of people working in the informal or "black" economy.

In summary, the effects of unemployment compensation on the functioning of labor markets are by no means clear-cut. While compensation schemes that guarantee a relatively high level of income at least in the short term almost certainly tend to increase the probability of someone moving from employment into unemployment as well as the time spent out of work, the magnitude of this effect and its relevance for the operation of the labor market are highly uncertain. Moreover, other important effects, for example, on labor force participation, also have to be taken into account.

From a macroeconomic perspective, an effective system of income protection for the unemployed stabilizes purchasing power; from a social perspective, it reduces divisions in society and provides some form of justice to those who lose their jobs through no fault of their own. A well-functioning compensation scheme is also of central importance in maintaining good industrial relations. If trade unions know that their members are adequately protected if they lose their jobs, they may be more cooperative in adjusting to structural change. In addition, the willingness of workers to be mobile or flexible in the labor market to retrain and to accept new jobs, which may involve a higher risk of unemployment, such as seasonal work, is likely to be greater if generous unemployment benefits are available.

In this respect, a generous compensation scheme can be regarded as an investment in a more flexible and efficient labor market. This is especially the case if it is combined with active measures to promote employment.

Unemployment Insurance and Active Labor Market Policy

There are obvious reasons for directing resources toward job creation or skill promotion (active measures) instead of pure income maintenance for the unemployed. Not the least important are persistent mismatches between supply and demand for particular skills and apparently increasing deficiencies in public infrastructure. In most member states, however, public expenditure on unemployment compensation continues to be considerably larger than expenditure on active policies.

In 1990, member states spent an average of 2.25 percent of GDP on labor market programs (Figures 3.8 and 3.9). Only 38 percent of this expenditure was devoted to active measures. Between 1985 and 1990, however, this proportion increased in all the countries, except for Denmark (Figure 3.10), the rise being particularly significant in the poorer, less developed countries of the Community—Greece, Portugal, and Spain—assisted by increased finance from the European Social Fund.[6]

There is marked variation among member states both in the overall size of labor market programs and in the proportion spent on active measures. On average, active policies on training, subsidies to integrate long-term unemployed, and special youth and disabled schemes, for example, accounted for 0.8 percent of GDP in the Community in 1990, though for 1.4 percent of GDP in Ireland as against only 0.4 percent in Luxembourg. Unemployment compensation, in contrast, ranged from 0.2 percent of GDP (Luxembourg) to over 3 percent (Denmark). Whereas spending on passive measures of income support is positively related to the level of unemployment, the proportion of total labor market policy expenditure spent on active measures varies inversely with unemployment—i.e., the higher the rate of unemployment, the lower the relative expenditure on active policy (Figure 3.11).

Figure 3.8 **Active Labor Market Policy Expenditure in Relation to GDP in the Member States, 1985 and 1991**

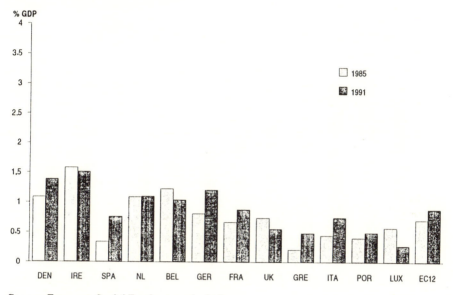

Source: European Social Fund; own calculations.

Figure 3.9 **Passive Labor Market Policy Expenditure in Relation to GDP in the Member States, 1985 and 1991**

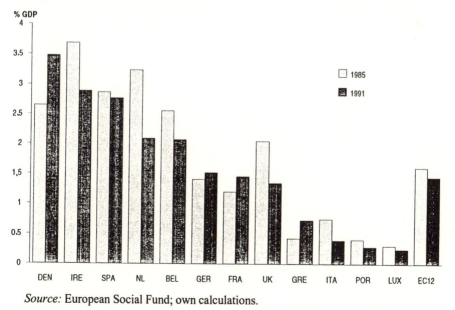

Source: European Social Fund; own calculations.

Figure 3.10 **Share of Labor Market Policy Expenditure Spent on Active Measures in the Member States, 1985 and 1991**

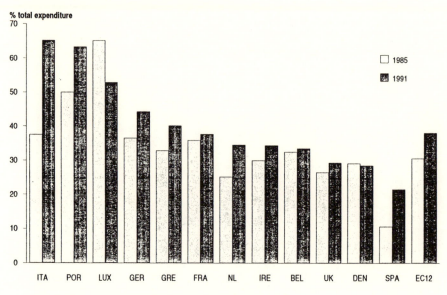

Source: European Social Fund; own calculations.

Figure 3.11 **Share of Labor Market Policy Expenditure Spent on Active Measures in Relation to the Unemployment Rate in the Member States, 1991**

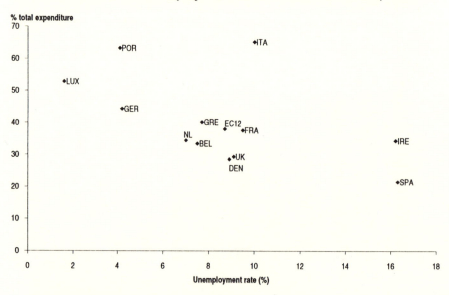

Source: OECD Employment Outlook 1992; own calculations.

This can be explained by the fact that spending on income maintenance tends to have priority over active policy. As unemployment increases, therefore, "passive" expenditure tends to crowd out active expenditure (especially in countries such as Germany, where both forms of expenditure are financed out of the same fund). Moreover, the higher the level of unemployment, the less effective are active measures likely to be in alleviating the problem, and the more relevant is macroeconomic policy.

The scale of public expenditure is, however, not a sufficient means of comparing the effectiveness and efficiency of labor market policies across the Community. It neglects, for example, fiscal policies that fall outside selective labor market programs, as well as nonfinancial measures and private initiatives. High expenditure on active measures is certainly no guarantee that the problem of unemployment is being addressed effectively. Whether or not this is the case can only be assessed by adopting a much wider perspective and by a more detailed analysis of individual programs.

Problems Arising Out of Differences in National Systems

The differences between member states described in the preceding sections show clearly that the Community is a long way from realizing a "unified social area in Europe" with regard to social security for the unemployed. A number of observers have expressed the fear that the juxtaposition of such diverse national security systems for the unemployed within a single labor market and economic area will (or could) lead to major problems. Three problem areas can be summarized as follows (cf. among others Chassard 1992; Walwei and Werner 1991).

(1) Mobility barriers: Workers who move from one member state to another in which the level of benefits is lower or entitlement conditions tougher face the risk of losing, partially or entirely, their acquired social protection. Thus, the differences in national systems of social security represent an obstacle to the mobility of labor—and thus to the optimal allocation of labor—within the Community.

(2) "Welfare tourism": The differences in social security systems might equally induce people to migrate to those countries in which benefits are particularly generous and entitlement conditions lax.

(3) "Social dumping": Increasing competitive pressure within the Single European Market may induce individual member states to reduce the benefits they offer to the unemployed, and thus the contributions paid by employers, in order to gain a competitive advantage over other member states. "Social dumping," as this is termed, could lead to a "race" between the member states to reduce social costs and so to a general deterioration in social standards within the Community.

Unemployment Support and Migration

With the aim of mitigating at least the first two problems—the obstacles to the mobility of labor and the danger of welfare tourism—in 1971 the European

Community passed a decree, based on Article 51 of the Treaty of Rome, which regulates social security for migrants within the Community. With respect to support for the unemployed, the decree, in its most recent form (cf. European Communities 1992; Altmaier 1992; van Raepenbusch 1991; Wanka 1991), makes the following stipulations:

- A worker migrating from country A to country B who, after a period of employment in the latter country, becomes unemployed there is entitled to unemployment support according to the provisions prevailing in that country. However, in determining whether the worker is entitled to benefits and the duration of any such entitlement, the period(s) of employment and the contributions paid in country A must be taken into account. The level of benefit, though, is determined solely with respect to the last earned income in country B.
- An unemployed person, registered as unemployed in country A, who migrates to country B, can retain his/her benefit entitlement in country A only if registered as unemployed in country A for at least four weeks and as unemployed in country B within seven days of taking up residence there. In that case the person would receive the same benefits in country B that would have been due in country A—for a maximum of three months. The costs are borne by country A. If the person returns to country A within three months, benefit entitlement there is retained; if the person remains in country B, all benefit entitlement will be lost after three months.
- "Cross-border commuters," those living in country A and working in country B, are entitled to unemployment support according to the regulations prevailing in their country of residence. Seasonal workers and those sent to work abroad can choose whether to register as unemployed in their country of employment or their original country of residence, whereupon they receive benefits according to the provisions of the country of employment or residence, respectively.

By means of these regulations, the Community enables employed workers to transfer their potential claims on the unemployment insurance system from one member state to another. For those already unemployed, on the other hand, the "export" of benefits is permitted for only a short period of time and is subject to restrictive conditions. Community regulations can thus be seen as an attempt to find a balance between two conflicting aims—to increase the mobility of labor and to prevent welfare tourism. They cannot completely fulfill either aim. The fact that, while an employed worker can transfer periods of employment and contribution-payments to another member state, the level of unemployment benefit would be that prevailing in the new country of residence, can, for instance, reduce mobility when benefit conditions are less favorable in the new country of residence than in the old (Simon 1990, 30). Equally, even the tightly circumscribed opportunity to export benefits (the aim of which is to enable the unemployed to seek work in another member state) will be exploited, at least to some extent, by those migrating for purely personal reasons, who are not really seeking work in their new place of residence. Such individuals can rely, it is argued (Wanka 1991, 99), on the fact that the employment office in the new country of residence (which, after all, does not have to bear the cost of the export of benefits) will not be in a position to verify nor have an interest in verifying whether they are actually available for work. In view of such problems (at least in theory), the efforts made by the EC Commission[7] and the southern member states to increase the scope for benefit export have so far been unsuccessful. They have met stiff resistance from a number of member states with relatively generous benefit conditions and a relatively large proportion of foreign workers, who fear that any extension of the right to export benefits would be to their disadvantage.

At the same time, the influence of differences in national social security systems for the unemployed on potential or actual labor migration within the Community should not, for a number of reasons, be overestimated. First, against the background of a gradual narrowing of living standard differentials in the Community, labor mobility between the member states has been declining since the 1970s: workers from other EC countries—some two million in all—account on average for less than 2 percent of national labor forces.[8] Even in the coming years, this share is expected (Simon 1990; Werner and Walwei 1992) to increase significantly only in isolated segments of the labor market (among trainees and young, highly skilled specialists and executive personnel, and in border areas). Second, empirical studies of labor mobility show that social security benefits are only a subordinate motive for migration (Walwei and Werner 1991). Third, the European Labour Force Survey shows that in the leading immigration countries workers from other EC countries constitute only a very slightly higher proportion of unemployment-support recipients than their share of the work force.[9] Fourth, national data indicate that the transfer of entitlement periods and the export of benefits are of relatively minor quantitative importance: the German unemployment insurance fund registered 16,275 persons in 1988 who had left Germany and made a request for confirmation of periods of insured employment in Germany in order to support a benefit claim abroad. In the same year the fund registered 6,803 unemployed persons who transferred their benefit entitlements to another country for a maximum of three months, and 665 unemployed individuals who transferred benefits acquired abroad, again for a maximum of three months (Walwei and Werner 1991, 87).

Social Dumping?

The question whether, and if so to what extent, national social security systems constitute a competitive advantage or disadvantage vis-à-vis other member states and thus constitute an incentive to "social dumping" is a subject of great controversy. From a macroeconomic perspective there is no evidence for the view that the existence of a comprehensive national system of social security has a negative impact on the competitiveness of the national economy. Rather, international comparison shows that economic performance and the level of social security correlate closely (Wilensky 1975; Chassard 1992, 17). This can be partly explained by the fact that social security not only incurs macroeconomic costs, but also generates macroeconomic benefits; for instance, by protecting workers from the consequences of structural economic change, it renders such structural change socially acceptable.

For individual firms or branches, on the other hand, a generous social security system can indeed represent a competitive disadvantage, particularly where social benefits are financed out of wage-related social contributions and the resultant high level of indirect wage costs cannot be offset by a correspondingly high level of labor productivity. From this point of view, it is interesting to note that the systems of unemployment support in the EC member states not only provide very different levels of benefit, they also have very different impacts on indirect wage costs. Contribution rates to the unemployment-insurance scheme range from less than 2.5 percent of wages (in Belgium, Denmark, Luxembourg, and the Netherlands) to more than 6 percent (in France, Germany, and Spain) (cf. synoptic table). Such differences place firms in certain countries—*ceteris paribus*—at a competitive disadvantage and give rise to demands for a downward adjustment and harmonization of benefit levels.

This situation is reminiscent of the genesis of the unemployment system in the United States in the early 1930s, when, initially, various states attempted to set up a contribution-financed unemployment-insurance system. That plan failed to gain approval in state legislatures, however, largely because of the argument that the burden of contributions on employers would put them at a competitive disadvantage against firms in other states. Not until 1935, when a federal law ensured that employer contributions would be the same in all states, did all the states set up their own unemployment-insurance schemes (cf. Schmid, Reissert, and Bruche 1992, 77–78).

Convergence of National Unemployment-Compensation Systems?

The differences between national social security systems for the unemployed in the EC member states create both positive and negative migration incentives and competitive advantages and disadvantages, the importance of which, though, as the above analysis has shown, should not be overstated. In order to narrow the benefit differences between national systems and to mitigate their problematic effects, the EC Commission is seeking to bring about a harmonization of social security systems in the member states by agreeing on minimum requirements. Those efforts are largely based on the Social Charter on Employee Rights, passed by the European Council (without the approval of the United Kingdom) in 1989, and the program of action aimed at implementing the charter published in the same year. By July 1992 the Commission had managed to persuade the Council of Ministers to make a recommendation on the "convergence of social protection objectives and policies" (Council of the European Communities, 1992) based on the program of action. It makes the following recommendation to all member states:

> a) in accordance with the provisions of the recommendations of 24 June 1992 and subject to their active availability for work, to guarantee minimum means of subsistence for employed persons legally resident in the territory of the Member State;
> b) to make available to the unemployed, particularly to young people arriving on the job market and to the long-term unemployed, a range of measures against exclusion designed to foster their integration into the labor market, subject to their active availability for work or for vocational training with a view to obtaining employment;
> c) to provide employed workers who have lost their jobs with either flat-rate benefits, or benefits calculated in relation to their earnings in their previous occupation, which will maintain their standard of living in a reasonable manner in accordance with their participation in appropriate social security schemes subject to their active availability for work or for vocational training with a view of obtaining employment.

Thus the recommendation conceives social security for the unemployed in terms of a combination of a minimum income (the welfare principle), active labor market policy, and the maintenance of living standards (insurance principle). The recommendation is not binding on member states, however, and it is at present impossible to judge whether it will create an impetus toward convergence between national unemployment-support systems.

Notes

1. For the most recent and best available review, see Atkinson and Micklewright 1991; a very informative complement to this is chapter 7 ("Unemployment Benefit Rules and Labour Market Policy") of OECD 1991; useful for German readers is also the survey by Stobernack 1991; an excellent analysis of the Swedish system has been provided by Björklund and Holmlund 1991.

2. An earlier and shorter version appeared as chapter 7 ("Help for the Unemployed: National Unemployment Compensation Schemes") in the yearly report by the Commission of the European Communities *Employment in Europe 1992*; the authors are indebted to John Morley for improving this chapter in style and content.

3. For comparative details on the history of unemployment insurance in Austria, France, Germany, Sweden, the United Kingdom, and the United States, see Schmid, Reissert, and Bruche 1992.

4. This methodology has been adopted from Clark and Summers 1982 and modified in terms of arguments.

5. For example, Meyer (1990, 780) reports that his results are toward the high end of the distribution of recent estimates: a 10 percentage point rise in the replacement rate

would be associated with an increase of around one and a half weeks in duration. A summary of the scattered evidence in Europe can be found in Atkinson and Micklewright 1991 (pp. 1710–15) and in Schmid et al. 1992 (pp. 154–59).

6. The European Social Fund (ESF) forms part of the Community Structural Funds and aims at supporting especially the reduction of long-term unemployment and helping young people into employment in the less favored regions of Europe. The member state in question always has to make additional funds of its own available.

7. Cf., for instance, the Commission's proposal of 9 July 1980, in: *Official Journal of the European Communities*, no. C 169.

8. The figures do not include immigrants in Italy (European Labour Force Survey 1990).

9. According to the European Labour Force Survey of 1990 foreign nationals from EC countries accounted for the following proportions of unemployment-support recipients and the national work force, respectively: Germany 3.7 percent and 2.7 percent; France 2.8 percent and 3.0 percent; United Kingdom 1.8 percent and 1.6 percent.

References

Altmaier, P. 1992. "Unemployment Benefits." In Commission of the European Communities, *Social Security for Persons Moving within the Community*, 38–45.

Atkinson, Anthony B., and Micklewright, John 1991. "Unemployment Compensation and Labor Market Transitions: A Critical Review." *Journal of Economic Literature* 29: 1679–1727.

Björklund, Anders, and Holmlund, Bertil. 1991. "The Economics of Unemployment Insurance: The Case of Sweden." In *Labour Market Policy and Unemployment Insurance*, eds., A. Björklund et al., Oxford: Clarendon Press, 101–78.

Burtless, Gary. 1983. "Why Is Insured Unemployment So Low?" *Brookings Papers on Economic Activity*. Washington, DC: The Brookings Institution 1: 225–49.

———. 1987. "Jobless Pay and High European Unemployment." In *Barriers to European Growth: A Transatlantic View*, eds., R.Z. Lawrence and Ch. L. Schultze. Washington, DC: 105–62.

Casey, Bernard, and Bruche, Gert. 1983. *Work or Retirement? Labour Market and Social Policy for Older Workers in France, Great Britain, the Netherlands, Sweden and the USA*. Aldershot: Gower.

Chassard, Y. 1992. "The Convergence of Social Protection Objectives and Policies. A New Approach." In Commission of the European Communities, *The Convergence of Social Protection Objectives and Policies*, 13–20.

Clark, Kim B., and Summers, Lawrence H. 1982. "Unemployment Insurance and Labor Market Transitions." In *Workers, Jobs and Inflation*, ed., M.N. Baily, 279–323. Washington, DC: Brookings.

Commission of the European Communities. 1992a. *The Convergence of Social Protection Objectives and Policies*. Luxembourg: Social Europe.

———. 1992b. Social Security for Persons Moving Within the Community. Luxembourg: Social Europe.

———. 1992. "Consolidated Version of Council Regulation (EEC) No. 1408/71 on the Application of Social Security Schemes to Employed Persons, to Self-Employed Persons and to Members of Their Families Moving within the Community." *Official Journal of the European Communities*, no. 325 (February 10, 1992): 1; also published in Commission of the European Communities 1992b, 74–113.

Council of the European Communities. 1992. "Council Recommendation of 27 July 1992 on the Convergence of Social Protection Objectives and Policies (92/442/EEC)." *Official Journal of the European Communities*, no. L245 (26 August 1992): 49; also published in Commission of the European Communities 1992a, 63–66.

Florens, Jean-Pierre; Fougère, Denis; and Werquin, Patrick. 1990. "Durées de chômage et transitions sur le marché du travail." *Sociologie Du Travail* 4:439–68.

Franz, Wolfgang. 1982. "The Reservation Wage of Unemployed Persons in the Federal Republic of Germany: Theory and Empirical Tests." *Zeitschrift für Wirtschafts- und Sozialwissenschaften* 1:29–51.

Hamermesh, Daniel S. 1977. *Jobless Pay and the Economy.* Baltimore: Johns Hopkins Press.

———. 1979. "Entitlement Effects, Unemployment Insurance, and Employment Decisions." *Economy Inquiry* 17, no. 3:317–32.

Johnson, George, and Layard, Richard. 1986. "The Natural Rate of Unemployment: Explanation and Policy." In *The Handbook of Labor Economics*, eds., O. Ashenfelter and R. Layard, vol. 2, 921–22. Amsterdam: North-Holland.

Kohli, Martin et al., eds. 1991. *Time for Retirement. Comparative Studies of Early Exit from the Labor Force.* Cambridge: Cambridge University Press.

Meyer, Bruce D. 1990. "Unemployment Insurance and Unemployment Spells." *Econometrica* 58, no. 4: 757–82.

Mortensen, Dale T. 1977. "Unemployment Insurance and Job Search Decisions." *Industrial Labor Relations Review* 30, no. 4:505–17.

OECD. 1991. *Employment Outlook.* Paris: OECD Publications.

———. 1992. *Employment Outlook.* Paris: OECD Publications.

Rothschild, Kurt W. 1988. *Theorien der Arbeitslosigkeit.* Munich: R. Oldenbourg Verlag.

Schmid, Günther; Reissert, Bernd; and Bruche, Gert. 1992. *Unemployment Insurance and Active Labor Market Policy. An International Comparison of Financing Systems.* Detroit: Wayne State University Press.

Simon, G. 1990. "Ein Standpunkt zur Mobilität der Bevölkerung in der EG: Tendenzen und Perspektiven im Vorfeld des Binnenmarktes." *Soziales Europa* (March 1990): 22–36.

Stobernack, Michael. 1991. "Der Zusammenhang von Arbeitslosenversicherung und Arbeitslosigkeit im Lichte der Empirie: Ein Literatursurvey." *Zeitschrift für Wirtschafts- und Sozialwissenschaften:* vol. 3, no. 2:251–71.

van Raepenbusch, S. 1991. *La sécurité sociale des personnes qui circulent à l'intérieur de la Communauté économique européenne.* Brussels: Verlag E. Story-Scientier.

Walwei, Ulrich, and Werner, Heinz. 1991. "Soziale Sicherung bei Arbeitslosigkeit im Europäischen Binnenmarkt—Konsequenzen für die Bundesrepublik Deutschland?" In *Beschäftigungsaspekte und soziale Fragen des EG-Arbeitsmarktes*, eds., U. Walwei and H. Werner, vol. 142:72–88. Nürnberg: Beiträge aus der Arbeitsmarkt- und Berufsforschung.

Wanka, R. 1991. "Wechselwirkungen zwischen dem europäischen Recht und den Vorschriften über das Recht der Arbeitslosenversicherung der Bundesrepublik Deutschland." In *Beschäftigungsaspekte und soziale Fragen des EG-Arbeitsmarktes*, eds., U. Walwei and H. Werner, vol. 142:89–103. Nürnberg: Beiträge aus der Arbeitsmarkt- und Berufsforschung.

Werner, Heinz, and Walwei, Ulrich. 1992. "Zur Freizügigkeit der Arbeitskräfte in der EG." *Mitteilungen aus der Arbeitsmarkt- und Berufsforschung* 25, no. 1:1–12.

Wilensky, H. 1975. *The Welfare State and Equality.* Berkeley: University of California Press.

4

Further Education and Training for the Employed

Systems and Outcomes

Peter Auer

Introduction

Today, vocational education and training is a widely discussed topic and is seen increasingly also as an important field of public policy intervention. The causes that have led to a certain shift of attention from general education and initial vocational training to further training of the employed (or company training, continuous vocational training, or other denominations that describe the same phenomenon) are by now familiar. Technological factors (accelerating technological and organizational innovation), combined with demographic factors (fewer young entering the labor market) result in a need to invest in training of the already employed. The "fourth pillar" of the education system is thus seen as an important factor for competition in an increasingly integrated world market.

For policy and research, the topic of further training has gained in importance, as is acknowledged by an increase in the number of studies (OECD 1991; (BMBW) 1990; Boot 1990; Géhin and Méhaut 1992; Office of Technology Assessment 1990; Osterman and Batt 1992, to name but a few) and the establishment of committees, institutions, and programs like, for example, the European Communities' FORCE program (the European Communities' Task Force on Human Resources), which explicitly has the task to support action in the field of vocational training for the employed.

However, possibly because of the recent emergence of the theme, most of the studies deplore the insufficiency of data and information on their object of re-

The author is grateful to Karin Wagner and Philippe Méhaut, who have commented on this paper, for their stimulating remarks.

search and, therefore, the limited possibilities of exploring the theme in depth. More than being studies of policy assessment, most of these studies have a normative orientation assuming a positive contribution of vocational training for the employed to productivity and growth, and—in line with human capital theories—the positive contribution of training investments to individual wage levels.

The present chapter, based on an explorative study in the field done by the labor market policy and employment unit of the Wissenschaftszentrum Berlin für Sozialforschung (WZB) for the Commission of the European Communities (Auer 1992), adds to the ongoing debate but has had to deal with the same problems of data limitation as other studies and can therefore only be regarded as one more partial contribution to a policy and research field that only slowly will unveil its concrete shapes.

Three main questions are addressed:

(1) How have countries organized their "systems" of further training for the employed, and how can one interpret the differences in the systems of the countries? Important also are the scope of (public) regulation in the field and the interface between private and public efforts for training.

(2) How many people are participating in further education and training for the employed (FETE) according to figures of the European Labour Force Survey and national data of other sources, and is there an influence of specific features (e.g., the private/public divide) of FETE systems on participation rates?

(3) Is there any obvious relationship between the extent of FETE participation and other educational variables on a macro (country) level and some macro-economic data measuring output?

This latter analysis has to be considered as highly tentative because of the uncertainty in data and methods used. As most arguments put forward today in support of investment in training are based on its alleged highly positive contribution to "competitiveness on the world market," such a consideration is, however, necessary. More than giving a precise answer to the question above, the objective of this part of the analysis is to draw attention of researchers and politicians to the virtual lack of information on the acknowledged output of training, which starts in the firms and is reproduced on other (meso, macro) levels of analysis as well. It is particularly difficult to grasp at an international comparative level focusing on macro-units (countries).

The chapter and the study on which it relies are based on five countries (Denmark, France, Germany, Italy, and the United Kingdom) with widely varying education and training systems.

The Organization of FETE Systems

The term *system* suggests that FETE consists of an ordered set of subsystems. However, FETE can hardly be characterized as an ordered system—it is more "a mixture of market elements and uncoordinated, isolated training interventions"

Table 4.1

Public Financing of Adult Training

Country	Vocational Training (in % of GDP)			Public Labor Market Training (in % of labor force)		
	Employed	Unemployed and at risk	Total	Employed	Unemployed and at risk	Total
Denmark	0.11	0.40	0.51	5.5	2.3	7.8
France	0.05	0.28	0.33	1.7[a]	2.5[a]	4.1[a]
Germany[c]	0.03	0.35	0.38	0.6	1.7	2.5
Italy	—	0.03	0.03	—	n/a	—
UK	0.03	0.20	0.23	0.04[b]	1.4[b]	1.9[b]

Source: OECD Employment Outlook 1992.
Note: Data for 1990 if not otherwise stated.
[a] 1989.
[b] 1989–90.
[c] Without former GDR.

(Centre Européen de devéloppement de la formation professionnelle [CEDEFOP] 1990). Still, to begin with comparative research, we have to assume some system properties like a certain order and specific functions among the subelements in FETE. The subelements and functions that we consider as parts of the FETE "system" and for which we assume a variety of possible combinations across countries are: the private and public element as well as the part of FETE run jointly by the social partners and the respective functions of these elements.

We then consider FETE as one subelement of the whole education and training system and look at the different articulations between, for example, initial and further training and again find different functions of FETE in regard to initial training across countries.

Public-Private Divide

In all five of our countries, with the possible exception of Denmark, the private segment of FETE is more important than the public segment. Firms provide for most of FETE in all countries, and direct public intervention (e.g., through financing of FETE) is rather marginal. Streeck's statement, made in an investigation into the matter of training in Germany (Streeck 1987), that public financing of training is still overwhelmingly geared toward the unemployed and those at risk of becoming unemployed, while private spending concerns the training of (already highly skilled) staff, is valid across our countries. For the public side, this is shown in Table 4.1.

Table 4.2

Distribution of Expenditures for Further Training Including the Unemployed
(numbers in %)

		GER	FRA	UK
CEDEFOP	public expenditure	25	53	20
	private firms' expenditure	50	43	51
	individuals (households)	25	4	29
		(1985)	(1986)	(1986)
Boot	public expenditure	12	34	16
	employers	87	66	76
	trainees	—	—	8

Sources: CEDEFOP, Flash 1/90; Boot 1990.

It appears that Denmark is the country in our sample that spends comparatively more than others for the employed, although it is also in Denmark that the unemployed receive by far the largest share of public funds. In Denmark a much higher percentage of the labor force than in other countries appears to pass through the public system of FETE. This is in line with other findings on Denmark's FETE system.

As far as the public-private share of financing for FETE is concerned, no consistent figures permitting a comparison exist, as the figures available usually include the unemployed (Boot 1990; CEDEFOP 1990). Given that public financing of training is geared toward the reintegration of the unemployed (those at risk to become unemployed being a marginal and hard-to-define group), the share of private financing is by far more important than suggested by the numbers given by those authors (see Table 4.2)

The marginality of public financing for training of the employed stays valid across all countries, with differences in degree more than in kind. Take, for example, France: according to Serfaty (1993), only 8.5 percent of public funding was used for the training of the employed. And for Germany, depending on the sources used, we come to a public/private divide estimate going from 1(public):3(private) to 1(public):9(private). Therefore, as far as the public/private share by country is concerned, no systematic comparison based on financial statistics can be undertaken, as financial data of training investment of firms and even more so the contribution of trainees themselves are particularly hard to collect. For the latter category it is not clear what the individual contributions cover:

Figure 4.1 **Extent of Public or Corporatiste Regulation of FETE**

Note: The chart should be considered only as a guesstimate of a country's position on the low-high regulation continuum, positions being based on an array of indicators, as, for example, public/private financial share, labor law regulation or collective agreements, training institutions, extent of certification, etc. Most of these indicators are themselves subject to imprecisions.
[a]Large regional variation.

foregone earnings or actual expenditure. British training statistics show that the largest part of individuals' contribution to (their) training consists in foregone earnings (9 billion pounds), whereas direct training expenditure accounts for only 0.5 billion pounds (data for 1986–87). Calculations should also include refinancing of public money via employers' and employees' contributions to training funds, as in Denmark, or to the labor market authority, as in Germany.

Free Market Approach or Regulation

However, governments do not intervene by direct financing alone. They can, for example, regulate curricula, introduce certification, impose a levy, or provide for training leaves. Not only governments, but also the social partners regulate training through collective bargaining agreements. If we take two extremes on a continuum going from a free market no-regulation approach to a regulatory approach and try to rank countries on this continuum, we would find the United Kingdom and then Italy on the free market side, Germany in the middle, and France and Denmark on the regulation side (see Figure 4.1). The ranking has of course to be specified. To illustrate our statement, we specify the position of the two extremely opposed countries by referring to what can be considered as the basic organizational features of the training system.

In the United Kingdom, during the reform of the training system undertaken by the conservative government, enterprise training, which has certainly not been the most regulated part in the British economy, was deregulated to a large extent. The Manpower Commission (a tripartite body responsible for the delivery of British employment and training programs) and its successor, the Training Agency, were dismantled progressively. These bodies were replaced by a network of local Training Enterprise Councils (TECs; LECs in Scotland), which are organized as private limited companies with only minor trade union representation on their boards. Although the TECs are supposed to enhance enterprise training, they still overwhelmingly deal with the delivery of government programs for the unemployed, with the effect that firms still handle their training alone. They are helped more by symbolic actions like the delivery of "best practice" certificates such as "Investors in People," which certifies firms to have excellent training, than by substantial financial aid. More important for enterprise training, all sectorally organized Industrial Training Boards established in the late 1960s, which raised a training levy among their member firms to enhance company training, have also been dismantled. They are replaced by sectoral Training Organizations for which membership and payment of fees are voluntary. A third element in the deregulation and privatization policy affecting British training is the present market orientation of local technical colleges (colleges of further education), which more and more are engaging to sell their services (formerly paid for by local public funds) to firms. Such a policy has pushed British FETE toward the free market end of our scale. Some authors believe that the handing over of training matters to business will not fundamentally change the chronic under investment in training, which is after all due—according to many critics—precisely to a firm's reluctance to invest in training in the absence of incentives or regulations that would prevent externalities like poaching (Rees 1993). The present effort to introduce nationwide certification for vocational skills (National Vocational Qualification Certificates) is also based on voluntary participation by firms (and is part of the market logic) and is rather different from publicly (or collectively) regulated certification as in Denmark.

On the other end of the scale is Denmark. In that country, a much larger part of enterprise training is regulated by the social partners and the state. A general (lump-sum) levy is raised from all employers and employees and goes into a training fund, which serves also to finance FETE (infrastructure as well as wage compensation). Moreover, branch training commissions and tripartite national commissions regulate curricula and certificates of nationwide validity. Special state and regional training institutions exist besides schools run by unions or employer organizations. Although there is a market-oriented change in the system, which strives to increase the firm's/individual's contribution to training, the public/corporatiste component is—comparatively speaking—more important than in the other countries of our sample. The countrywide introduction of a "second chance" training (organized by the Ministry of Education) with the possibilities of public funding of such compensatory training for the employed—which are trained mostly outside working time—is another proof of the importance of public intervention in the area of FETE. However, the social partners play a dominant part, which gives the whole system more of a corporatiste stance.

The ranking in Figure 4.1 is certainly not entirely satisfying and is subject to debate. For example, the share of FETE that takes place in public institutions in the United Kingdom (e.g., in the local technical colleges) is quite substantial, as is indicated by the U.K. labor force survey. But how much of this training is actually paid for by the employers, and what part is paid by the (local) authorities? The trend clearly goes toward a firm's buying of such services, but in that respect the United Kingdom could possibly be placed somewhat more to the regulation end. On the other hand, France, through the levy imposed on employers, has a regulation that now covers the majority of firms and enforces them to establish training plans and report results to the authorities, all factors that legitimize the position of France on the regulation end of Figure 4.1. However, this means neither that training provision is regulated nor that company training is certified. Quite the contrary, a substantial training-provider market has developed. The existence of this "training market" would shift France somewhat back toward the low regulation end of the figure. The Danish position is legitimized because it has the most regulated FETE system in all respects: collective bargaining agreements, laws (the state playing, however, a subsidiary role), certification, levy system, and public or semipublic providers.

An additional difficulty in comparing training systems is the existence of institutional dynamics. The example of the United Kingdom and Denmark shows this difficulty. Here one is to compare a rather stable system (Denmark) with a system that has recently undergone tremendous change. Although in all training systems there is a clear shift from regulation to the market, the goals set and position arrived at are very different from country to country. The "market share" in "regulated" FETE is as yet rather marginal (but growing) in Denmark but is becoming more and more dominant in the United Kingdom. In terms of institutional dynamics the training systems of Denmark, Italy, France, and particularly of Germany—although all are affected by change—are more stable than that of the United Kingdom. For further research, the dimension of institutional dynamics in training could be an important field of analysis.

"Output" of Training I: Training Participation

Once we have established such a ranking, we have to compare it to some "output" variable that tells us something about the ways in which the specific systems work. For example, we could ask if a system that is more regulated leads to higher and possibly also to more evenly distributed participation as a "free market system." Here the problems really start because of a set of difficulties with which research into the topic has to deal. To name but the most important difficulties:

- the data on FETE are particularly hard to collect. This is due to the relatively vague definition of further training in some countries (if there is no specific initial vocational training system, no further vocational education system can—by definition—exist) and the fact that FETE is often done more or less informally by firms that often do not systematically collect data. Even public accounts often lack clear definitions in regard to what has been spent on initial or further training. What is needed here, for example, are large-scale enterprise surveys made on a comparative basis, which do not exist for the moment.

- a general restriction of all research on further training is that "measures of training are input—rather than output—based" (OECD 1991, 142), that is, usually incidence rates showing the number of people who have received training over a certain period in the past, or money spent on training. It is clear that such quantitative indicators do not tell us anything about the quality of education and training received, and even if there were two countries spending the same amount on training or having the same number of participants in FETE, one cannot assume equal quality. Still more important, the output of a training system, that is the qualification produced, is already hard to grasp statistically and systematically. This is even more true for the output in an economic sense, the increase in the quality and quantity of products and services produced because of investments in training.

However, as limited as data and information of FETE are, our analysis has to start with some quantitative indicators.

Training Participation According to ELFS

First we used unpublished data of the European Labour Force Survey, where several questions on vocational training received in the four weeks preceding the survey are included. The survey concerns about 600,000 households in the Community and is a good starting point for cross-national research. However, both restrictions given above apply, as the definitions of training differ across countries, and the same question may lead to different answers in the different systems. French workers might, for example, only report training of a certain formality but not informal on-the-job training, whereas British workers would report such training, as this is a typical form of training for British firms. Institutional differences, more than real differences in participation, could hence show in the figures. There are other problems that have to do with survey methods in general: training effort is supposed to be underestimated because the period considered was only four weeks before the survey (longer reference periods usually show higher participation rates), and data are based on self-assessment of individuals (or even on responses given by someone else in the household). Some of these restrictions we simply have to accept, as the social sciences and empirical economics in general deal not with reality itself, but with "reality" as (re)presented by data sets. Some of these restrictions can, however, be dealt with by referring to multiple sources and an analysis of institutional differences in the different countries.

Table 4.3 gives an overview of training participation incidence rates for those dependently employed who had received any kind of vocational training during the four weeks preceding the date of the survey in 1989. By definition, these are the numbers relevant for our topic. However, there are different possibilities of defining those in "further education and training." For the *Employment in Europe* report of the Commission, data based on adult vocational training (training

Table 4.3

Incidence Rates According to Different Definitions of FETE (1989)

	Total number of trainees 14–49[a]	14–49[a]	25–49[b]	14–49[c]	Rank order of all incidence rates
DEN	248,470	13.5	16.2	17.7	1
UK	1,074,809	11.4	12.3	13.2	2
GER	903,870	5.0	5.1	6.3	3
FRA	325,334	2.1	2.7	3.4	4
ITA	237,005	1.9	1.9	2.3	5

Source: European Labour Force Survey.

Note: Rates reflect the percentage of those having declared to have received training in relevant population.

[a] Excluding those having declared to be in initial training.

[b] Without apprentices.

[c] Including those having declared to be in initial training without apprentices.

for ages twenty-five to forty-nine, column 3) was used. Because of the uncertainties of the definition of further vs. initial training and to account for the fact that people younger than twenty-five years are also in further rather than initial training, we included in the subsequent analysis all fourteen- to forty-nine-year-old trainees, excluding apprentices or young people in programs like the Youth Training Scheme in Great Britain. An additional advantage is the larger numbers of trainees in that category, which makes an analysis on lower levels of aggregation (branches, regions) easier. However, a very strict definition of FETE should be based on column 1, which excludes—in addition to the apprentices—all those having declared to be in initial rather than further training. For all definitions, rank orders of countries are the same.

If we compare Table 4.3 with data of national sources on the extent of FETE in the economy, we must conclude that the ELFS figures grossly underestimate participation. This seems to be due very much to the short reference period of four weeks, all other surveys or administrative data being based on longer reference periods (see Table 4.4). However, the reference period being equal in all five countries, incidence reported by ELFS is of some worth if we are to compare countries. Still, because of all that we have said on definitions, incidence *levels* are not a very reliable source for comparison (see below).

Macro-Organization and Training Participation

The possible influence of the "macro-organization" of FETE systems (e.g., the extent of regulation, trade union, and employers' involvement in the system) on participation rates must therefore rely on qualitative judgment, which can only

Table 4.4

Participation Rates in FTE According to Different Sources

	International sources					National sources		
	ELFS 1989	OECD[a] 1989	OECD[b]	Boot	Force	Germany BMWB	Germany Mikrozensus	France
DEN	17.7	NA	—	NA				
GER	6.3	5.3	—	(1985) 25.0	(1987) 32.6	(1985)[d] 17.0 (1988)[d] 25.0	(1985)[e] 11.2	
FRA	3.4	3.5	26.6	(1986)	(1987)			(1985)(1987) 12.4[f] 26.0[g]
ITA	2.3	NA	—	21.0[c] (1986)	33.5 (1986–87)			
UK	13.2	14.4	—	37.0	30.0			

Sources: Labour Force Survey, data provided by Eurostat, *OECD Employment Outlook 1991*, Boot 1990, BMWB, Ministry of Education and Science, FRG; Serfaty 1992

Note: FTE = Further Vocational Training for the Employed.

[a] Based on national LFS, excluding apprentices' reference periods: F=time of survey, other surveys last four weeks.

[b] Administrative data, reference period 1 year=1988.

[c] Job-related further adult training (FETA) (25+). Boot's estimates are based on different national sources and personal calculations.

[d] Employed German nationals in FETE 19–64 on all employed 19–64 (representative survey of 3,500 persons in 1985 and 7,000 in 1988). Reference period: last year before survey.

[e] Mikrozensus 1985: those in FETE on all employed 15–64. Reference period: last two years.

[f] Enquete Formation Qualification 1985; reference period five years.

[g] CEREQ, Declaration 2483, employed in firms with ten or more employed (administrative source) year of declaration.

very partially be based on statistics. From Table 4.3 we can infer that a regulated system with a high degree of involvement of the social partners and a general levy as in Denmark "achieves" good participation levels. However, a deregulated system as in the United Kingdom without much government or social partner involvement and only a partial levy (not all Industrial Training Boards [ITBs] were discontinued in 1989) also has high participation levels. Moreover, despite the French obligatory levy of 1.2 percent (1.5 percent from 1993 onward), participation according to ELFS is lower than in Germany, where no such levy (but more social partner involvement) exists. A decentralized (regionalized) system, as in Italy, seems to draw the smallest proportion of the labor force into FETE. It should be clear that such an analysis stays on shaky grounds as long as no reliable indicators exist. If we based our assumed relationship on other figures (e.g., those on off-the-job training compiled by FORCE in Table 4.4), other configurations would appear. Estimates about the influence of a system (that is a set of policies) on participation in FETE will therefore remain uncertain for some time and leave much room for diverging interpretations as both the independent (system) and the dependent (here participation rates) variables remain unspecified.

The particular shape of a FETE system might influence not only the level, but also the structure of participation by sex, age, qualification level, and job status reached, by industry and firm size. A general observation is that participation in FETE in all our countries is biased in favor of those that have already reached the highest job status. This is best illustrated by two inverse pyramids: one shows job hierarchies, the lowest grades being on the bottom, the highest on the top; the other shows FETE participation, lowest participation at the bottom, highest at the top. Although there might be other configurations (it has been suggested during our case studies that very top management rarely participates in training), for the bulk of FETE the inverse pyramid holds true. A closer look at that distribution among countries does, however, reveal some differences: participation of the unskilled and semiskilled being higher, for example, in Denmark, the United Kingdom, and France than in Germany. Does that mean that public intervention (government or trade union) stimulates participation of those groups in those countries? The evidence is again not clear-cut if we stick to what we have said about the public-private divide, and higher participation of those groups in the United Kingdom and France seems to be due to higher shares of unskilled and semiskilled in the work force. Only for Denmark, where a lower share of unskilled in the work force goes together with a higher share of unskilled in FETE, can such an influence be acknowledged. According to ELFS figures, if women are still underrepresented in FETE levels for 1989 in Germany and the United Kingdom, women's incidence rates showed higher increases in three of our countries (Denmark, the United Kingdom, Italy). National sources seem to confirm the leveling off of men's and women's differences in FETE participation also for Germany (Bunderministerium für Bildung und Wissenschaft [BMBW] 1992). This trend is not due to active policies stimulating women's participation, however, but rather to increases in the participation of women in employment.

A second general feature of FETE distribution is the skewed participation between small and big firms, participation being usually a continuous positive function of firm size. There is partial evidence of country differences in that regard, too: data for France show a participation of only about 11 percent for firms with twenty to forty-nine employees but about 50 percent for firms with more than two thousand employees. For the same size classes British figures are 38 percent and 48 percent, indicating a much more even participation in the United Kingdom (OECD 1991). A more even distribution is also shown by a German sample survey (Bundesinstitut für Berufsbildung [BIBB]/Institut für Arbeitsmarkt und Berufsforschung der Bundesanstalt für Arbeit [IAB] special survey; see Géhin and Méhaut 1989).

The influence of FETE systems on that distribution is, of course, subject to debate: in France, the skewed distribution in regard to firm size is a policy concern, and paradoxically a uniform levy across all sizes of firms (except the very small firms with fewer than ten employees and as of 1993, have to spend only 0.15 percent of their wage bills for training) has not changed the uneven distribution.

It has to be added that FETE is only a subsystem ("the fourth pillar") of the whole ET system, and the interrelations among the four elements (general primary and secondary education, higher education, initial training, and further training) are also important for interpreting the functions of FETE. The crucial question (and the crucial intervening variable) here is whether FETE has to compensate for deficiencies on lower levels or is cumulative and adds up on existing knowledge. We will come back to that later.

"Output" of Training II: Economic Growth and Productivity

Up to now we have been mostly concerned with input considerations; even our "output I" measure is in fact an input measure: how the system is structured and how many participants there are. We should, however, also ask about the purpose of FETE: What is aimed at with FETE, and how can we evaluate the fulfillment of goals in a cross-national perspective? Although we are aware that the goals of FETE are manifold, we restrict our subsequent analysis mainly to economic considerations, and not without cause. Today, despite claims that training not only has to fulfill economic (efficiency) goals but is important also for equity reasons (e.g., equal access for all), most authors concerned with an analysis of FETE do, in fact, assume that the main goal of FETE is the enhancement of competitiveness on world markets—in other words, that FETE has—ceterus paribus—a positive impact on economic variables such as productivity (together with enhanced product quality) and stimulates the growth potential of the economy.

The Relationship between FETE, Economic Growth, and Employment

The argument refers to both initial and further training and includes general education of all levels (Porter 1989; Denison 1988; Finegold and Soskice 1988; Ostermann and Batt 1992; Office of Technology Assessment of the U.S. Congress 1990). While it has to be acknowledged that training and education fulfill other and wider functions (e.g., personal development), the "training as competitive factor" in an increasingly integrated and competitive world clearly dominates the debate in recent economic and socioeconomic literature concerned with training.

Work-related training (including the vocationally relevant parts of general education), although only one of the factors affecting competitiveness, is said to be a crucial factor and determine partly whether a country enters a vicious circle of low skills, low-quality products, low profitability, low tech, and so on, or instead a virtuous circle of high skills, high-quality products, high productivity, and high tech (Boot 1990; Rubenson 1987; *Employment in Europe*, Commission of the European Communities 1991).

It is also argued that the market segments in which industrialized market economies have a competitive advantage are precisely the upper segments of high-quality goods and services needing for their production a highly skilled work force (Matzner and Streeck 1991). Sectors (and countries) that have a large share of such products have, for example, fared much better during structural adjustments of the mid-1970s to the mid-1980s (Auer 1992).

In comparative sectoral studies that heavily stressed vocational training systems, it has been demonstrated, for example, that compared to Germany and even to France, the United Kingdom has a lower-skilled work force in many sectors and that this adversely affects products (lower standard, mass-produced goods) as well as processes and productivity (Steedman and Wagner 1987; Prais 1989; Campbell, Sorge, and Warner 1989). Other authors found Great Britain in a "low skill equilibrium" (Finegold and Soskice 1988). Porter's work on the "competitiveness of nations" (1989) stresses the importance of the vocational (and general) training and education system as a factor affecting national competitiveness. Edward F. Denison has repeatedly argued that education (a residual factor once land, capital, and labor are taken into account) is a major contributor to economic growth (1967, 1988). He has shown that a large part of U.S. economic growth between 1929 and 1969 was due to increases in the education levels of the U.S. population and that education contributed even more to the rise in productivity than advances in technology.

Usually these authors underline the importance of training as an independent variable that in turn favors competitiveness, economic growth, and eventually employment growth, although it seems as hard to quantify the actual impact of training and learning in the production function for labor as to account for the exact contribution of technology on the capital side.

This difficulty seems to increase if the contribution of education to growth is compared across countries. Look, for example, at Denison, who is one of the most renowned experts in accounting for the causes of economic growth and someone for whom education is of utmost importance for growth. In *Why Growth Rates Differ* (Denison 1967), a cross-national analysis of the factors contributing to economic growth was undertaken. The basic assumption was that the contribution of training can be studied by the "upward movement of the distribution of the labour force by amount of formal education" (p. 78), which shows also in earning differentials by years of education. "The more educated groups earn more and contribute more to the national product" (p. 79). This is in line with arguments of the Human Capital school (Becker 1964), which assume that investment in education leads to an increase in earnings, which is the rationale for individuals to engage in education and training.

However, after making complex calculations and ranking countries according to a quality index based on years of schooling and comparing it to a ranking of growth rates across several countries, Denison states that "the reader will note that there is no correspondence between a ranking of the countries by increases in education quality indexes and a ranking by growth rates of national income per person employed, so that education in the labour force is not a factor that *systematically* helps to explain differences in growth rates" (p. 78). He adds, "Education does not help to explain why growth rates in Europe were higher than in the United States but, on the contrary, adds to the differences that must be explained by other sources" (p. 104).

In the subsequent lines we will show that for our very limited sample (and the limited time span), we cannot but agree with Denison.

Output and Training: The Puzzle

For our subsequent analysis of the relationship between FETE incidence rates and some macroeconomic variables, we have taken into account the figures of the ELFS. This is because even if *levels* are misleading, incremental changes over time can be of some value if the outline and questions of the survey have not changed over time. Average annual change rates of FETE participation between 1983 and 1989 are therefore a more reliable indicator of country differences than levels. Definitions can be assumed to be constant over time, and incremental changes can therefore not be due to variation in definitions: for example, even if French data are grossly underestimated by the survey, they will be grossly underestimated at both dates.

The growth rates for FETE thus found can then be put in relation with economic output indicators such as annual average change rates of GDP, of GDP per employed, and of total employment over the same period.

Change rates alone, however, might not adequately represent a country's rank, as it might well be that for "leading" countries starting levels were already very high and incremental change low, but for followers the contrary can hold

Table 4.5

GDP Per Employed

	Level	R	Level	R	Level	R	Average annual change (in percent)			
	1970		1983		1989		70–89	R	83–89	R
Denmark	7,984	4	24,570	5	31,340	5	15	5	4.6	4
France	9,234	1	31,160	1	42,922	1	19	2	6.3	2
Germany	9,003	2	29,450	3	38,990	3	18	3	5.4	3
Italy	8,720	3	29,705	2	41,765	2	20	1	6.8	1
UK	7,756	5	25,017	4	31,599	4	16	4	4.4	5

Source: OECD National Accounts 1960–90; own calculations (Purchasing Power Parities, in US$).
Note: R = rank order.

true. The follower tends to catch up to the leader, and, as Baumol (1986) argued, for productivity the larger the gap between leader and follower, the faster the follower's potential rate of (productivity) advance. For our FETE data we do not have long historical series, but the rank orders for levels and growth rates (for the period considered) are the same: that is, countries with high incidence levels in 1983 had bigger growth rates and ended up with higher levels in 1989, too. No catching up is visible, rather a falling behind (e.g., see Italy).

For productivity (GDP per employed) the starting levels in 1970 are repro-duced in Table 4.5. The table shows that France already had a (slightly) higher GDP per employed level in 1970 than, for example, Germany and that the FETE "leaders" from 1983 to 1989 had a significantly lower level of productivity. Some catching up between 1970 and 1989 (e.g., between Italy and Germany and Denmark) the United Kingdom seems to have taken place, and the rank order has changed somewhat between the two dates. However, arguing with levels does not fundamentally alter the unsystematic relation-ships found below.

FETE participation is also influenced by the business cycle, firms tending to cut expenditure on training during recessions and expand it during recoveries. However, because the period between 1983 and 1989 corresponds in all our countries to the recovery period after the second "oil shock," we did not assume any major business-cycle influence on FETE participation. For FETE, the years 1983 to 1989 are also of particular importance, as this period coincides with the increasing importance of "human resource development" policies in firms, that is, internal strategies of work force adjustment to structural change, in which FETE is an important part (Auer 1992).

No time lag was allowed for in measuring the impact of FETE on our low level of analysis: In contrast to initial training, which is more long term in nature

Table 4.6

Gross Domestic Product, Employment, Unemployment, Productivity, and Training (average annual change 1983–89 in percent)

	GDP1[a]	R	Employ- ment[a]	R	Unemploy- ment[b]	R	Produc- tivity[a]	R	Train- ing[c]	R
UK	3.4	1	2.0	1	-6	1	1.3	4	6.7	3
Italy	3.1	2	0.4	4	4.8	5	2.7	1	-1.9	5
Germany	2.8	3	0.8	3	-1.3	3	1.9	3	(7.8)[d]	2
France	2.6	4	0.2	5	2.3	4	2.4	2	1.0	4
Denmark	2.1	5	1.2	2	-3.6	2	0.9	5	8.1	1

Note: R = rank order.

[a] *Source: OECD Economic Outlook,* no. 48, December 1990: Productivity = GDP per person in employment; Employment = total employment.

[b] *Source: Employment Outlook 1991*, p. 257; own calculations, rounded.

[c] *Source:* European Labour Force Survey, WZB: Training = FETE, dependently employed in training/all dependently employed (14–49).

[d] *Source:* BMBW 1989 (period 1982 to 1988).

and might show its impact only after some time, we assumed that the impact of FETE, which is usually of short duration, will show immediately. This, of course, is only a plausible assumption and not a proven fact, as the "incubation period" might be longer and is certainly different for the various types of FETE (e.g., firm-specific or general). However, the time span considered being six years, productivity changes should show not in year one but in the subsequent years of the period.

The story of Table 4.6 is a simple one: On this level of aggregation, with our data and for the period 1983 to 1989, no straightforward and systematic positive relationship between increases in the participation of FETE and economic growth and productivity can be shown. If a consistent pattern can be developed out of such a small sample, an inverse rank order must be acknowledged for productivity and training (which stays valid if one extends the analysis to ten EEC countries for which we have comparable data; see Auer 1992): countries with high increases in participants in FETE are not those with corresponding increases in productivity (and growth).

Vocational training for the already employed as an assumed major contribution to competition and growth has only rather recently come to the fore. For most economists dealing with the links between education and training and growth, the developments of general education, as measured by higher attainment levels and corresponding wage increases, have played a much larger role. It can therefore be argued that general education or initial vocational training is of more importance for economic output than FETE.

Table 4.7

Compound Indicators of Education and Training (rank orders)

	Educa-tion 1	Educa-tion 2	Educa-tion 3	Educa-tion 4	Training 1	Training 2	Compound ranking (average)
Denmark	1	1	1	2	2	1	(1.3)	1
UK	4	4	2	5	4	2	(3.5)	3/4
Germany	2	2	4	1	1	3	(2.1)	2
France	5	3	3	3	3	4	(3.5)	3/4
Italy	3	5	5	4	5	5	(4.5)	5

Notes: Education 1 = Share of population 14–49 having received education and training during last four weeks. *Source:* ELFS 89.

Education 2 = Attainment levels in 1987 (except DK figures for 1983–84), countries are ranked according to their achievement in providing the population with more than secondary schooling. *Source: OECD Employment Outlook 1989;* for DK: Kristensen 1989; for France: Möbus and Sevestre 1991.

Education 3 = Attainment levels in 1987 (except DK figures for 1985–86) countries are ranked according to the number of people receiving higher education. *Source: OECD Employment Outlook 1989;* proxy for DK calculated from Höcker 1992; for France: Möbus and Sevestre 1991.

Education 4 = Ranking of participation levels of 16 to 18 years old in ET (1986). *Source:* training statistics 1990, Employment Department Training statistics, (HMSO).

Training 1 = Ranking of initial vocational training (number of participants in dual or vocational training). *Source: OECD Employment Outlook 1989;* Kristensen 1989; Höcker 1992; Möbus and Sevestre 1991.

Training 2 = Further Education and Training for the Employed 1989 participation levels. *Source:* European Labour Force Survey, 1989.

For compound ranking all indicators are assumed to have the same value.

To allow for general education to be taken into account, we have computed a compound indicator of education and training of the five countries in our study. Table 4.7 shows the ranking of our countries according to different measures for education and training, as well as the compound indicator. (For details and sources see notes in Table 4.4.)

If we compare our compound ranking with the ranking obtained for FETE participation incidence rates for 1989, we see that Denmark is still the country with the "best achievements" (*n.b.*: all indicators are input based) in education and training, and that Germany comes second, followed by France and Great Britain (*ex aequo*), while Italy remains "last" even if we take into account multiple elements of education.

Again, if we now relate our compound education indicator to our three productivity measures (average annual changes in overall GDP per employed 1983–89 and,

Table 4.8

Compound Indicators of Education and Training, Economic Growth, and Productivity (rank orders)

	Compound ranking	GDP	Productivity		
			1	2	3
Denmark	1	5	5	4	5
Germany	2	3	3	3	3
France	3/4	4	2	2	2
UK	3/4	1	4	5	4
Italy	5	2	1	1	1

Notes: GDP = Average annual change 1983–89.

Productivity 1 = GDP per person in employment average annual change, 1983–89, OECD 1990.

Productivity 2 = Output per hours, manufacturing only, average annual change, long-term trend 1960–87. *Source:* Bureau of Labour Statistics, 1988; *Monthly Labour Review,* December 1988.

Productivity 3 = GDP per employed in current prices and current Purchasing Power Parities (PPP's) in US$, average annual change trend 1970–89 (own calculations based on data from *OECD National Accounts 1960–1990,* OECD 1992).

to account for long-term trends, average annual change in GDP per employed 1970–89, and hourly manufacturing productivity 1960–87), the relationship between ET and productivity initially found remains valid (see Table 4.8).

Long-term productivity trends are considered here only to show that productivity differences among countries in 1983–89 are not only short-term phenomena but seem to hold true with slight changes also over the long term. We have not dealt with intertemporal problems (like lags and changes over time) and assume that national institutions like ET systems have a certain stability over time. However, it must be acknowledged that a more dynamic analysis considering institutional change and lags could produce more reliable results.

As far as the static analysis of the relationship between education and growth in the sample of five countries is concerned, no systematic positive relationship between education and growth appears. However, GDP per employed, one of the usual indicators to measure macroeconomic performance, might not be adequate because it is not measuring the success of a national economy to integrate its population into the labor market.

GDP per head might be a better indicator of a country's wealth than GDP per employed, because it could well be that the national product of, say, Italy, known for its low labor force participation rate, is relatively high if only the employed are taken into account, but low in relative terms if the whole population is considered. Taking into consideration level and increase of GDP per head (on a

Table 4.9

Rank Orders GDP per Head (in PPP and US$)

Country	Level 1970	Level 1989	Change 1970–89	Comp.Ind ET
Denmark	2	3	5	1
France	3	2	2	3/4
Germany	1	1	4	2
Italy	5	4	1	5
UK	4	5	3	3/4

Source: OECD National Accounts 1960–1990, Paris 1992.

Purchasing Power Parities [PPP] basis in US$) would in effect change the level ranks somewhat (e.g., Germany taking rank one before France, Italy coming only fourth) and also show that levels and increments of GDP per head do not correspond in ranks (Italy being first in long-term change from 1970 to 1989 but fourth in level; for Germany the inverse relationship holds true). Again, with regard to our analysis, which tries to find a systematic link between ET and economic growth and productivity, a first analysis of national divergency of GDP per head figures and training indicators reveals that even a more appropriate performance indicator does not solve the puzzle. Although our compound ET indicator shows a better correlation with GDP per head in 1989 levels, it does not tell us much on long-term growth rates.

The questions remain as to why it was possible for Italy to achieve the highest growth rates over the long-term (nineteen years) with, according to some accepted standards, a deficient education system, and why Denmark's highly rated ET system did not push the country onto a more marked growth path.

The very limited data put forward here suggest that ET does not explain why growth rates or productivity between the countries considered differ. We cannot but agree with Denison's conclusion of the very unsystematic contribution of education to growth across countries and also with his statement that rather than solving the riddle, it adds to the difficulties of determining the causes of growth (Denison 1967, 78).

Table 4.6 shows not only the differences in ranking of countries between FETE incidence increases and corresponding increases in productivity but also changes in employment and unemployment. A first observation is that countries with higher employment growth have higher FETE participation rates than countries with low employment growth. A simple bivariate regression analysis with all EEC countries for which we had comparable figures (only ten, but almost the whole entity of twelve) confirmed that statement (Auer 1992) (see Figure 4.2). Evidence suggests that employment seems to be the independent variable, explaining partially why FETE participation rose: over the period, FETE participation increased particularly for women, as did employment participation. Both FETE leaders (Denmark and the United Kingdom) had by far the highest increase in women's labor force participation rates: from 73 to 89 plus 25 percent for Denmark and plus 22 percent for the United Kingdom according to the OECD (1992).

Also, unemployment has decreased slightly more in countries with high(er) participation rates in FETE, although that seems to be due to the fact that in those countries the participation rates of the unemployed in FETE have increased more than in the others and that employment was on the increase: FETE seen as prevention against unemployment might therefore be only of minor influence.

From our figures we can infer that employment-led growth leads to higher participation rates in FETE than productivity-led growth. Without developing that point here fully, some observations can be made: There was and is a wide-spread debate about whether employment-led growth or productivity-led growth is desirable. This debate concerns mostly the U.S. job-miracle vs. the European "scelorosis" on the job-creation side (e.g., between 1970 and 1992, for each percentage point in growth, there was a 0.7 growth in jobs in the United States compared to only 0.11 for Europe). It has been stated that while the United States had to pay for employment-led growth by a slowdown in productivity and an increase in low-paid jobs, Germany had to pay for high productivity by comparatively higher unemployment and transfer payments (see Schettkat 1992).

An analysis too strictly concerned with productivity could miss the fact that employment development, even when it is not paralleled by productivity increases, can be judged a positive contribution to welfare and growth if the jobs created are of an acceptable standard.

Other Evidence of Uncertain Links between Training and Economic Output

The many uncertainties in both input and output data (e.g., how to measure productivity in the highly training-intensive public sector), especially at a high level of aggregation, the limited number of cases, the limited time span, and so on could certainly be used to simply reject the results found. But more important, as the input nature of education and training data does not tell us much about achievements anyway, how can the link with outcome on the product (or services) side be established?

Moreover, as even firms do not know much about the translation of training efforts into quantity and quality of products (this is a clear result of our own case studies, Auer 1992, and is confirmed by other—national—studies, e.g., Koning and Gelderblom 1992), how could one know these things at higher levels of aggregation?

These are certainly fundamental questions. However, even if we would never go as far as to contend having grasped the reality of the relationship between ET and growth (only one possible representation of this relationship through fairly limited data), we contend that one should take the results seriously in order to

Figure 4.2 **Employment Growth and Training Participation**

% of workforce in training (1989)

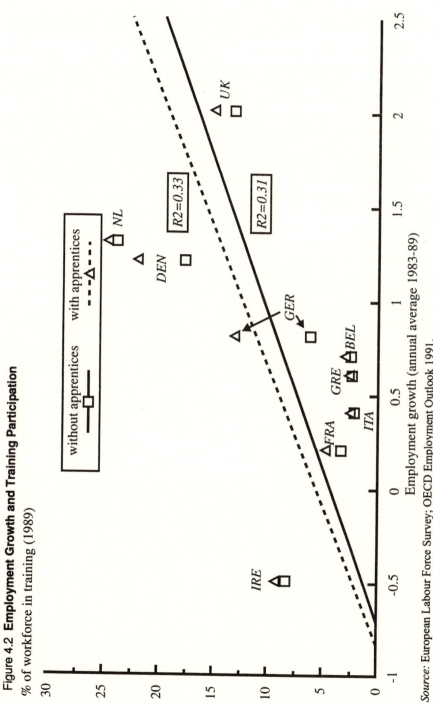

Source: European Labour Force Survey; OECD Employment Outlook 1991.
Note: Luxembourg excluded (data nonreliable).

enhance further research on the topic and attract the attention of policymakers to problems that go beyond the easy assumption that "more is better" in education and training.

Other researchers have come to equally puzzling results in using much more sophisticated methods. We have already mentioned Denison, who found no systematic relationship between education and training in an international comparison. A (national) study on company training and productivity in fifty-one Dutch firms that had also taken participation rates in company training as a measure showed "that training efforts make no significant impact on productivity" (Koning and Gelderblom 1992, 72), although the enhancement of productivity was the main reason the firms engaged in such training. And the authors of *The Machine That Changed the World* (Womack, Jones, and Roos 1990) confront us with puzzling data on the link between education and productivity. Their data suggest that in Japan a car is assembled in 16.8 hours, and 60 defects per 100 cars are detected. Newly recruited automobile workers get an average training of 380 hours. In the United States, new recruits get only 46 hours of training, and average productivity stands at 25.1 hours per car with 82 defects per 100 cars. In Europe, with training hours standing at 173, the productivity average is 36.2 hours and 97 defects. That is to say that with less training than their European counterparts, U.S. workers are more productive and produce better quality. Certainly, different training systems play a role (Japan relying heavily on on-the-job training), and again (as for all studies, by and large) we can have doubt about the figures presented. But they indicate at least a very unsystematic relationship between productivity and training.

It should not be pretended that all studies show such unsystematic or even negative relationships. On the contrary, the general wisdom (and the general intuition) is to assume a positive contribution of education to growth, and Denison (1967, 1988) has demonstrated it empirically for the United States. Also, Schultz (1961), Psacharopoulos (1984), Bowman (1967), and Rosen (1977) found such a relationship for general education. In summarizing the work of growth-accounting studies, the OECD shows that such studies have all assumed and found a positive relationship but have failed to account for nonformal training like on-the-job experience (and one can add further vocational training in general: the German and the Danish apprenticeship systems did not enter into Denison's comparison, thus he ranked Denmark and Germany last in educational achievement, a mistake that shows how much general education has been mystified as a factor supporting economic growth). However, doubts are also expressed here as to the straightforward links between the two variables: "Overall, the evidence accumulated over the past two decades does underline the importance of educational attainment as a variable influencing economic performance. It affirms the association between schooling and labour productivity and is linked in turn to positive impacts on macroeconomic performance and individual well-being. . . . However, the evidence is not definitive about the precise nature

of the relationship between educational attainment and labour productivity. . . .
thus there are obvious dangers in relying too much on any one of the theories of
the economic significance of education. . . . It may be concluded that education
is a necessary, although not a sufficient condition for economic growth. . . .
Educational attainment of the labour force is an important indicator of an
economy's *potential* for economic growth" (OECD 1989, 51 and 52). In his
paper "Training too much? A Sceptical Look at the Economics of Skill Provision
in the UK," J.R. Shackleton raised some doubt on the alleged contribution that
training can make to restore the competitiveness of the U.K. economy. He sees
training as only one other item on a list of proposals that have been made in the
past to restore the United Kingdom's economy, among which were "inadequate
investment in new technology, high marginal tax rates, too much state involvement in industry (or too little, or the wrong kind) . . . combative or subversive
trade unions, the lack of an incomes policy, the burden of the welfare state . . . ,"
and he clearly thinks that the role of training to boost an economy is overestimated. Among many others he cites a study of the Central Policy Review Staff, a
British think tank, on the links between training, its quality, and productivity.
Their conclusion reads as follows: "It is difficult, if not impossible, to prove that
particular features of a country's training and education system are associated
with high or low levels of productivity" (cited by Shackleton 1992, 17).

Possible Reasons for Training's Low Impact

The evidence seems to point toward a rather skeptical estimation of the impact of
education and training on economic performance, which does not concord with
the recent views (hardly ever empirically assessed) of so many authors and
policymakers. In the following lines, some arguments as to why there might be
no straightforward link between training and performance are discussed.

There is no doubt that company training can enhance the development potential of firms. There is, however, no reason to believe that there is a straightforward link between training (that is, FETE) and economic performance. Different
factors have to be considered:

* Training and absenteeism
    A first factor is the quantity of groups within the labor force participat-
    ing in FETE at any moment in time. The more people who participate in
    education and training, the fewer who participate in production itself. For
    example, in Denmark in 1983 10 percent and in 1988 more than 7 percent
    of all absences from work were due to training (OECD 1991). If train-
    ing is of comparatively long duration (data of a representative survey
    made by Anker and Andersen show an average duration of 127 hours
    per participant in 1991, by far the longest average duration in Europe),
    high participation rates could result in losses of production (which
    could lead—via replacements—to employment-enhancing but produc-

tivity-slowing effects). And even on-the-job training, not involving absence from work, can result in losses in productivity, as trainees are assumed to be less productive during training. One may assume that over the long term the workers trained are more productive and contribute positively to productivity and growth, but no data are available to show the net result in such a balance, and nobody knows the break-even point—i.e., the point where the positive contribution of job-related training exceeds the negative impact of absences or the lower productivity of trainees.

- Inefficient allocation of training in internal labor markets or losses due to high mobility

In a macro perspective the contribution to growth of firm-specific vocational training for internal labor markets and of vocational training that enhances external mobility (e.g., general training for the labor market) should be considered equal. (This does not hold true for a micro perspective, where clear differences in the returns of firms to specific and general training can be distinguished; Becker 1975). However, one can question the contribution to performance in both kinds of training: in internal labor markets, especially in the training-intensive public sector and in large firms, training participation can often be linked to the "social" administration of internal labor markets and not to productivity enhancements (see, for example, Dayan, Géhin, and Verdier 1986). This, of course, is even more so if training received is not job related. There is no clear evidence about the differences in the share of employed in internal labor markets among our countries. However, low productivity because of inefficient training in internal labor markets seems to be less a problem than low productivity because of employment instability and high labor turnover. In fact, training that enhances external mobility (general training) might not push the economy into a productivity-enhancing path because transaction costs (Williamson 1985) of high mobility might be important and might result in productivity losses not offset by productivity gains through training investment.

Moreover, high mobility could make (induction) training even more necessary without leading necessarily to additional productivity. Although there is mixed evidence on micro and meso levels (some sectoral data showing high participation in sectors with high employment stability), FETE participation rates as shown by ELFS figures tend to be higher in countries with high (external) labor mobility (Denmark, the United Kingdom) than in countries with lower external mobility like France and Italy (Auer 1992). The same applies to job-creation capacities. Between 1983 and 1989, EEC countries that have created more jobs, also have higher FETE participation rates (see above).

- Insufficient quality of training

In the field of company training the quality aspects are often not known. Our own case studies show convincingly that firms themselves know little about the quality of their training, as they have only "soft" methods of evaluation. This is, however, an area of change as firms become increasingly aware of the necessity to evaluate training investments. A thorough assessment of the quality of training hidden behind a quantitative measure like FETE participation might reveal that it is not the quantity of training that is important for competitiveness but the quality of training.

- Compensatory training

    Moreover, if company training has to compensate for a lack of initial (or general) training, its contribution to performance has to be assumed to be less important, as in the case of a FETE system building skills upon an existing vocational training system. Among our countries, the United Kingdom's high incidence rates seem to indicate also the need for compensation of insufficient initial training. Empirical "proof" for such a compensatory role could be the extent of initial training as reproduced in Table 4.7, columns 2 (percentage of population of working age with more than secondary-level education), 4 (ET participation levels 16 to 18 years old), and 5 (share of initial vocational training). If high FETE incidence goes with low rankings in each or any of these categories, some compensation can be assumed. This is, for example, the case in the United Kingdom. Also, Italy has a poor ranking in all of these categories. However, despite the provision of a training leave for compensation purposes ("150 hours"), no major effort of compensation through FETE seems to take place in Italy, as FETE participation is low (Forlani 1992; Goldin 1992). In Germany, compensation seems not to be a major problem, and this holds true for Denmark, which has, however, an "inbuilt" compensation in its FETE system in the form of widespread institutionally assured training for unskilled and semiskilled workers (Anker and Andersen 1991; Höcker 1992).

Another way to look at the extent of compensation is to look at the distribution of training according to training participation of different occupational groups. In all the countries under consideration, the chances to participate in FETE increase with the amount of training already received and the occupational status reached (see above). This would suggest that FETE in general is cumulative more than compensatory. However, there are differences among countries: the share of unskilled and semiskilled workers participating in FETE is especially low in Germany but is more important in the United Kingdom (CEDEFOP 1990), so that we can assume more compensation there.

Conclusion

To conclude, it has to be recalled that the present article dealt mostly with one particular kind of training—further training for the employed work force—and the main questions asked were how the training systems of five selected countries are shaped and if some of the countries have ET systems that help to better enhance the output (in services or products) on a macro level than those of others. For FETE the question of the links between productivity and training systems is crucial also because in a globalizing economy, there is not much shelter against competitors that might have superior production systems (it might not be as crucial for other types of education and training that are less concerned by immediate performance). The question seems relevant because there is a widespread belief "that human capital in technology-driven economies is becoming a decisive factor in contributing to economic performance" (OECD 1990, 64). The main finding of our partial research is that by examining the systems and performance indicators on the macro level, such a relationship cannot easily be assessed on empirical data, and the general evidence is that the links between education and training and economic performance are not clear at all, especially in a cross-national comparative view.

Idiosyncrasies of training systems are important, and it is difficult to talk about country "models" serving as examples for other countries. It seems as if productivity can be reached with several types of ET systems, and there is a correspondence between the training system and the economy in general. The studies of Steedman and Wagner (1987) and Prais (1989) have shown this convincingly for Germany and the United Kingdom: in diverse branches of the economy (kitchen furniture and the metal industry, for example) the two countries engage in different market segments and this also because of their training systems. In the United Kingdom, firms seem to produce more for the mass consumption segment, whereas in Germany up-market products for specific market niches are common. This is also due, according to these authors, to differentials in the skill levels of the two countries.

However, once we widen our analysis to questions of productivity it is not very easy to put forward appraisals of different systems. According to our data, it is true that Germany has a higher overall productivity rate than Great Britain, and one can show that vocational training (particularly initial vocational training) is one of the explanations for such productivity differentials (see Steedman and Wagner 1987). But if we compare another pair of countries, such easy statements of one system being better than the other become more difficult. For example, according to certain accepted standards, the Danish system of further vocational training, organized by the social partners and the state, which tops up an initial vocational system in part comparable to the German system and gives the possibility of combining many short-time modules into a certified career, thereby serving the interests of firms and workers alike and resulting in high participation, looks like a "best practice" system. However, while it surely has contributed to turning Denmark into a developed economy, it seems that it has contributed less well to enhancing relative performance over the last fifteen or twenty years. On the other hand, the Italian way of organizing FETE on a heterogeneous regionalized basis with low FETE participation and a school-based initial vocational system has not prevented the country from having comparatively high long-term growth rates.

Such results make us believe that much more research is needed to solve the training-productivity puzzle. In part, our problem is surely a problem of data and the problems that arise if one is to argue on a macro level using a broad macro productivity measure. Therefore, to begin with, the problem of data inadequacy and unavailability should be tackled. The present efforts of the European Commission's FORCE program (together with Eurostat and CEDEFOP) to carry out a major representative survey of firms' participation in FETE might bring about a more reliable data base by the end of 1994. Further research, we believe, should be done much more on the micro (company) level, where the detailed elements of efficient or less efficient training "systems" can be more adequately grasped than on a very aggregate level where too many variables intervene. However, if one is to argue in cross-country comparative terms, a dynamic analysis level should be introduced, because the requirements for training and the demands put on training institutions change over time, and a system, once adapted to support growth in the economy in a certain period, might be less well adapted to do so in the following period. Adaptability of training systems might be—above and beyond productivity—another indicator of success for training systems.

Other indicators are the success or nonsuccess of a country to provide for regulation of externalities: for training investments such externalities arise if employers who train their work force have their trained staff "poached" by other employers before they are able to recoup their training investment. If this occurs frequently, employers who train (and therefore create positive externalities for others) might invest only the minimum necessary in training that would lead, according to economic reasoning, to a general underinvestment in training. The problem can be coped with by providing publicly financed and organized training, by the introduction of a levy system, or by incentives for those firms that train. It has to be assumed that "market" systems would have more of this sort of problem than regulated systems; for example, a "low skill equilibrium" (Finegold and Soskice 1988) is said to be experienced by the U.K. economy because of the nonexistence of much regulation that spreads cost for training (high FETE participation does not directly contradict such a statement if one accepts that this is done in the United Kingdom often to compensate for a lack of initial training). Again, the Danish system, because of its regulatory frame and "socialized" costs through the levy, protects better against the negative effects of poaching.

Because of the limited scope of our analysis, only some very broad recommendations can be given as far as training policy is concerned. In general, a clarification of targets for private or public policies in FETE could be helpful. As Becker has already observed in his seminal book *Human Capital* (1964), companies are rather unwilling to engage in such general training when they are not sure to recoup their costs of training investment. This would be an argument for public intervention in this area, as the market seems not to offer enough incentives to firms to invest in training. This is even more so for compensatory training.

It must be assumed that companies always provide for their specific training, which should accordingly never be financed publicly. However, the distinction between general and specific training is rather blurred in a growing number of branches and occupations. For example, information technologies are now widely used in many areas of the economy, and training on computers being very much a basic skill in labor markets nowadays is therefore highly transferable among companies (Auer and Schmid 1993).

Still, it seems rational that public policy be clearly targeted on areas that help firms where they have to fulfill tasks that should have been fulfilled in other levels of society. We have singled out compensatory training as being one that is preventing companies (and countries) from reaping all the benefits of FETE. Therefore, public policy should help companies with compensatory kinds of training, or, still better, reform basic education and initial vocational systems in order to allow firms and workers to engage in further training that will top up effectively sound basic and initial training. If previous skill levels are high, FETE becomes more effective, as an educated work force is more receptive to further training.

Especially during recessions, companies, even if they get public funds, might be unwilling to fulfill any "social" role like the organization of compensatory training. And yet it is exactly in downturns that such training should take place, because employees are partially freed from production work: An active use of public funds could help to organize this kind of training. For example, "passive" allowances like short-time work compensation could be used more actively and linked to training. During recessions many qualified workers are freed from direct production work and can act as trainers for those needing compensation training. In compensatory training at least, efficiency and equity goals could be met at the same time.

References

Anker, N., and Andersen, D. 1991. *Efteruddannelse*. Copenhagen: Socialforskings-instituttet.

Auer, P. 1992a. *Workforce Adjustment Patterns*. Luxembourg: Commission of the European Communities.

———. 1992b. *Further Education and Training for the Employed (FETE): European Diversity*. Discussion paper FS I, 2–3. Wissenschaftszentorium Berlin für Sozialforschung.

Auer, P., and Schmid, G. 1993. *Challenges and Possible Responses. Further Education and Training for the Employed in Europe*. Discussion Paper FS I 93–202, Wissenschaftszentrum Berlin für Sozialforschung.

Baumol, W.J. 1986. "Productivity Growth, Convergence and Welfare: What the Long-Run Data Show." *American Economic Review* 76, no. 5 (December): 1072–85.

Becker, G.S. 1964, 1975. *Human Capital*. New York: National Bureau of Economic Research.

Boot, P.A. 1990. *Further Education and Training of Adults. Provision, Participation, Economic Impact and Policy Options.* Netherlands, The Hague: Ministry of Social Affairs and Employment.

Bowman, M.J. 1967. "Education and Economic Growth." In *Economic Factors Affecting the Financing of Education in the Decade Ahead*, eds., R.L. Johns et al., 83–120.

Bundesministerium für Bildung und Wissenschaft. 1990a. *Berichtssystem Weiterbildung 89, Integrierter Gesamtbericht.* Bonn.

——. 1990b. *Betriebliche Weiterbildung Forschungsstand und Forschungsperspektiven, zwei Gutachten.* Bonn.

Campbell, A.; Sorge, A.; and Warner, M. 1989. *Microelectronic Poduct Application in Great Britain and West Germany: Strategies, Competence and Training.* Aldershot: Avesbury.

Commission of the European Communities, Task Force Human Resources, FORCE. 1991. "Managing Chart," unpublished mimeo. Brussels.

CEDEFOP. 1990. Flash 1/90 (bulletin). Berlin.

Dayan, J.L.; Géhin, J.P.; and Verdier, E. 1986. "La formation continue dans l'entreprise." *Formation Emploi*, no. 16 (Oct.-Dec.): 7–35.

Denison, E.F. 1967. *Why Growth Rates Differ: Postwar Experience in Nine Western Countries.* Washington: Brookings Institution.

——. 1988. *Accounting for United States Economic Growth.* Washington: Brookings Institution.

Doeringer, P., and Piore, M. 1971. *Internal Labour Markets and Manpower Analysis.* Lexington, Mass.: Lexington Books.

Employment Department. 1990. *Training Statistics 1990.* London.

Finegold, D., and Soskice, D. 1988. "The Failure of Training in Britain: Analysis and Prescription." *Oxford Review of Economic Policy* 4, no. 3.

Forlani, L. 1993. "Further Education and Training for the Employed: The Case of Italy." In *Challenges and Possible Responses. Further Education and Training for the Employed. A Workshop Reader*, eds., P. Auer and G. Schmid. Wissenschaftszentrum Berlin.

Géhin, J.P., and Méhaut, Ph. 1989. *La formation continue en RFA, Production et usage de la formation par et dans l'entreprise.* Paris: Tome III.

Goldin, R. 1992. *Berufliche Aus-und Weiterbildung in Italien.* Manuskript, Berlin.

Höcker, H. 1992. *Berufliche Weiterbildung für Beschäftigte in Dänemark.* Wissenschaftszentrum Berlin, Discussion Paper FS I 92–8.

"International Labor Productivity in Manufacturing." *Monthly Labor Review*, December 1988.

Koning. J. D., and Gelderblom, A. 1992. *Company Training: Volume, Underinvestment and Return.* Fourth (EALE) European Association of Labour Economists Annual Conference Paper, Madrid, pp. 63–74.

Kristensen, P.H. 1989. "Country Report Denmark." In *Education, Technical Culture and Regional Prosperity. Interim Report*, ed., G. Sweeney. Dublin: Sica Innovation Consultants Ltd.

Matzner, E., and Streeck, W. 1991. *Beyond Keynesianism. The Socio-Economics of Production and Full Employment.* Aldershot: Elgar Publishing.

Möbus, N., and Sevestre, P. 1991. *Formation professionnelle et emploi: un lien plus marqué en Allemagne. Economie et Statistique*, no. 246–47 (September-October).

OECD. 1989. "Educational Attainment of the Labour Force." In *Employment Outlook 1989*, pp. 47–93.

——. 1990. *Labour Market Policies for the 90s.* Paris.

——. 1991. "Enterprise Related Training." In *Employment Outlook 1991*, 135–75.

————. 1992. "National Accounts 1960–1990." Paris.

————. 1992. *Employment Outlook 1992.*

Office of Technology Assessment of the U.S. Congress. 1990. *Worker Training: Competing in the New International Economy.* Washington, D.C.

Osterman, P., and Batt, R. 1992. *Employer Centered Training for International Competitiveness.* Cambridge, Mass.: Massachusetts Institute of Technology, Sloan School. Manuscript.

Porter, M. 1989. *The Competitive Advantage of Nations.* New York: Free Press.

Prais, S.J. 1989. "Productivity, Education and Training: Britain and Other Countries Compared." *National Institute Economic Review*, February 1989.

Psacharopoulos, G. 1984. "The Contribution of Education to Economic Growth." In *International Comparisons of Productivity and Causes of the Slowdown*, ed., J.W. Kendrick, 335–60. Cambridge: Ballinger Publishing.

Rees, G. 1993. "Further Education and Training for the Employed: The Case of the UK." In *Challenges and Possible Responses. Further Education and Training for the Employed. A Workshop Reader*, eds., P. Auer and G. Schmid. Wissenschaftszentrum Berlin.

Rosen, S. 1977. "Human Capital: A Survey of Empirical Research." In *Research in Labour Economics*, ed., R.C. Ehrenberg, 3–39. Greenwich, Conn.: JAI Press.

Rubenson, K. 1987. *The Economics of Adult Basic Education.* Vancouver: University of British Columbia.

Schettkat, R. 1992. *Productivity Trends in Germany and the US: Some Speculations on the Impact of Institutions.* CEPR Workshop on Institutions and Economic Growth, London, November 1992.

Schultz, T.W. 1961. "Investment in Human Capital." *American Economic Review* (March): 1–17.

Serfaty, E. 1993. "Le rôle de la puirsance publique law le système de la formation professionnelle en France. In *Challenges and Possible Responses. Further Education and Training for the Employed, A Workshop Reader*, eds., P. Auer and G. Schmid. Wissenschaftszentrum Berlin.

Shackleton, J.R. 1992. *Training Too Much? A Sceptical Look at the Economics of Skill Provision in the UK.* Hobart Paper 118, Institute of Economic Affairs, London.

Steedman, H., and Wagner, K. 1987. "A Second Look at Productivity, Machinery and Skills in Britain and Germany. Productivity, Education and Training: Britain and Other Countries Compared." *National Institute Economic Review* (November 1987).

Streeck, W. et al. 1987. *Steuerung und Regulierung der beruflichen Bildung.* Berlin: Sigma.

Williamson, Oliver E. 1985. *The Economic Institutions of Capitalism.* New York: Free Press.

Womack, J.P.; Jones, D.T.; and Roos, D. 1990. *The Machine That Changed the World.* New York: Rawson & Associates.

5

Institutional Regimes of Part-Time Working

Friederike Maier

Introduction

One of the changes in the structure of labor markets in the industrialized Western countries has been the increase in forms of employment that differ from permanent full-time employment. Part-time employment, i.e., working time arrangements with a usually shorter working time than the full-time volume of hours, is one form of atypical work, and it often includes both shorter working hours and different employment status, such as fixed-term employment.

Part-time work is often women's work, but it is only one form of female employment, and its increase seems to be a general trend but not a uniform process. It reflects a variety of changes in the labor market:

- changing structures of labor supply, i.e., a growing proportion of women searching for paid employment. Due to time restrictions set by family responsibilities, some women want or need paid employment with shorter working hours than regular full-time employment offers;
- changing employment patterns in certain sectors of the economy, i.e., firms using "working time" variations as an instrument of gaining flexibility and higher productivity.

The general assessment of part-time employment is rather contradictory: on one side, part-time employment opens employment opportunities for those who want or need reduced working time, and is, therefore, sometimes favorable to continuous labor force attachment; on the other side, part-time employment means less income (compared to full-time employment), and a restricted choice concerning sectors and occupations where part-time employment is offered, and it is often incompatible with occupational progression, as full-time permanent employment remains the norm.

Part-time work is far from being a new phenomenon. As early as the 1960s there was a growth of employment relations with reduced working time in many industrialized countries. This usually took the form of offering married women special employment possibilities, in both manufacturing and service sectors. Conceived as an employment to top up family income and introduced at a time of labor shortage and the expansion of the service sector, part-time employment opportunities reflected the tightening of the labor markets and the societal norm that dictated women's place as primarily in the family.

Since the mid-1970s, however, the development of part-time work has changed fundamentally: the diffusion of part-time work has increased, and whole sectors of national economies have reorganized their employment/working-time patterns around various forms of part-time work. The combination of the general employment crisis with mass unemployment, the rising aspirations of increasingly well-qualified women regarding paid employment, and the pressure on both private and public employers to rationalize and cut costs led to a widespread use of part-time work as an important instrument of economic and labor market adjustment.

This chapter deals with the factors influencing the growth of part-time employment in six EC countries (Belgium, West Germany, Denmark, France, the Netherlands, and the United Kingdom). It is based on a more detailed study finished in 1991 and updated (see Maier 1991). By using European Labour Force Survey data, which provide a common data base, the chapter looks on the demand side and the supply side of the labor market, analyzes the underlying institutional regimes of the gender-specific division of labor, and highlights the influence of legal regulations concerning labor law and social security on the level and structure of part-time work. The chapter concludes with some tentative ideas on the future developments of working time and employment in the European Community.

Changes in the Labor Market

Demand Side Developments

The demand for part-time labor by employers must be seen in the context of new enterprise strategies to cut labor costs and increase labor productivity. Uncertainties in product markets, the expansion of the service sector, especially in private services, and the new scope for decoupling individual working time from plant operating time have accelerated the introduction of flexible working-time regimes, of which part-time work is only one of many forms (including shift work, overtime/short-time work, weekend work, etc.). In this context part-time work provides employers with a variety of advantages:

- The cost-output relation is generally more favorable in part-time than in full-time employment, as part-timers work more intensively—for shorter time periods—than full-time employees. In other words, enterprise performance requirements and individual capabilities and work capacity are more effectively combined than is the case with full-time workers.

- The relation between enterprise labor requirements and individual work performance is far closer for part-time employees: actual working hours correlate closely to paid hours. Work breaks and periods of inactivity are reduced, and fluctuations in work loads and operating times can be handled more flexibly.
- The institutional regimes of part-time work may be such that part-time work at nonstandard times such as the weekend, and before or after normal daily working hours is particularly cost-effective, as full-time workers receive bonuses for working at such hours; part-time workers are usually not entitled to such bonuses.

These advantages apply in principle to all industries with short-term fluctuation in work load during the day or the week (e.g., retailing, banking, public transport), where it might be expected that part-timers are used to cover such peaks, and to all industries with both seasonal and short-term work load fluctuation (e.g., hotels, catering, tourism and leisure industries, construction industry) that might be expected to resort to working-time patterns and contracts that embody part-time and casual or temporary employment relations.

As we can see from Table 5.1, part-time employment, and especially female part-time work, is highly concentrated in a few economic sectors. These sectors are other services, including a broad variety of private services like cleaning, medical services, domestic services, cultural services, and personal services; retail and wholesale trades, hotels, catering; followed by banking and finance, insurance, business services, renting; and public administration. In the six countries studied in detail (see Maier 1991), part-time employed women sometimes accounted for as much as 40 percent of all employees of the "other services" sector in 1987. The general increase of employment in services contributes substantially to the increase of part-time work, a situation quite different from the late 1960s, when part-time work was offered more frequently in the manufacturing industries.

However, the fact that certain industries produce goods and services with a work force employed to nearly 40 percent at part-time contracts is not gender-neutral. Industries subject to the same type of fluctuation (for instance, public transport and retailing) make different use of part-time. In public transport, part-time employment is relatively insignificant; this sector is dominated by male workers, whose traditional employment relation is permanent and full-time. Working-time flexibility is achieved through complex shift systems. Short-term demand peaks are handled with the help of well-paid overtime work (see, for detail, Rubery and Fagan 1992). In retailing, on the other hand, whose gender composition has increasingly been "feminized," the flexibility and working-time

154

Table 5.1

Part-Time Employed Women As a Proportion of all Employees in the Economic Sectors, 1987

	FRG	France	Netherlands
less than 5%	energy/water (2.4%) building/engin. (3.8%) metal (3.9%) mineral/chem. (4.8%)	mineral/chem. (1.6%) metal (1.6%) building/engin. (1.9%) energy/water (2.6%) other manuf. (4.6%)	energy/water (2.8%) building/engin. (3.4%) other manuf. (4.6%)
5% to 10%	agriculture (7.8%) transp./comm. (8.4%) public ad. (9.7%) other manuf. (9.8%)	transp./comm. (6.1%) agriculture (7.1%) banking/fin. (8.8%)	mineral/chem. (5.0%) transp./comm. (7.9%)
10% to 15%	banking/fin (13.5%)	public ad. (12.0%) trade/hotels (12.1%)	agriculture (10.3%) public ad. (10.3%) banking/fin. (13.7%)
15% to 20%	trade/hotels (18.4%)	other serv. (18.8%)	
20% to 30%	other serv. (22.1%)		trade/hotels (24.2%)
more than 30%			other serv. (40.9%)

	Belgium	United Kingdom	Denmark
less than 5%	energy/water (1.2%) building/engin. (1.4%) mineral/chem. (1.8%) transp./comm. (2.1%) metal (2.7%) other manuf. (3.7%)	energy/water (2.6%) metal (4.5%) mineral/chem. (4.7%)	building/engin. (3.4%) energy/water (3.5%)
5% to 10%	public ad. (8.0%) banking/fin. (9.9%)	transp./comm. (5.5%) building/engin. (5.6%) other manuf. (9.7%)	metal (5.3%) transp./comm. (5.6%) agriculture (8.8%) mineral/chem. (9.4%)
10% to 15%	agriculture (10.0%)	public ad. (10.9%) banking/fin. (13.8%) agriculture (14.0%)	other manuf. (12.5%)
15% to 20%	trade/hotels (18.5%) other serv. (18.9%)		banking/fin. (15.6%) public ad. (19.4%)
20% to 30%			trade/hotels (23.2%)
more than 30%		trade/hotels (34.8%) other serv. (37.8%)	other serv. (37.5%)

Source: European Labour Force Survey; Maier 1991.

pattern is quite different. The fixed-term part-time employment contract is wide-spread, often organized on an "on-call basis" (with a limited set of hours, days, or weeks in advance). Permanent and full-time employment is likely to be the exception for women in retailing in some countries. Gender-specific working-time regimes are even to be found within a single industry: the men employed in the retailing sector, for example, are usually employed full-time; the few part-time working men of this sector are often students or retired persons. Neverthe-less, there remain country-specific differences in the absolute level of part-time working women in retailing, a fact that can be explained by the different institutional regimes concerning working time (for a detailed study on retailing, see Gregory 1992).

This means that the beneficial effects on enterprise flexibility inherent in part-time employment are exploited in a way that is not independent of the institutional regimes of different countries. But the gender composition of the work force exerts a common influence in all countries observed: Male-domi-nated industries and occupations are generally characterized by a low proportion of part-time workers, while in those with a high share of female workers part-time employment tends to play an important role.

To turn the argument the other way round: In all Western industrialized countries labor markets are segregated by sex. Women's employment is highly concentrated in certain industries and occupations. Part-time work is concen-trated in female-dominated sectors and occupations and—looking deeper into the vertical segregation—is often restricted to a limited range of low-paying, low-status work. The concentration of part-time employment on poorly paid low-skilled jobs at the bottom of enterprise hierarchies and the almost complete absence of part-time employment in high-skilled and executive positions is a consequence of the hierarchical nature of work organization. Within the concepts of work organization, working time is an important factor in the allocation of status, income, and power. A process of differentiation is occurring whereby actual working hours are on the increase in high-skilled and managerial positions and simultaneously on the decline among workers performing low-skilled or unskilled activities. The hierarchical differentiation of working time, which is also occurring within the full-time "normal" employment relation (for experi-ences from Germany, cf. Kurz-Scherf 1989), combined with the strong gender-specific component discriminates not only against high-skilled women, but also against the small number of male "working-time pioneers" who voluntarily work part-time (cf. Bielenski and Strümpel 1988).[1] Well-qualified women (and men) who want to work fewer hours have the choice either of taking full-time posi-tions in order to remain at an appropriate level, or of accepting an inferior part-time job.

A recent study for the EC (Rubery and Fagan 1992) calculated the occupa-tional segregation for full-time and part-time working women, showing that the level of segregation in most of the EC countries is lower for full-time working women (compared to all employed women), indicating that women working part time are employed in a narrower range of occupations and are even more underrepresented in higher-status and professional jobs than female full-timers.

Employers' use of part-time work is often based on the argument that there is a functional incompatibility of part-time work with jobs that involve a large degree of coordination, problem solving on a group level, or process-based production. The majority of part-time work is therefore offered in the low-paid and low-skilled segments of a firm's internal labor markets even when it represents nearly half of all employees. It often includes a highly diversified internal division of labor or the segregation of part-time work in separate working groups or units. Part-time working women are often captured in this segment and often excluded from firms' internal career paths and promotion procedures. Only in very few cases, specially trained women are offered part-time jobs as a means of retaining them in employment. Employers facing severe recruitment problems sometimes offer their skilled female employees the option of part-time employment during a transitional period in their careers, but this offer is usually connected to childbearing periods; other reasons for individual reductions in working time are hardly ever recognized by employers.

As most studies reveal, the growing proportion of part-time employment is allocated within the service sector. Labor demand in this sector, and particularly in certain subsectors, seems to use the advantages of part-time work extensively and highly concentrated on women, a development that can be explained by the growing labor supply of women.

Supply-Side Developments

The interest in part-time employment on the part of the labor force can be the result of a variety of needs and wants. Workers may wish to provide their skills and knowledge in paid employment without having to withdraw from other life-spheres (such as child care, housework, education, leisure) because of long working hours. Labor market participation may be a source of additional or temporary income, while other roles (e.g., education) predominate. Older workers may wish to leave the work force gradually rather than abruptly.

For women the most important aim is often the compatibility of family and work. This compatibility is being sought less and less in terms of successive stages (education and training, labor market entry, withdrawal from the labor market upon childbirth, reentry); the emphasis in most countries is increasingly on parallel family and work biographies. This consciously "two-track" pursuit of family and employment interests is a relatively recent development. With every new cohort entering the labor market, women become more and more geared toward paid employment. The orientation of women toward creating individual income security via continuous paid employment has become a characteristic of all industrialized countries. This is because direct income provision via a "breadwinner" in paid employment has become increasingly uncertain in recent years—a consequence not only of unemployment and decreasing real income but also of the increase in divorces and single parents—and because of the improvement in general and vocational education for women, and the desire of women for social recognition and social integration outside private (family) life. The role models for women in modern industrial societies have shifted in such a way that the "housewife and mother" without paid employment no longer exerts the dominant influence.

Part-time employment can be an element in a temporary or permanent reduced-level integration into the labor market, which for women is often linked with "overtime" in the private sphere. For many women, part-time work seems to be the ideal solution to the problem of combining family life and employment. For other groups, such as school-leavers and young people still in the educational system, part-time employment can represent the model of entry into the employment system. Depending on the extent of the overlap between training/education and employment, part-time work can be part of the development of the vocational skills or merely a source of additional income in a biographical phase marked by other interests and time structures. For older workers part-time employment can offer the opportunity of a staged transition from employment to retirement, avoiding the disadvantages of a sudden end of working life.

The different needs, wants, and wishes of the work force can be studied in surveys and panels—they are only partly reflected by the existing labor market and employment structures as we find them today. The majority of part-time employment relations, concentrated as they are in the most poorly paid jobs, is far away from the wishes and the interests of the workers concerned. The result of the market constellation where employers write the rules, which has been confirmed in numerous studies, is often a discrepancy between the wishes of part-time workers and the reality of their employment. This applies in particular to the volume of hours, the weekly and daily distribution of the working time, the underutilization of skills, the low pay, and the missing integration into plant-level training and occupational promotion processes.[2]

While in principle part-time employment could represent an extension of choice, increasing the scope for individual action, in the real context of labor markets under prevailing economic conditions, it means that workers have to adjust to the predetermined structure of enterprise working-time regimes.

The concrete forms taken by part-time employment cannot, of course, be explained "autonomously," i.e., separate from the economic, social, and institutional conditions prevailing in a given society. To analyze the institutional factors behind both the similarities and the differences in part-time employment trends in the EC countries, the following parts of the institutional framework that shapes labor market supply and demand will be analyzed:

- the gender-specific division within the paid and the nonpaid sectors of societies, and

- the economic and social policies developed by governments, trade unions, and employers.

The study takes the idea of "institutional regimes" as a broad concept, including institutional forms of regulation concerning family, employment, and gender relations as well as labor law, social security regulations, and collective agreements.

Institutional Regimes of Gender-Specific Labor Division

In the 1980s women's paid employment grew more rapidly than men's employment in all European countries. Most of the increase in the labor force in the EC member states is due to a growth of women's activity rates. The general assumption that higher female labor force participation is automatically combined with an increase in part-time work is true only for some EC member states. This assumption is based on the argument that more women will enter paid employment if part-time rather than full-time jobs are available.

The data for the EC countries displayed in Table 5.2 show a more diverse picture. The overwhelming majority of part-time workers are women. They account for between 90 percent (West Germany) and 70 percent (the Netherlands) of all part-time employment. Over time this gender-distribution has remained relatively constant, varying only marginally in some countries (Belgium, France, West Germany) and falling lightly in those countries with an already high part-time employment share (Denmark, the United Kingdom, and the Netherlands). The integration of male workers into part-time employment grows in the youngest and the older age-groups.

The importance of part-time employment for women varies considerably in the different countries. In the Netherlands almost 60 percent and in the United Kingdom over 40 percent of working women are employed part-time. In Denmark part-time shares among women decline in the years 1981 to 1991, whereas in Belgium, France, and Germany the share increases. The level of female part-time employment varies considerably among the six selected EC member states (and even more when looking at the other six member states), so that it is difficult to make out a single consistent pattern of trends in female employment across all the countries studied. There is no straightforward relationship between high rates of part-time employment and high activity rates in all countries. France, for example, has a higher female labor force activity rate than the Netherlands but one of the lowest part-time work rates.

Figure 5.1 gives data on activity rates, unemployment rates, and part-time rates. Calculating activity rates, unemployment rates, and rate of part-time work for women aged 20–59 years in 1990 for all twelve EC member states produces a picture that is even more diverse. The patterns of female labor force integration show a broad variety, from Denmark at the top of labor force participation with a falling share of female part-time work to the Netherlands with a medium partici-

Table 5.2

Part-Time Shares Men/Women

	Belgium					Germany					Denmark				
	1975	1981	1985	1987	1991	1975	1981	1985	1987	1991	1975	1981	1985	1987	1991
Part-time employed as a proportion of:															
-total employed	4.9	6.4	8.6	9.9	13.3	11.2	12.0	12.8	12.7	15.3	21.2	23.7	24.3	24.2	24.1
-male employed	1.0	1.3	1.8	1.9	2.2	1.9	1.6	2.0	2.0	2.2	4.7	5.6	8.4	9.3	10.9
-female employed	12.9	16.3	21.1	24.2	31.8	26.7	28.9	29.6	29.5	34.0	45.1	46.5	44.0	42.2	38.3
Women's share in all part-time employed	85.1	85.8	86.1	87.5	89.9	89.6	91.9	90.5	90.5	91.5	86.8	86.9	81.1	79.2	76.5

	France					United Kingdom					Netherlands				
	1975	1981	1985	1987	1991	1975	1981	1985	1987	1991	1975	1981	1985	1987	1991
Part-time employed as a proportion of:															
-total employed	8.2	8.3	10.9	11.7	12.3	17.1	17.9	20.9	21.9	23.1	8.7	21.8	22.4	29.4	32.0
-male employed	3.0	2.3	3.2	3.5	3.2	2.3	3.1	4.3	5.3	5.4	2.4	9.7	7.6	13.8	15.5
-female employed	16.7	17.4	21.8	23.0	23.6	41.0	40.0	44.3	44.6	43.7	28.8	49.0	51.0	57.2	58.6
Women's share in all part-time employed	78.0	83.3	83.0	82.5	85.5	91.5	89.6	88.0	86.2	87.7	81.4	69.4	77.6	70.0	70.1

Source: European Labour Force Survey; Maier 1991.

pation but extremely high share of part-time work and France with a high activity rate and a low share of part-time work. On the basis of these disparate trends it has to be said that the relationship between part-time employment and labor force participation of women is clearly not monocausal. Series of other factors obviously exert an influence on changes in employment trends in general and part-time employment in particular.

As mentioned before, family responsibilities may influence women's position in the labor market. In all industrialized countries women are seen as responsible for child and other dependent care as well as household duties. The private division of labor in the households has remained remarkably stable over time. This division of labor is common to all industrialized countries, but it shapes the integration of women into the paid economy quite differently: employment rates of women with children under ten varied in 1988 between Ireland at 23 percent and Denmark at 79 percent.

This means that phases in the life cycle where there are small children in the household are not in general connected with a withdrawal from the labor market or a reduction in the individual's working time. There is no uniform pattern in Europe for combining family and paid work. How women combine children and paid employment depends heavily on child-care provision, regulations for maternity and parental leave, and cultural and social norms.

Having a child under ten years old is more likely to be connected with no paid employment in Ireland, Spain, the Netherlands, Luxembourg, and Germany, whereas women with children in Portugal, Denmark, and France are more likely to be found in paid employment. Concerning full-time or part-time employment in phases where the children are under ten years old, there is another split: nearly all mothers with children under ten years in employment work part-time in the Netherlands; in the United Kingdom and Germany two-thirds of all employed mothers are in part-time jobs. This rate is different in France, Italy, Belgium, Ireland, and all the Mediterranean EC member states. (See Table 5.3.)

The decision to take up paid employment depends on the family's social status, the labor market situation, and the availability of and access to child-care facilities. Families of low-paid workers often have to rely on two incomes in the household and on private and free-of-charge child care. "Choice" is therefore limited to work undertaken at times when other household members can look after the children without financial compensation. Women with small children coming from households with a low income are therefore searching for jobs in the mornings (especially in countries like Germany, where schools are only part-time), in the late evenings, or on weekends, when fathers or other relatives can look after the children. The women's employment has to fit in with the family care systems, and these are influenced by two factors: the publicly provided child care and school systems and the inflexible working-time patterns of the male employees. Typical male working-time patterns impose an external constraint on families' time-budgets, and women provide the flexibility both in

162

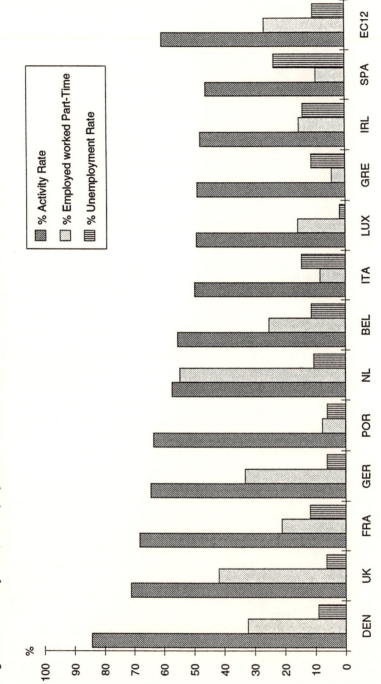

Figure 5.1 Activity Rate, Unemployment Rate, and Rate of Part-Time Work for Women Aged 20–59, 1990

■ % Activity Rate
▨ % Employed worked Part-Time
▥ % Unemployment Rate

Source: Bulletin on Women and Employment in the EC, No. 1.

Table 5.3

Employment and Parenthood, 1988

	% employed women with child under 10		% employed men with child under 10		% employed women aged 20–39, without children	
Germany	38%	(21%)	94%	(1%)	75%	(15%)
France	56%	(16%)	93%	(1%)	75%	(11%)
Italy	42%	(5%)	95%	(2%)	55%	(4%)
Netherlands	32%	(27%)	91%	(9%)	68%	(30%)
Belgium	54%	(16%)	92%	(1%)	68%	(13%)
Luxembourg	38%	(10%)	98%	(–)	69%	(5%)
U.K.	46%	(32%)	88%	(1%)	83%	(20%)
Ireland	23%	(7%)	79%	(1%)	67%	(6%)
Denmark	79%	(32%)	95%	(2%)	79%	(6%)
Greece	41%	(5%)	95%	(1%)	52%	(3%)
Portugal	62%	(4%)	95%	(1%)	69%	(6%)
Spain	28%	(4%)	89%	(1%)	44%	(5%)
EC	44%	(17%)	92%	(2%)	71%	(13%)

Source: CREWS Reports 1992.
Note: Key figures in brackets = % employed part-time.

the family and in paid employment. Men's general unwillingness to take parental leaves and to provide some flexibility within the families' time-budgets, and the social norm of men's work being full-time explains the dominance of women in part-time employment. Men's working lives are rarely affected by family responsibilities, as Table 5.3 shows. Women's decision to work part-time does not change the internal division of labor: Since they allegedly have more "free time," they are often burdened with housework, and their partners in full-time employment do not feel the urge to help out.

Women forced to work part-time in "unusual" hours or to withdraw from the labor market face severe problems. Withdrawal creates high barriers of reentering the labor market (a problem that is particularly severe in Germany and the Netherlands). The skills gained in child care or other family work command no or only a small market price and are recognized in paid employment only in caring work or in household-related, subordinate work. Women seeking part-time employment, especially in "unusual hours," depend on the jobs offered in this segment. These jobs are heavily concentrated in low-paid traditional female occupations like cleaning, retail trade, hotel and restaurant work, private households, and the subordinate occupations of the care sector. This means that women seeking part-time work in unusual hours or seeking to reenter the labor market via part-time employment end up, despite their professional skills, in unskilled or semiskilled low-paid work.

The situation is different in France and the Scandinavian countries, where child-care facilities are publicly provided and the decision to have children does not necessarily include a withdrawal from the labor market or working at unusual hours. Women with small children remain in the labor market and are more likely to work full-time. Part-time work is characterized as a transitional or temporary stage within the professional career. It is easier for women to combine family and paid work in a skilled profession on a full-time basis, when there is a well-developed public child care and school system or a guaranteed right to return to full-time employment (see Näsman 1992, for the Swedish experience).

The sexual division of paid and unpaid labor, the myth of the male breadwinner and his dependent wife who earns some supplementary income, is still alive and is reflected in institutions like child care and school systems and preferential treatment of "housewife"-families in tax systems (compared to dual-earner families), for example.

In these circumstances, part-time work can be characterized as a female coping strategy between paid work and family responsibilities in societies where the social and institutional norms are still based on the breadwinner-family model. Part-time work allows the sexual division of labor and society to remain intact even with more women in the paid economy. There is certain evidence that this basic institutional regime is changing only slowly as the supply side of the labor market has changed. More women than ever before have access to training and education, more women have an increasingly strong orientation toward paid employment, and more women want and need paid employment as a source of income and social status.

If male employees have changed their attitudes toward working time, it is not reflected in their actual time allocation. While female participation in the labor market has increased, men's working time in the core age-groups has—despite overall reductions in working time—not decreased.

In summary: Part-time work seems to be a coping strategy to combine family and paid work, especially to provide flexibility in both the household sphere and the labor market. Depending on access to public child care, women combine caring for children and paid work differently: they withdraw from the labor market and try to re-enter some years later; they switch from full-time to part-time employment; and they seek employment with work times that fit in with the family-care system. Compared with their male counterparts, all part-time working women face severe disadvantages in terms of wage and career prospects. Women still bear the risks connected with the flexibility needs of both families and employers.

The outmoded concept of women's employment is deeply embedded in the social norms of the societies and is not only reflected in the institutional provisions of child care and the treatment of men and women in the tax system but is also included in the institutional regimes of employment relations and labor law and social security legislation.

Regulation by Labor Law and Social Security Legislation

Employers' Costs and Benefits

Legal provisions, especially those of social security and labor law, exert an influence on the level and, in particular, the structure of part-time employment: in some countries legal systems integrate part-time employment as a regulated form of labor market participation, other legal systems exclude part-time contracts and therefore construct part-time work as a marginalized means of generating some extra income. Depending on the structure of these legal provisions, part-time employment may be more or less attractive (higher or lower relative wages and costs for employers and higher or lower net wages for employees) compared with full-time employment.

For employers the relative incentive to employ part-time workers may be influenced by the relative costs of part-timers compared with full-timers. It makes a considerable difference if employers' contributions to statutory or collectively bargained systems of social security have to be paid—

- irrespective of the individual employment contract, or
- only for employees with working times above a minimum of hours or who receive a certain monthly wage, or vary individually in proportion to income or the number of hours.

The scope for increasing flexibility by the use of part-time employment depends, among other factors, on statutory or collectively bargained regulation concerning flexible part-time work ("on call," overtime payments, dismissal protection, and the regulations concerning pay, bonuses, fringe benefits, etc.). Among other factors, the availability of functional equivalents to part-time work may be important, too, such as the willingness of full-time employees to work overtime in peak periods and regulations allowing reductions of work time in recessions or seasonal downs (e.g., short-time working, seasonal subsidies for certain sectors like the construction industry).

The aim of this section is to describe the provisions of labor law and the systems of social security in six EC member states (Belgium, Denmark, France, West Germany, the Netherlands, and the United Kingdom), not in their entirety, but to the extent that they contribute to the regulation of part-time work (for more details, see Maier 1991).

Studying the different systems of social security, a main distinction can be drawn between health insurance, maternity benefits, and old-age insurance (pension schemes) on one hand and unemployment insurance on the other hand.[3] Within Europe, we find a broad variety of employers' financial obligations concerning social security: in Denmark, France, and Belgium employers' contributions to health insurance, maternity benefits, and old-age pensions are based on the taxable income of the firm (Denmark) or the overall enterprise payroll

(France and Belgium). Employers' contributions to the social security system are not influenced by the working time (full-time or part-time) of the employees.

In West Germany, the United Kingdom, and the Netherlands contributions to social security are paid as a percentage of individual earnings and therefore linked to individual employment contracts. In all three countries contributions have to be paid above a certain threshold with an associated minimum working time (Germany, fifteen hours a week; Netherlands, fourteen hours a week) or a pay level below which employers are not obliged to make contributions (Germany, 480 DM; the United Kingdom, 48 £ a week).

In these three countries part-time employment below the threshold level is not subject to social security contributions, with the result that employers have neither to pay insurance contributions nor to grant employer-paid benefits (like sickness pay, maternity pay, etc.), which are part of the social security systems.

All countries examined have in common, however, that employer-provided benefits (such as continued wage-entitlement during sickness or maternity, and obligatory/voluntary supplementary pension schemes), based on additional collective bargaining at national, regional, or firm level, often exclude part-timers with less than 50 percent working time. While the provisions of such systems vary considerably within the countries studied, national and EC-wide studies indicate that collectively bargained and company-based pension schemes often exclude part-timers in general, or those working less than 50 percent of standard hours or below a certain level of income (see Meulders and Plasman 1989; Hohenberger, Maier, and Schlegelmilch 1989; Kravaritou-Manitakis 1988).

As discriminatory treatment of men and women in the statutory and collectively bargained systems of social security is forbidden within the EC and the exclusion of part-time workers disproportionately affects women, the European Court has made a number of judgments calling on employers to cease discrimination by integrating part-time workers into such systems. In most countries, however, governments are very reluctant to change the statutory system and point frequently to the fact that the partners to collective bargaining have exclusive rights of regulation in their spheres, so that legal changes appear to be unlikely. Nevertheless, the court's decisions exert some pressure on national legislation and collective bargaining, so that we can assume that in 1994 more collective agreements include part-timers than in the late 1980s.

To summarize these findings: Whereas in some countries part-time workers are included in the statutory social security schemes and it is, concerning employers' contributions to social security, irrelevant which form of employment is chosen, in other countries "marginal" part-time workers, i.e., workers with a low volume of hours or income, are excluded even from statutory social security schemes. In both groups of countries part-timers often do not participate in employer-provided benefits, neither in collectively bargained systems nor in voluntary ones.

As to unemployment insurance systems, it is only in Denmark, France, and the Netherlands that employers have to pay the same (proportional) contributions for part-time and full-time employed, whereas in Germany, Belgium, and the United Kingdom employees working less than a minimum level of hours or receiving minimum pay are excluded from contributions to unemployment insurance. These thresholds are sometimes higher than in the other social security systems (for example, in Germany) and exclude a higher proportion of part-time working people. Despite this exclusion, there are no other financial incentives within the unemployment insurance system for employers to choose part-time instead of full-time employment.

Concerning the position of part-time employees within the legal framework of labor law, there are specific statutory regulations in France, Belgium, and Germany. In these countries labor law regulation guarantees equal (pro rata) pay for work of part-timers, and equal holiday and dismissal-protection entitlements for part-time and full-time workers. Moreover, all three countries stipulate minimum periods of weekly hours and of notification for irregular part-time work ("on call") and the obligation of employers to set out working hours in a labor contract. In France and Belgium employers also are obliged to give priority to already employed part-timers when seeking to fill full-time job vacancies.

National legislation in these countries is of recent date and can be regarded as a response to the rise in flexible, irregular part-time employment, associated with substantial income and working-time insecurity for the workers affected. To this extent, these legal provisions have placed restrictions on the flexible use of part-time employment, creating "time-corridors" within which flexible working time could oscillate.

With the exception of France and Belgium, the use and remuneration of overtime for part-time employees is treated very "flexibly" in labor law. Only in these two countries the number of additional hours part-timers can be made to work without an overtime premium is limited to a fixed level below the standard number of (full-time) hours. In West Germany overtime is not subject to statutory regulation; this is left to collective bargaining. Usually overtime of standard pay rates can be worked up to regular full-time hours; only then does an overtime premium become necessary (for details, see Bispinck 1992). Part-time working employees are often not covered by special premiums for work in the evenings and weekends and are sometimes excluded from internal career regulations (as in the German public service, where part-timers needed twice the length of employment to be entitled to automatic promotion until 1992).

This pattern is broadly followed in the other countries, where part-time employment is not explicitly covered by legislation. In Denmark, the Netherlands, and the United Kingdom only some legal provisions exist for part-time workers. Most of these legal provisions exclude part-timers from "standard" regulations: statutory dismissal-protection regulations apply only to those working more than fifteen hours per week (Denmark), fourteen hours per week (Netherlands), and sixteen hours per week (after two years' employment) or eight hours per week (after five years' employment) in the United Kingdom. In the Netherlands part-timers with less than fifteen hours a week are excluded from passive and active electoral rights in the system of workers' representation and have no legal entitlement to the statutory minimum wage.

In Denmark the majority of working conditions not covered by legislation are dealt with in collective agreements, where, in most cases, part-time and full-time workers enjoy equal rights. In the Netherlands, on the other hand, collective agreements often reveal extensive gaps in the coverage of part-time workers, and in the United Kingdom unequal treatment of part-timers is widespread. In both countries employers have a greater freedom in their treatment of part-time workers, not only regarding the extent and variation of individual part-time work, but also with regard to equal pay, dismissal protection, and minimum wage regulation.[4]

But even in countries where part-time work is included in statutory labor law, some of the regulations state explicitly that the employer is obliged to treat part-time employees in the same way as full-time employees "unless objective reasons justify different treatment." Especially in rights that exceed the legally guaranteed minimum, like additional bonuses, additional paid holidays, special premiums for shift work or work at "unusual hours" and night work, part-time workers in general or those with less than 50 percent of the standard full-time working time are often excluded. This exclusion has a substantial effect on the real wage of part-timers, even in countries where employers are obliged to pay equal hourly wages to full- and part-timers.

Several studies report that there are pay differentials between female full- and part-time employees: in Germany semiskilled and unskilled manual part-time working women with more than fifteen hours a week earned 97 percent of the full-time employed women, marginal part-timers (less than fifteen hours a week) only 90 percent. Full-time employed women earned 78 percent of the men's hourly wage in the same group (Büchtemann and Quack 1989).

The earnings gap was even higher in the United Kingdom: in 1989, female part-timers earned only 75 percent of the hourly wages of full-time employed women. Differentiated by occupations the female part-time/full-time earnings gap was highest in nonmanual occupations and lowest in painting and assembly work, and it has widened since the early eighties (Rubery 1991).

In another study, including the influence of skill and content of work on payments, Horrell, Rubery, and Burchell (1989) came to the conclusion that in the United Kingdom "gender differences arise from quite wide and systematic differences between male and female full-time hourly pay, and further differences between female full-timers' and female part-timers' pay, although the gaps between full-time and part-time pay are both narrower and less consistent."

In general, the earnings gap between female full-time and part-time employees is less pronounced than the female/male wage gap. But it seems to be a quite stable phenomenon, and the differentials between female part-timers and full-timers have to be explained in part as a result of more or less direct wage discrimination against part-timers by excluding them from relevant parts of the overall effective remuneration (like shift-work premiums, premiums for work in the late evenings or weekends, overtime premiums, and employer-provided benefits like cheaper meals).

It is difficult to calculate the exact cumulative effect of the statutory and collectively bargained forms of regulation on the cost-burden or cost-incentive faced by the employer of part-time labor:

- As far as financial contributions to the system of social security are concerned, there are no financial incentives to the expansion of part-time employment in Denmark, France, and Belgium, whereas in the Netherlands, the United Kingdom, and West Germany employers of part-time labor below a set number of hours or a set level of income are exempted from this cost burden. This applies in particular to health insurance, maternity benefits, and unemployment insurance. As to old-age insurance it is in Germany and the United Kingdom where employers may be exempted from contributions for part-timers of certain types, especially marginal part-timers.
- Equal treatment of full-time and part-time employees in labor law is guaranteed by labor law in France, Belgium, and West Germany, and by collective agreements in Denmark. These forms of regulations place restrictions on employers' flexible use of part-time employment. Nevertheless, the use of "overtime" by part-time workers remains cost effective for employers in most countries. As part-timers are cheaper when employed on weekends and evenings or on call, the use of part-time employed might be attractive for employers that produce and offer goods and services in these times. Moreover, in the United Kingdom and the Netherlands the legal position of part-time workers is less secure (dismissal, workers' rights), facilitating the cost-effective and flexible use of part-time employment.
- Gender-specific wage differentials in general, and wage differentials between full-time and part-time employees reduce the wage costs for employers. This is especially true for most of the fringe benefits, voluntarily paid social security and pension schemes, bonuses for overtime and shift work, etc. Trade unions and works councils still widely accept the exclusion of part-timers from these collectively bargained parts of the remuneration.

Part-Timers' Costs

Employees may see part-time employment as a desirable or necessary form of labor market participation for a number of reasons. Frequently, financial, social, or legal disadvantages are recognized and accepted when making the decision to work part-time. The fact that part-time workers are sometimes excluded from the obligation to pay social security contributions, coupled in some countries with tax exemption on low income, may provide a certain incentive to accept such forms of employment. For certain groups, such as married "secondary" earners, young people still in education, or pensioners, the freedom from social security and tax payments, implying a higher hourly net income, may constitute an attraction to take up part-time employment.

This exclusion from the system of social security may, however, become risky and problematic if the social or individual arrangements on which this freedom is based show signs of disintegration. Examples of this are situations when income security via another breadwinner is no longer guaranteed, or when the precarious forms of employment are no longer a short-term option but become the only chance of finding employment at all.

The fact that especially marginal forms of part-time work are excluded from contributions means that these employees are excluded from transfers paid by the social security system. In the cases of sickness or maternity, unemployment, and retirement, no financial compensation for losing income is made. Part-time workers with few hours are—in all countries examined—no better protected against income risks than those completely outside the employment system. Given that the decision between nonemployment and (partial) employment is linked to the economic position of the household, part-time workers are often dependent on the earned (part-time) income but simultaneously inadequately (if at all) protected from the effects of the loss of such earnings. The financial opportunities offered by part-time work are often built on sand, as the balance of incentives (higher net income) and risks (no financial compensation in cases of unemployment, sickness, and old age) is unequally distributed and only in a short-term perspective favorable for part-time workers.

Depending on the national systems, there are differences in the degree of risks: whereas the basic rights to get medical treatment are independent from employment status and marital status in most countries, transfers-benefits are bound to a certain minimum level of hours worked, a certain income earned, and a given period of employment. The exclusion of employed part-timers from transfers-benefits and employer-paid benefits has recently been seen as an indirect form of discrimination against women by the European Court, which ruled that a West German employer had to pay sickness benefits to a noninsured female part-time worker.[5]

In the old-age insurance/pension schemes the level of transfers is even more connected not only with the income earned but also with the duration of employment. A sufficiently high pension can be attained only with a thirty- to forty-year period of steady full-time income; even a working life with a low full-time income leads to a situation of a pension near subsistence level. In some countries, like Denmark, France, the Netherlands, and the United Kingdom, all citizens are entitled to a minimum state pension, which is granted irrespective of employment status. In other European countries, like Germany and Belgium, however, the pension schemes are based only on contributions paid and length of employment. All supplementary pension schemes, adding up to "people's pensions" in Denmark, France, the Netherlands, and the United Kingdom, also are geared toward the principle of lifelong, continuous full-time employment.

Significant cuts in pensions occur if employment is interrupted or is not subject to contributions, or if earned income decreases due to the part-time nature of the employment. It is not only that marginal part-time workers are excluded from the schemes altogether, but also that those with regular part-time work who pay contributions end up with more than proportionately reduced pension entitlements. The different systems of providing for old age have serious effects on the financial situation of part-timers after retirement: While in Denmark and the Netherlands elderly people receive a minimum pension independent of their employment biography, and in the United Kingdom and France at least a basic pension if they were employed a minimum period, in Belgium and Germany a working life of marginal part-time employment ends without an individual entitlement to a pension. In these two countries marginal part-time workers are totally dependent either on support from the families or on public welfare. But even regular part-time employees receive individual pensions below the minimum living standard. It does not come as a surprise, therefore, that poverty among pensioners is highly concentrated in women—resulting from the generally lower earnings, the interrupted work careers, and the insufficient coverage of part-time workers by the old-age pensions.

Regarding unemployment insurance, the national systems are even more heavily oriented toward the principle of standard full-time work, with the result that unemployment benefits have even higher thresholds for benefit entitlement. Part-time people who work fewer than eighteen hours a week (Germany), fifteen hours a week (Denmark), three hours a day (Belgium), or earn less than forty-eight pounds a week (United Kingdom) are excluded entirely from receiving benefits. Even those who do pay contributions do not always receive benefits proportional to their contributions; this is true for part-timers with an hours-volume between marginal levels and around two-thirds of the regular standard working time (for details, see Maier 1991). In two countries, Germany and the United Kingdom, those receiving unemployment benefits must declare themselves willing and able to take up full-time employment. In other countries, like Belgium, Denmark, and France, workers with a "full-time entitlement" (having worked full-time before unemployment) receive reduced unemployment benefits if they take up part-time employment to increase their real income. These provisions were introduced in the late 1970s in order to encourage the unemployed to take up part-time employment.

The legal position of part-time workers in statutory or collectively bargained labor law regulations is—as shown—weaker than that of full-time employees. In particular, irregular, short-term, or marginal part-time work is obviously less protected against the employers' will to dispose of labor. These gaps of regulations are most obvious in the regulation of flexible part-time, overtime pay, premiums, and dismissals. These, of course, are precisely the areas in which the interests of employers and part-time workers most immediately conflict. Flexible working time, often changing by week, obligatory overtime on demand, and working hours inconvenient with the family-care system conflict directly with the commitments that induced some people to take up part-time work in the first place. Given the unequal power relations between employers and employee, it is the employer who will be in a position to define the legal "space" left open by labor law. The scope for the employer to modify the working time arrangement is hardly limited by restrictions in the United Kingdom and the Netherlands.

Summarizing the findings, it remains a common feature of all countries investigated that the significant gaps in legislative and collective regulation of part-time work divide this form of employment into a "more protected sector" consisting of those working more than 50 percent of the standard working time ("long" part-time) and a widely "unprotected sector" below this level ("short" part-time). Especially in this precarious segment, the balance of incentives would appear to lie in favor of the employer, with workers bearing considerable additional risks.

Increased Polarization of Part-Time Work

With respect to institutional regulations of social security and labor law, short and long part-time work are two distinct forms of employment. As Tables 5.4 and 5.5 show, short part-time working is growing more rapidly in some countries than the total growth of part-time working. For the period 1983 to 1988, in Denmark, the United Kingdom, Belgium, and the Netherlands, the expansion of short part-time exceeded that of long part-time for both men and women, whereas in Germany the increase was true only for men, and in France long part-time grew faster than short part-time. In 1988, the Netherlands and the United Kingdom had a proportion of short part-time work among all part-time workers of more than 45 percent, for both men and women. In Denmark, however, short part-time work accounts for 75 percent of all male part-timers and only 25 percent of all female part-timers, whereas it accounted for less then 30 percent of the male and female part-timers in West Germany, Belgium, and France.

Data on the social status of short part-time workers show that men are typically students and pupils in the Netherlands, the United Kingdom, and Denmark. The majority of short part-time working men are single and under twenty-four years old and live as a "dependent child" with their families.

The vast majority of short part-time working women are married, classifying themselves as dependent spouses. But a growing proportion are said to be the head of the household, i.e., the main breadwinner.

The growing polarization has two dimensions: it shows a gender-specific pattern of short part-time working and an uneven growth of part-time working

Table 5.4

Development of Part-Time Employment by Groups of Hours, 1983–88

	FRG[a]		France		Netherlands		Belgium		U. Kingdom		Denmark	
	male	female	male	female	male	female	male	female	male	female	male	female
Short part-time												
1–15 hours	185	118	143	104	423	157	168	148	186	124	200	139
16–19 hours	231	145	165	114	326	203	60	152	187	132	224	82
Long part-time												
20 hours and more	72	112	152	153	159	136	105	137	165	116	98	102
Total	98	114	151	134	237	149	105	141	176	120	155	106

Source: European Labour Force Survey; Maier 1991.
Note: Index 1983 = 100.
[a] FRG figures 1984.

Table 5.5

Short and Long Part-Time (male/female), 1983–88

Proportion part-time employees with:	FRG 1983 male	FRG 1983 female	FRG 1988 male	FRG 1988 female	France 1983 male	France 1983 female	France 1988 male	France 1988 female	Netherlands 1983 male	Netherlands 1983 female	Netherlands 1988 male	Netherlands 1988 female
1–10 hrs.	15.0[a]	11.2[a]	17.7	9.8	7.7	14.0	7.0	10.4	20.0	27.5	38.0	31.0
11–15 hrs.			12.2	8.6	6.3	11.1	6.2	9.1	6.7	15.8	9.6	14.5
16–19 hrs.	40.2[a]	50.0[a]	11.5	5.4	5.9	10.8	6.4	9.3	4.8	7.7	6.6	10.4
20–29 hrs.	24.9	33.2	44.4	62.3	31.6	37.1	41.6	40.1	32.2	38.0	33.3	32.2
30 hrs. and more	19.8	5.6	14.2	13.9	28.2	16.6	18.7	21.3	16.0	10.4	12.4	11.9
no reg. working time					18.2	9.2	17.5	8.4				
Short part-time (1–15 hrs./week)	15.0[a]	11.2	29.9	18.4	14.0	15.1	13.2	19.5	26.7	43.3	47.6	45.5
Long part-time (>20 hrs./week)	44.9	38.8	58.8	76.2	59.8	53.7	60.3	61.4	48.2	48.4	45.7	44.1

Proportion part-time employees with:	Belgium 1983 male	Belgium 1983 female	Belgium 1988 male	Belgium 1988 female	U. Kingdom 1983 male	U. Kingdom 1983 female	U. Kingdom 1988 male	U. Kingdom 1988 female	Denmark 1983 male	Denmark 1983 female	Denmark 1988 male	Denmark 1988 female
1–10 hrs.	9.5	10.1	18.0	10.2	31.7	22.2	34.3	22.8	33.9	8.6	52.5	17.0
11–15 hrs.	6.7	9.1	8.0	9.9	16.2	17.2	16.5	17.8	21.3	11.8	19.1	9.7
16–19 hrs.	22.0	17.5	12.4	18.9	9.5	12.4	10.1	13.6	3.3	6.1	4.8	4.7
20–29 hrs.	33.6	51.5	39.9	47.9	27.2	37.0	29.8	35.3	25.3	50.3	16.9	41.9
30 hrs. and more	27.7	11.0	21.3	12.7	13.9	10.5	9.0	10.3	11.1	20.0	6.1	26.0
no reg. working time	0.5	0.8	0.5	0.4					5.1	0.0	3.2	0.0
Short part-time (1–15 hrs./week)	16.2	19.2	26.0	20.1	47.9	39.4	50.8	40.6	55.2	20.4	71.6	26.7
Long part-time (>20 hrs./week)	61.3	62.5	61.2	60.6	41.1	47.5	38.8	45.6	36.4	70.3	23.0	67.9

Source: European Labour Force Surveys; Maier 1991.
[a] 1983 in the FRG 11–19 hours in one category.

with different hours-volume. In most countries the recent increase of short part-time work is highest among young men who are not married and are living in the households of their parents, typically doing part-time work combined with education and training. Nevertheless, short part-time working men are a very small minority in the labor market, and their part-time employment is bound to specific parts of their working lives or entry into the labor market. For women, short part-time work forms an important part of employment, especially in the core age-groups. The vast majority of women employed in short part-time earn additional income to the household, and, as we know, household dependency on women's income has increased. These women are not "middle-class" women whose husbands earn medium or high wages. The vulnerable position of short part-time workers affects the situation of these households substantially, even if there is another breadwinner. The uneven growth of part-time work, especially in the unprotected and unregulated part of the labor market, most pronounced in the Netherlands, the United Kingdom, Denmark, and Belgium and constituting in the Netherlands and the United Kingdom nearly 50 percent of all part-time employment, raises concerns about the adequacy of the predominant forms of social security and labor law.

It does not come as a surprise that the polarization is most pronounced in the two countries (the Netherlands and the United Kingdom) with the most flexible labor law regulations concerning short part-time work.

Explaining the Findings

To examine whether the social security and labor law regulations exert an influence on the level and the development of part-time work, the six countries are grouped into categories—high and low part-time rate. Table 5.6 gives a rough picture. It seems that the construction of the social security system itself does not play a major role in whether a country has a high or a low rate of part-time employment. Comparing development in the United Kingdom and Germany, countries with similar regulations concerning marginal part-time employees, there is substantial difference in the level of part-time employment. What seems to be of more importance is the degree of coverage by labor law regulations: both the United Kingdom and the Netherlands have low coverage and a high proportion of part-time work, especially of marginal part-time work. Combined with a tax policy that exempts low income from tax payments, a low degree of child-care provisions, and a growing employment rate of women (partly as a result of decreases in male earnings), employers in both countries seem to employ female part-time workers in the most flexible and cost-effective way. Employers and employees in France, Belgium, and West Germany seem to be more reluctant to increase marginal part-time employment.

Labor law regulations reflect (to a certain degree) the power relations between employers and trade unions. In most industrialized countries, trade unions had

Table 5.6

Part-Time Employment and Policy Regulations

Employers' Contributions to Social Security Systems

	high part-time rate	low part-time rate
Independent of volume of hours and work contract	Denmark Netherlands	France Belgium
Depending on volume of hours, minimum wage, and Individual work contract	United Kingdom	Federal Republic of Germany

Integration of Part-Time Employment in Labor Law Legislation

	high part-time rate	low part-time rate
Independent of volume of hours	Denmark (collective agreement)	France Belgium Federal Republic of Germany
Dependent on volume of hours and minimum wage	United Kingdom Netherlands Denmark (legal status)	

Source: Maier 1991.

been strongly opposed to the introduction of part-time work because they feared the weakening of contractual and economic power of employees and unions. Unions sometimes accepted the introduction of part-time work as long as it was organized in a way that it either protected the relative power of core workers or, at least, did not affect them negatively. Negative trade union attitudes toward part-time employment resulted in its noninclusion in collectively bargained rights and in the development of a peripheral and unprotected work force, which, in return, saw no advantage in joining the union.

Employers used nonunionized part-time workers and their exclusion from collectively bargained rights to expand these segments of "cheap" labor, especially in the feminized parts of the trade and service sector industries. In these sectors, where trade unions had been less powerful than in male-dominated core sectors, the increase in part-time work created segments of low-skilled and low-paid jobs. The negative alliances between trade unions and employers were especially popular in the sixties and seventies. Trade union attitudes changed in some countries in the early eighties, when unions discovered that part-time work is no longer confined to a small proportion of women and that it is not a transitory phenomenon of the seventies. The need to regulate part-time employment increased, and in some countries governments and trade unions were able to improve the position, the wages, the employment rights, and the working conditions of part-time employees.

The high proportion of part-time work and its low level of integration into the collectively bargained or statutory guaranteed rights reflects a weakness of the trade unions in the Netherlands and the United Kingdom, whereas the low proportion of part-time work and its, at least, partial integration reflects a certain influence of trade unions in France and Germany. But the low proportion of part-time jobs influences women's labor market position quite differently: whereas in France the female labor force participation rate is rather high, with a high proportion of full-time employed women and continuous labor force attachment, it remained relatively low in Germany. The Nordic countries show a third development: high level of part-time work, highly integrated into collectively bargained rights, and high labor force activity rates.

Whether a better integration of part-time work in the overall regulations of employment results in improvements concerning women's position in the labor market, in a higher or a lower labor market integration of women, depends on the institutional regimes of the gender-specific division of labor within a society. Germany is, within the group of highly industrialized countries, in its basic societal norms, the norms inherent in social policy and welfare policy, broadly based on the model of the breadwinner family, in which the male breadwinner earns a sufficiently high family wage. Despite recent erosions of this model, trade unions and employers are able to push productivity in the core sectors of the economy to maintain high (male) wages. Flexibility is gained by variations in the working time of the full-time employed with regulations concerning overtime work, short-hours work, complex shift systems, and subsidies for sectors with seasonal employment variations. In recent years the German private service sector developed more slowly than in other countries, and although the feminized parts of the service sector suffer from lower earnings (compared to the manufacturing industry), the expansion of a low-paid, marginal part-time job market was rather modest compared to other countries. At the end of the 1980s, Germany did not have a high labor force activity rate of women like the Nordic countries, France, and the United Kingdom; a rapid increase in unprotected part-time work like the United States, the United Kingdom, and the Netherlands; or an increase in protected full-time work as in France and the Nordic countries.

The German model of women's labor market integration, which avoided an erosion of the labor market regulations by a rather restrictive regulation on part-time work, limited women's employment chances, as it did not provide sufficient full-time employment positions or the Nordic option of choosing part-time employment as a temporary solution in a woman's working career (for details, see Näsman 1992; Quack 1992).

The institutional welfare system in Germany did not expand as it did in the Nordic countries, so women still provide more services unpaid at home and find less employment in the service sector than in other countries. Rather restrictive regulations concerning shop-opening hours reduce employers' demand for shop-keepers, and the limited (and rather expensive) supply of child-care facilities forces women out of the labor market instead of searching for part-time employment. As neither the trade unions nor the employers feel the need to campaign for women's increased labor market participation, the results are contradictory: on one hand, more women in Germany want paid employment, and the institutional restrictions are such that many of them search for part-time employment to reenter the labor market; on the other hand, the expansion of part-time employment is rather slow and is concentrated in a restricted number of low-paid and unskilled jobs. Neither employers nor trade unions take initiatives to push for part-time employment in higher-paid or skilled jobs or to improve the situation in the provision of child-care facilities.[6]

Some Tentative Conclusions

Part-time employment has become a growing and stable part of the labor market and employment structures of industrialized countries. It is often women's work, although it has a quite different relevance for women's overall employment in different countries. It is heterogeneous, and it includes a variety of different situations for both employers and employees. For women, part-time employment may provide the flexibility both in the family and in the firms, as men's working-time patterns are inflexible and an "external" constraint to the families. In most countries part-time employment represents only a restricted choice, as women searching for part-time jobs are confronted with poorly paid, low-skilled jobs, often combined with a precarious status concerning benefits, social security regulations, and employment rights. The fact that many part-time working women do not want to work full-time does not imply that they prefer to do the part-time jobs offered nowadays.

Part-time work provides flexibility to the employers and is an instrument of cost-saving and increasing productivity—and it is used only by certain service sectors and in certain occupations, especially in those countries where the legal restrictions concerning pay and working-time regulations are weak. Only in a few countries the legal system and the social partners have reacted to the emerging part-time employment by making efforts to guarantee part-time workers social security and employment rights. Some governments consider the surge of more precarious jobs as a by-product of an increasing need for flexibility and cost savings, thus strengthening the competitiveness of the national economy. The fact that most part-timers are married women seems to strengthen the notion that part-time employment does not need the same level of payment, working conditions, and employment protection as the work of the "primary" earner. Part-time working women are worse paid than full-time working women in most countries, which seems to be the consequence of two factors: first, employers can impose wages, work conditions, and employment relations that men would not accept; and, second, employers offer part-time employment especially in the nonunionized sectors at the bottom of the occupational hierarchy. They make use of the weak positions of trade unions concerning equal treatment of men and women and full-time and part-time employees.

As far as the impact of the Single European Market is concerned, the EC tried to take initiatives to regulate equal conditions for part-time work in the EC member states. First initiatives date back to the end of the 1970s; a first draft of an EC directive was published in 1981. Since then, no directive on part-time employment has passed the Council of Ministers, as even the minimum regulation of the last draft was blocked by the British and German governments (see Maier 1991). The last draft aimed at improving working conditions of atypical employees with respect to access to companies' vocational training schemes, payments made under the auspices of welfare or noncontributory social security schemes, and coverage under compulsory social security schemes on a pro rata basis. This draft did not include part-time workers with fewer than eight hours a week. But even this still restrictive definition would have put more pressure on the national legislations of Germany and Britain to extend social security and labor law coverage to part-time workers. Some pressure concerning the legal situation and the working conditions is developing in the European Court. As some cases brought to court under the Equal Treatment Directive concerned part-time employment, the court made some substantial decisions on equal treatment of full-time and part-time employees and on men's and women's wages, work conditions, etc. But success on national legislation was limited until now.

Strategies to upgrade part-time work would include campaigning for equal pay and equal benefits for jobs of equal skills and job content. It would include the evaluation of women's work and pay in general to close the female-male wage gap, and a redefinition of social security and labor law standards. Trade unions are confronted with the task of integrating part-time work in the bargaining policies and in collective agreements.

To the extent that part-time work expresses people's desire for a more flexible combination of work and family, it seems to be necessary to consider men's work times. At present, part-time work follows the flexibility demands of employers. Women seeking solutions to combine family and work adapt to employers' rules, which often do not reflect women's preferred working-time arrangements. A general redistribution of labor within the labor market and the private household may be difficult to achieve, but it seems to be necessary to put more emphasis on the overall reduction of working time and more equal distribution of working time and pay among men and women.

Notes

1. Men wishing to work part time in the core age groups are called "working-time pioneers." In general, male part-time employment is concentrated among young and old men, reflecting an increasing number of students being employed part-time, new forms of professional entry systems organized in a combination of part-time work and training, and early retirement trends. The overall proportion of male part-timers is low but slowly rising.

2. The traditionally used labor market survey question to study the mismatch between employment reality and the demands of the employees is whether respondents work part-time because they had been unable to find full-time employment. The answer is often taken as a measure of whether part-time work is chosen voluntarily or not, but it is in fact misleading concerning the question of whether the existing part-time employment meets women's demands or not.

3. This distinction is not true for the United Kingdom, where all social security systems are integrated in the National Insurance, which includes health insurance, the state pension scheme, and unemployment insurance.

4. The Dutch government announced in 1992 a new law that entitles part-time workers to claim the same hourly wage as full-time workers in the same job.

5. This decision has not yet led to a change in the legal regulation.

6. The growing importance of paid employment for women is even more true after the German unification, as unemployment rises fast among women in East and West Germany; for details, see Maier 1993.

References

Bielenski, H., and Strümpel, B. 1988. *Eingeschränkte Erwerbsarbeit bei Frauen und Männern,* edition sigma Berlin.

Bispinck, R. 1992. *Tarifliche Regelungen zur Teilzeitarbeit, WSI: Elemente qualitativer Tarifpolitik* no. 17, Düsseldorf.

Büchtemann, Chr., and Quack, S. 1989. *"Bridges" or "Traps?" Non-Standard Forms of Employment in the Federal Republic of Germany.* Discussion paper FS I 89–6, Wissenschaftszentrum Berlin für Sozialforschung, Berlin.

CREWS Reports. 1992. *Childcare Recommendation Adopted, Reports* 12, no. 5 (May 1992).

Gregory, A. 1992. "Part-time Working and Patterns of Working Hours in Large Scale Grocery Retailing in Britain and France." In *Aspects of Part-time Working in Different Countries*, ed., U. Ebbing, 49–78. Arbeitspapier 1992–7, Arbeitskreis sozialwissen-schaftliche Abeitsmarktforschung (SAMF), Gelsenkirchen.

Hohenberger, L.; Maier, F.; and Schlegelmilch, C. 1989. *Regelungen und Förderprogramme zur Teilzeitarbeit in Schweden, Norwegen, Großbritannien, Frankreich, Niederlande, Belgien und Österreich, Dokumentation des Bundesministeriums für Jugend, Familie, Frauen und Gesundheit.* Materialien zur Frauenpolitik 3/19989, Bonn.

Horrell, S.; Rubery, J.; and Burchell, B. 1989. "Unequal Jobs or Unequal Pay?" In *Industrial Relations Review* 20, no. 3:176–91.

Kravaritou-Manitakis, Y. 1988. *New Forms of Work—Labour Law and Social Security Aspects in the European Community.* Luxembourg: European Foundation for the Improvement of Living and Working Conditions.

Kurz-Scherf, I. 1989. "Teilzeitarbeit: Individuelle Notlösung und/oder Vorbotin einer neuen Zeitordnung?" In *Frauen Sozialkunde*, eds., U. Müller and H. Schmidt-Waldherr, 42–57. AJZ-Verlag Frauenforschung Band 3 Bielefeld.

Maier, F. 1991. *The Regulation of Part-Time Work: A Comparative Study of Six EC Countries.* Discussion paper FS I 91–9, Wissenschaftszentrum Berlin für Sozialforschung, Berlin.

———. 1993. "The Labour Market for Women and Employment Perspectives in the Aftermath of German Unification." In *Cambridge Journal of Economics*, no. 17 (September): 267–80.

Meulders, D., and Plasman, R. 1989. *Women in Atypical Employment, Report of the European Commission.* V/146/89, Brussels.

———. 1992. "Part-Time Working in the EEC Countries—Evolution during the Eighties." In *Aspects of Part-time Working in Different Countries*, ed., U. Ebbing, 5–22. Arbeitspapier 1992–7, Arbeitskreis sozialwissenschaftliche Arbeitsmarktforschung.

Näsman, E. 1992. "Parental Leave in Sweden—A Workplace Issue." In *Aspects of Part-time Working in Different Countries*, ed., U. Ebbing, 139–60. Arbeitspapier 1992–7, Arbeitskreis sozialwissenschaftliche Arbeitsmarktforschung.

Network of Experts. 1992. *Network of Experts on the Situation of Women in the Labour Market, Bulletin on Women and Employment in the EC.* No.1, October 1992.

Quack, S. 1992. "Continuous and Transitory Part-Time Working in West Germany." In *Aspects of Part-time Working in Different Countries*, ed., U. Ebbing, 95–116. Arbeitspapier 1992–7, Arbeitskreis sozialwissenschaftliche Arbeitsmarktforschung.

Rubery, J. 1991. *Pay, Gender and European Harmonisation: Some Societal Effects in the Determination of the Gender Pay Differentials.* Manuscript. Manchester School of Management (UMIST).

Rubery, J., and Fagan, C. 1992. *Occupational Segregation amongst Women and Men in the European Community.* Report of the EC, Manchester/Brussels.

6

Self-Employment Schemes for the Unemployed in the European Community

The Emergence of a New Institution, and Its Evaluation

Nigel Meager

Introduction

The 1980s saw a notable increase in self-employment across EC countries, in absolute terms and as a proportion of total employment. Within this overall picture, however, the experience of individual countries was variable, with the United Kingdom experiencing by far the greatest increase, in contrast to others (such as France and Germany) where the level of self-employment was stagnant, and still others (such as Denmark and Luxembourg) where it continued to decline.

These varied trends occurred against the background of a governmental policy stance broadly and increasingly supportive of self-employment in all EC countries. This was influenced by two rather different forces: the general trend toward deregulation in the industrial and labor market spheres; and the widespread belief in the face of persistent mass unemployment that small businesses could be an engine of job creation. Without exception, since the late 1970s, EC countries introduced labor market schemes designed to encourage members of the labor force (particularly unemployed members) to become self-employed, and to support those who did so. The near universal existence of such schemes in EC and other developed economies justifies us in describing them as a new labor market institution.

The chapter begins with some definitional and theoretical discussions. Following this we take comparable data on EC countries and briefly examine recent trends in the extent and composition of self-employment and the explanations that have been put forward for such trends. We present in particular new empirical evidence on inflows to and outflows from self-employment, since it is an important part of our argument that such flows data have a useful role to play in comparative evaluations of policy measures. Finally, we look in more detail at these policy initiatives and address some of the comparative evaluation issues that they pose. The chapter draws on other work by the author, including a comparative study of self-employment in the United Kingdom and Germany (Meager, Kaiser, and Dietrich 1992) and research conducted at the Wissenschaftszentrum Berlin (WZB) during 1991–92 (Meager 1992a, 1992b, and 1993) on behalf of the Commission of the European Communities (DGV).

Some Definitional Considerations

Our focus is on self-employment as a *labor market* phenomenon. Traditional labor market analysis typically fails to distinguish between *employees*, who sell their labor for a wage or salary; and the *self-employed*, who do not. Most analysts of self-employment agree that this distinction, based on "the degree of autonomy and control these workers have over their labor" (Aronson 1991, xii), is the crucial distinction (from a labor market viewpoint) between the self-employed and other workers. Such definitions of wage employment and self-employment "also imply different institutional contexts and, even more important, different responses to such labor market signals as relative earnings and employment opportunities" (ibid.).

At an intuitive level, then, and taking this labor market perspective, the definition of self-employment is clear. *The self-employed are those who work on their own account (or "for themselves") rather than for an employer in a conventional (dependent) employment relationship.* Once one attempts to operationalize this definition, however, the boundaries around the concept of self-employment are neither clear nor necessarily fixed. What counts as self-employed and what counts as employee status may depend very much on who is doing the counting. In principle, it seems that in most EC countries, the various *official* definitions (in employment law, in tax liability, and in social security) are broadly consistent with each other. Such definitions may not be consistent with individuals' perceptions, however, particularly where the latter are linked with notions of independence and autonomy, and such inconsistencies may explain the differences between Labour Force Survey estimates of self-employment and those based on administrative sources. A particularly important inconsistency relates to the distinction between *incorporated* and *unincorporated* businesses. As Hakim 1988 notes in the U.K. context,

> In strictly legal terms, the self-employed are restricted to owners (sole proprietors and partners) of unincorporated businesses. Working proprietors or managers of incorporated businesses are classified as employees . . . because that is their status in law and for tax and social insurance purposes. (Hakim 1988, 422)

A similar point applies in most countries. When a business becomes an incorporated company, its working proprietors are usually reclassified as employees. The decision to incorporate a business may be one of administrative convenience, or tax advantage, or simply the desire to reduce personal financial risk. The crucial point is that there is no clear set of criteria implying that businesses of certain sizes, types, and stages of growth will be incorporated. It is perfectly feasible to find two proprietors or directors of otherwise identical small businesses, one of which is incorporated and the other not, with the former officially classed as an employee, and the latter as self-employed. It is possible also, however, that both would *regard themselves* as "self-employed" and would identify themselves as such in responding to social surveys.

A further difficulty is that even many people whose official status is "self-employed" do not correspond in reality to the model of independence, autonomy, and control over their labor that is implicit in our notion of self-employment (Rubery and Burchell 1992; Rainbird 1991). Such groups might include "labor only" construction workers (a category that has expanded considerably in the United Kingdom in recent years), operators of franchises (an expanding group during the 1980s in several EC countries (see Felstead 1991; Kneppers-Heynert 1992), and certain groups of homeworkers (Hakim 1987; Allen, Truman, and Wolkowitz 1992).

The data used in this study derive from the European Labour Force Survey (ELFS), which together with its component surveys in individual EC countries, uses a concept of self-employment based on respondents' self-definition. This raises some difficulties of comparison, since the ways individuals define themselves in response to a survey interview may vary between countries because official definitions differ, or because different cultural norms affect the social "value" attached to self-employment. Indeed, this may also vary *within* a country over time. In the United Kingdom, for example, it is argued that one effect of the post-1979 Thatcher government's emphasis on the "enterprise culture" generated "a new climate of opinion which encourages the entrepreneurial spirit, values entrepreneurial endeavours and produces a more positive public image for self-employed workers as a result" (Hakim 1988, 428).

Given this more positive public image, it is plausible that some workers whose activities lie close to the border between employment and self-employment may have become more willing to identify themselves as self-employed during the Thatcher era.[1] Hence the upward trend recorded in U.K. self-employment may contain an element of reclassification as well as genuine growth.

In the light of these difficulties, and the limitations of available data, there is little point in imposing *ab initio* a more precise definition of self-employment than that offered above. Rather, as with most internationally comparative studies, we need to take account of the complexities of definition and meaning and exercise due caution when interpreting the data. In attempting to explain differences between countries, or trends over time, we must always be prepared to ask how far the data indicate real differences, or real changes, and how far they simply reflect definitional differences or changes.

Finally, we should note that a key feature emerging from almost all previous studies of self-employment is that however they are defined, the self-employed constitute an extremely diverse category in terms of their individual characteristics, the skill levels they deploy, and their degree of "independence." The "typical" self-employed person does not exist. Self-employment covers a wide range of types of individuals and activities, which in most countries include, for example: the proprietors of small businesses; farmers; independent, highly skilled professional workers (in liberal professions and the arts, for example); manual craft workers; some categories of homeworkers or "outworkers"; and a wide range of "own account" workers of varying degrees of skill. They may have little in common other than the fact of their self-employment, and the influences of policy and of economic and structural forces may be very different between these different "segments" of self-employment.

Some Theoretical Considerations

In addressing questions about the nature and causes of recent self-employment trends in Europe, the theoretical social science literature does not provide us with a firm base. Self-employment has not, until recent years, attracted significant attention from social scientists. As other recent authors have noted (e.g., Steinmetz and Wright 1989), since the 1950s labor *sociologists* either ignored self-employment, or treated it as a residual segment of the labor market, associated with agriculture, small-scale crafts, and an archaic "petit bourgeois" section of society. While a strand of sociological literature examines the characteristics of the self-employed as individuals and as members of a distinct social stratum (see Burrows 1991), beyond the notion that this stratum is a declining one, there has been little aggregate analysis (for recent exceptions, see Steinmetz and Wright 1989; Bögenhold and Staber 1990). Thus, while much is known about the social and economic characteristics influencing individual propensities to become self-employed, these analyses provide only a weak basis for explaining macrolevel trends.

The treatment of self-employment in the *labor economics* literature is even more limited. Again, this is partly due to its having been seen as an obsolescent mode of employment, largely characterizing preindustrial societies. Most modern labor economics texts provide no more than passing reference to self-employment. One reason for economists' neglect of self-employment is that as a topic it falls uneasily between two subbranches of the discipline. It is often unclear whether it is rightfully within the purview of labor economics or is better treated within the framework of industrial economics. From a labor economics perspective (see Rees and Shah 1986; Blau 1987), it is common to model entry into self-employment as a problem of occupational choice, with individuals maximizing utility across various combinations of income and leisure, and the "nonleisure" options including dependent wage employment and self-employment. A problem inherent in such approaches is that it is implausible to treat self-employment analogously to dependent employment, with the income received by the self-employed seen purely as a return to labor input. Introducing more realism into such models typically makes for greater complexity and less tractability, since it is clear that income in self-employment also includes some elements of a return to capital. The way in which this should be treated may depend on whether the capital in question is owned by the self-employed person or is supplied through the capital market (in which case, the question of the degree of perfection of capital markets facing potential entrepreneurs must also be considered). The model may also need to be broadened to allow for the fact that a return to self-employment is also in part a return to risk bearing.

Compared with the labor economics tradition, there is a more significant literature on the subject in *industrial economics*. Much of this, however, concentrates on the creation and death of firms, barriers to entry, limit pricing, etc. It typically fails to allow for the fact that self-employment is in significant part a labor market phenomenon, and that the self-employed may not always be best characterized analytically as "entrepreneurs" or as very small businesses. The mainstream models of industrial economics and the "theory of the firm" suggest that given scale economies and technological requirements, the optimal size of an "enterprise" invariably implies an employment level greater than one. Thus the self-employed are treated as an (extreme) case of "small enterprises," and self-employment is of interest primarily as a transitory stage through which (some) newly emergent enterprises might pass on their way to becoming fully fledged small businesses. Some of the more recent economic literature, however, has begun to develop models of entrepreneurship (Evans and Jovanovic 1989; Blanchflower and Oswald 1990b), integrating many of the factors discussed above at a microtheoretical level and taking some steps to bridge the theoretical gap between labor economics and the theory of the firm. Again, however, these approaches lack an exposition of self-employment as a labor market phenomenon and do not allow for the possibility that a significant proportion of the self-employed are not independent entrepreneurs but may be highly dependent on larger organizations.

In any event, the linkage between such theories and aggregate models remains weak, and they provide a poor starting point for explaining observed trends in self-employment at a macro level across countries and looking for policy impact at that level. In the absence of an adequate theoretical framework, the research strategy adopted in the work reported here was not to attempt to develop one, but rather to draw in an eclectic manner on theoretical and empirical work in all of the above traditions, in order to identify the main factors influencing the development of self-employment at an aggregate level. In place of a single theoretical framework, therefore, a looser, analytical schema was used, tracing the links and relationships between these various factors in order to construct as far as possible a coherent account of the recent changes, and intercountry differences, consistent with the available evidence.

This schema is presented in detail elsewhere (Meager 1993; Meager, Kaiser, and Dietrich 1992), but the essential point relevant to the present discussion on policy evaluation is that any attempt to isolate and evaluate the impact of public labor market policies for self-employment cannot consider these policies in isolation. They are but one of a set of interrelated external influences on the level and composition of self-employment, of which others include:

- macroeconomic developments (issues of "unemployment push" and "prosperity pull," which we consider in more detail below, are relevant here);
- structural change, in particular the ongoing shift from manufacturing to service sector employment in most advanced nations;
- changes in the organizational structure and behavior of employers (e.g., the shift to "contracting out" of service functions, the growth of franchising, etc.);
- changing demographic structures, given the different propensities to enter self-employment found in different sections of the work force (in many EC countries, growing female labor market participation and an aging labor force are relevant here).

We would argue, further, that the combined effects of these external influences on developments in self-employment are conditioned or mediated by the influence of a constellation of factors concerned with the institutional environment in which the self-employed and the potential self-employed operate. It is *differences in these institutional environments*, we argue, that are crucial in explaining different self-employment patterns between some countries that we might otherwise expect to perform rather similarly in self-employment terms. Two of the most important of these factors are:

- the institutional and regulatory framework governing business start-up and occupational entry;
- the structure, regulation, and functioning of capital markets facing potential entrepreneurs.

The role of these factors can be illustrated through a comparison of the United Kingdom and Germany (see Meager, Kaiser, and Dietrich 1992). Institutional differences between these countries led, in the 1980s, to U.K. self-employment being more "dynamic" and more unstable, with higher rates of both entry and exit, than its German counterpart. Taking the first of the two factors, it appears that despite deregulation in both countries during the 1980s, regulation over entry to certain occupations and over business start-up in general remained higher in Germany than in the United Kingdom. This is particularly true in *Handwerk* (crafts), which covers a wide range of activities (from bakers and hairdressers to dispensing opticians)—see Doran 1984. To set up in self-employment in Handwerk one must be a *Meister* in the occupation concerned (or to employ such a Meister), which means having served an apprenticeship and having acquired certain postapprenticeship experience and training. There is no such requirement in the United Kingdom. Thus, to a greater extent in Germany than in the United Kingdom, entry into self-employment in many occupations is dependent on prior, long-term career choices, and insofar as entry into self-employment responds to short-term macroeconomic fluctuations, such responsiveness tends to be less in the more regulated German environment.

Turning to the second factor, it was generally easier for entrepreneurs to obtain start-up finance in the United Kingdom than in Germany in the 1980s. Financial deregulation in the United Kingdom led to a credit boom, with financial institutions keen to lend directly to potential entrepreneurs, or indirectly through loans for consumption or house purchase, which could be recycled for other purposes. This contrasts with a tighter credit environment in Germany and was reinforced in the United Kingdom by the large and growing rate of home ownership, which, coupled with house price inflation, led to growing personal housing wealth, which could be used as collateral for business start-up (further, capital gains from housing often leaked into other areas via "equity withdrawal"). There is also evidence (Danish Technological Institute 1991) that the venture capital industry specializing in high-risk financing of new business is more developed in the United Kingdom than in Germany, and expanded in the 1980s.

Thus, a lower degree of regulation in the United Kingdom over many occupations and businesses, as well as a looser lending environment than in Germany, is consistent with our evidence below of lower inflow rates to self-employment in Germany than in the United Kingdom. It seems, further, that new German entrepreneurs in this period were better placed to survive in business than their U.K. counterparts because: (a) German self-employed were more likely to be qualified in the relevant occupation; (b) they were more likely to have their proposed business scrutinized by a lending institution; and (c) those entering regulated sectors (e.g., Handwerk) enjoyed relatively protected markets. Further, having set up in business, self-employed Germans face a wider array of publicly funded support and advice (Bannock and Albach 1991); thus Anglo-German differences in policy stance reinforce the institutional differences. As a result, new entrants to self-employment in Germany are more likely to come from dependent employment than from unemployment or economic inactivity (as confirmed by the ELFS data below), since the former are better endowed than the latter in terms of both financial and relevant human capital. A further consequence is that self-employment outflows run at a lower rate and are less responsive to recent inflows in Germany than in the United Kingdom (again confirmed by the ELFS). Hence, international comparisons of self-employment trends must take account of the way different institutional and legislative contexts condition the response of self-employment to economic variables. We now turn to examine these recent trends.

Recent Self-Employment Trends in the EC

Since the early to mid-1970s, EC self-employment has grown absolutely and relative to the level of total employment. Thus, taking the nine EC member states in 1975,[2] the ELFS shows that total self-employment grew by nearly a quarter between 1975 and 1989 to over 15.5 million. The total number of people in employment grew by only 8.9 percent over the same period.

This trend is also observable in industrialized countries outside the EC (see OECD 1986 and International Labour Office—ILO—1990), representing an apparent reversal of a long-term secular tendency for self-employment to decline. An important and as yet unresolved question (OECD 1992) is how far such a change is merely a short-term deviation from trend, associated with cyclical or one-off factors, and how far it represents a more permanent shift toward smaller units of employment (see Sengenberger, Loveman, and Piore 1990).

Beneath this overall picture, however, lies considerable intercountry variation. Figure 6.1 shows total self-employment trends since 1973 in four countries (Denmark, France, Germany, and the United Kingdom) selected for detailed examination in the study on which this chapter is based, which diverged sharply after 1979, with self-employment taking off into strong and sustained growth in the United Kingdom at one extreme, and continuing to fall at an accelerated pace in Denmark, at the other. France and Germany lie between these extremes, exhibiting slight growth of self-employment during the 1980s. This wide variation was one of the main criteria for selecting these four countries for study (another was that they also exhibited important variations in the policy regimes for self-employment—a point taken up later in the chapter). As far as the remaining EC countries are concerned, none match the extreme trends in the United Kingdom and Denmark, but they nevertheless exhibit considerable variation (Meager 1993).

We have noted the considerable variation in recent self-employment trends in EC countries. The *relative importance* of self-employment compared with wage also varies considerably across the EC. Thus, looking at the most recent year for which we have comparable data (1989), we can divide the EC countries into three broad groups (see Figure 6.2):

- five countries (the four southern EC countries—Greece, Italy, Portugal, and Spain—plus Ireland) with much higher than average self-employment rates (over 20 percent);
- three countries—Belgium, France, and the United Kingdom—that have self-employment rates within a few points of the EC average (between 12 and 16 percent); and
- the remaining countries (Denmark, Germany, Luxembourg, and the Netherlands), which all have self-employment rates much lower than the average (below 10 percent).

Figure 6.1 **EC Self-Employment Trends, 1973–89** (all sectors)

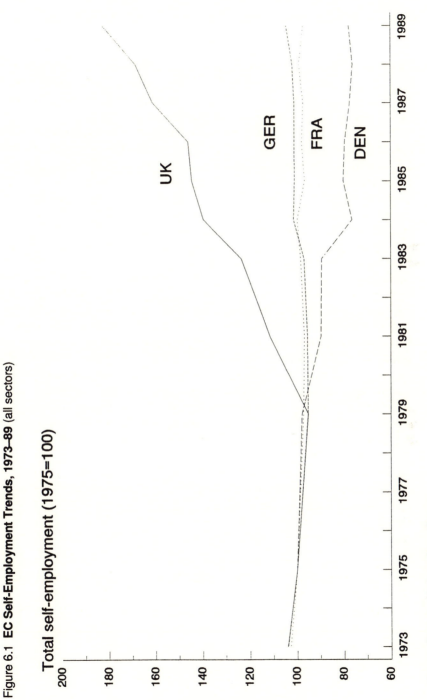

Total self-employment (1975=100)

Source: European Labour Force Surveys.

192

Figure 6.2 **EC Self-Employment Rates and Growth Rates, 1983–89** (all sectors)

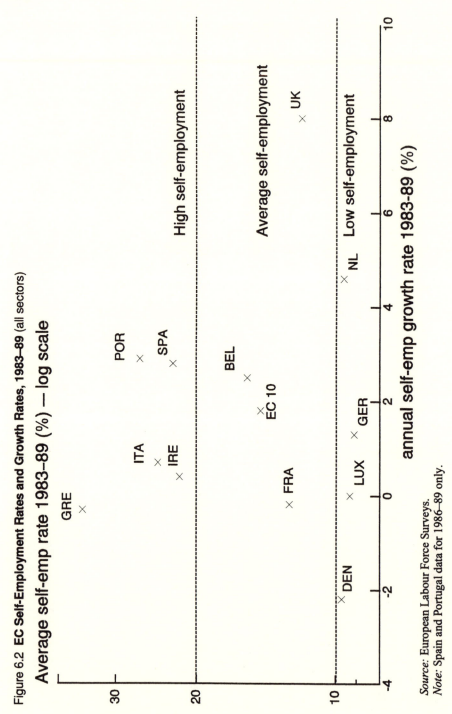

Source: European Labour Force Surveys.
Note: Spain and Portugal data for 1986–89 only.

One possible explanation for the variation in self-employment rates is associated with the role of agriculture (self-employment rates in agriculture are, in most countries, higher than those in other sectors). Further breaking the data down (see Meager 1993), however, shows that in practice agriculture plays little role in determining this ranking of countries. Thus while self-employment rates in countries with a large agricultural sector (particularly the southern European countries and Ireland) are reduced somewhat by the exclusion of agriculture from the data, these countries' nonagricultural self-employment rates remain for the most part considerably higher than those in northern Europe.

Figure 6.2 also shows that there is no clear relationship across EC countries between the extent of self-employment and its rate of growth. It is not the case that countries with relatively high self-employment rates have also experienced relatively fast growth in self-employment in recent years, or vice versa.

An alternative explanation for intercountry self-employment differences, however, is that there is an inverse relationship between national income and self-employment:

> In non-agricultural activities, self-employment exhibits a declining trend with higher income. As income grows in the course of economic development, markets expand, output shifts to more capital intensive products and production is organized in larger-scale enterprises, all drawing workers away from self-employment. The share of self-employment in total non-agricultural employment is generally high in low-income countries (ILO 1990, 8).

This relationship and its theoretical basis are discussed more extensively in Acs, Audretsch, and Evans 1992, drawing on empirical evidence from OECD countries and a selection of developing economies. Figure 6.3 apparently supports the existence of an inverse relationship between self-employment rates and GDP per capita in Europe. One problem with this argument, however, is that it suggests an inexorable trend toward declining self-employment as national incomes grow. While the argument may be valid when comparing developing with developed economies (as in ILO 1990), it is less clearly the case when comparing countries *within* the EC, which are, in terms of the ILO comparison, all relatively "high-income" countries. Within the EC, among both the generally richer northern countries and the generally poorer southern countries, we can find countries exhibiting self-employment growth and decline. Such an argument based on income levels is, therefore, clearly an insufficient explanation for recent trends in EC countries. A more detailed analysis, taking account of the short-term dynamics of self-employment and allowing for the possibility that self-employment rates in some countries may, in the short run, *increase* with economic development and GDP growth, is required. In the following section, therefore, we examine the evidence on the relationship between self-employment and the economic cycle.

Figure 6.3 **EC Self-Employment Rates and GDP**

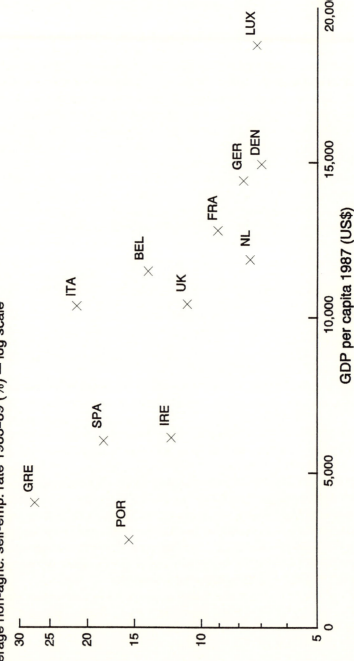

Average non-agric. self-emp. rate 1983–89 (%) — log scale

GDP per capita 1987 (US$)

Source: European Labour Force Surveys/International Labour Organisation.
Note: Spain and Portugal data for 1986–89 only.

Cyclical Fluctuations in Self-Employment

The relationship between self-employment and the economic cycle has been extensively explored elsewhere, and the previous literature is critically reviewed in Meager 1992a and 1992b. Much recent research, including the important work of Bögenhold and Staber (1990, 1991), argues that labor market pressure combined with slow or stagnant economic growth following the oil shocks of the 1970s and 1980s has played a crucial role in the slowing or reversal in the previous self-employment decline. This line of theorizing sees growing self-employment as a response to sustained mass unemployment and lack of opportunities in wage unemployment.

As we have argued elsewhere, however (Meager 1992a and 1992b), while this kind of "unemployment push" is indeed likely to have played some role in contributing to observed aggregate self-employment trends, the dynamics of self-employment are more complex than this. There is, for example, likely to be a relationship between unemployment and the economic cycle acting in the *opposite* direction, with growing unemployment acting as a dampening factor on self-employment due to poorer market opportunities and higher risks of small business failures (in what follows, we refer to the argument that economic growth and falling unemployment lead to growing self-employment as the "prosperity pull" hypothesis).

There are, furthermore, two major methodological problems in the time-series correlations between self-employment and unemployment and/or GDP observed by authors such as Bögenhold and Staber. As a result of these problems, such analyses cannot adequately test for or discriminate between the various arguments (unemployment push, GDP pull, etc.) that purport to explain the cyclical behavior of self-employment.

The first problem is the tendency in such work to examine the relationship between the self-employment *rate* (self-employment as a proportion of total employment) and unemployment, GDP growth, etc. It is clear that any observed relationship between the self-employment rate and other aggregate variables (e.g., the positive relationship between the self-employment rate and unemployment of Bögenhold and Staber 1990) will be dominated by the cyclical relationship between these aggregate variables and the *denominator* of the self-employment rate (i.e., total employment). An observed positive relationship with unemployment may not be confirmation of an unemployment push hypothesis but may simply reflect the fact that total employment fluctuates procyclically.

The second problem is that such analyses typically examine a relationship between unemployment and the self-employment *stock*. This is inappropriate for examining hypotheses such as unemployment push, which are concerned with the influence of unemployment and other economic variables on workers' propensities to *enter* (or to *leave*) self-employment and are thus hypotheses about *flows*. In particular, it is straightforward to show that even if the unemployment push hypothesis were valid, and increasing unemployment acted as a stimulus for self-employment entry, this would not even constrain the *sign* on the relationship between unemployment and self-employment stocks, since the latter is a net effect from both inflow and outflow relationships and is not predictable *a priori* (Meager 1992a).

The first problem is addressed in Meager 1992a, where time-series evidence for ten EC countries is presented, showing that when the *level* rather than the rate of self-employment is used in the analysis, there is in most countries *no clear positive relationship* over time between the self-employment stock and unemployment. Indeed, for several of the countries, and much of the period examined (1970–88), the data suggest that any underlying relationship between the self-employment stock and unemployment is a *negative one*. One interpretation here would be that any unemployment push tendency has been more than outweighed by the dampening effect of high unemployment and low economic growth on self-employment.[3]

As suggested by our discussion of the second problem, however, this does not invalidate the unemployment push argument, but implies that flows data are required to examine it adequately. To establish how unemployment and the macroeconomy influence the numbers entering and leaving self-employment, we need flows data. Similarly, we need such data to establish how labor market policies for self-employment influence these entry and exit flows, which must be a key element of any comparative evaluation of such policies. More specifically, for both purposes we need not only aggregate gross flows data, but also, for example, inflow data to self-employment broken down by the source of the inflow.

Thus when examining the unemployment push hypothesis, there are good reasons to expect that increasing unemployment will affect rather differently the propensities of unemployed, employed, and economically inactive people to enter self-employment (see following section). Equally, when looking at the impact of policies targeted at encouraging the unemployed to take up self-employment (pages 208–10), we need to be able to identify separately inflows to self-employment that originate in unemployment. In the next section, therefore, we consider the possibility of constructing internationally comparable flows data of this type from the ELFS.

The Dynamics of Self-Employment: Flows Analysis from the ELFS

As previous studies have shown (see Meager, Kaiser, and Dietrich 1992), while such dynamic analyses are seriously constrained by the paucity of adequate self-employment flows data, it is possible to use retrospective questions from the ELFS to construct flows data. The ELFS contains questions on respondents' employment status one year prior to the survey. We can, therefore, identify people who have changed status during the year (for example, by entering or leaving self-employment). In what follows we make use of these data to construct estimates of annual inflows to and outflows from self-employment in EC countries.

There are several deficiencies in this approach, which are discussed in detail in Meager 1993, but the most serious is that the data do not yield true "flows" data, since they fail to pick up multiple changes of status during the year, hence underestimating the full extent of mobility. Despite these deficiencies, however, it is likely that major changes in the dynamics of self-employment flows will show up in these data, and they are increasingly used as the principal source of data on self-employment flows (see, for example, OECD 1992).

Aggregate trends in self-employment inflows and outflows for a number of EC countries are presented in Meager 1993, for the period 1983–89, showing that *annual inflows exceeded outflows* in most countries throughout the period. The main exception is Denmark, where outflows exceed inflows by a considerable margin (consistent with the recent strong decline in Danish self-employment). The excess of inflows over outflows is particularly marked in the case of the United Kingdom, where, as we have seen, self-employment grew faster during the 1980s than in other EC countries. Meager 1993 also relates (for those six EC countries for which we have five or more observations during the 1980s) trends in inflows and outflows to trends in aggregate unemployment, and the observed pattern is a very mixed one. In Germany, for example, there is some relationship (in the direction predicted by unemployment push) over most of the period, but the relationship breaks down at the end of the period, with self-employment inflows increasing between 1987–88 and 1988–89, at a time when unemployment was falling. In the United Kingdom, however, any relationship would appear to have been in the "wrong" direction throughout the period, with inflows to self-employment increasing when unemployment has been falling, and vice versa.

Overall, the patterns observed in Meager 1993 do not provide any clear evidence of a push relationship between unemployment and the aggregate flow into self-employment. One possibility, however, is that the push hypothesis holds not for the *aggregate* inflow, but for one or more of its subcomponents (see Meager 1992a). Thus, if the unemployment push hypothesis held, we might expect to observe a positive relationship between the unemployment rate and the *subflow from unemployment to self-employment*. In the case of the *subflow from dependent employment*, however, the picture is less clear. On one hand, increasing unemployment (and declining employment opportunities) might result in an increased flow into self-employment among some involuntary job-losers (choosing self-employment rather than unemployment). On the other hand, a certain proportion of the subflow from wage employment to self-employment consists of voluntary quitters, opting for self-employment for economic or life-style reasons. A deteriorating economic climate would, *ceteris paribus* (consistent with the "pull" hypothesis), tend to reduce the size of this group. Similarly, when we consider those labor market (re)entrants moving from economic inactivity to self-employment, an economic downswing might push more of these toward self-employment; but equally among those for whom it is an option, the downswing might have a "discouragement" effect, resulting in postponement or abandonment of labor market entry.

Given these likely differences in the way in which the economic cycle affects different types of inflow to self-employment, it is not surprising if no strong push effect is picked up in the aggregate inflow data, and there is a strong case for disaggregation according to the various components of the inflow—a task attempted below.

Similarly, the evidence in Meager 1993 on the relationship between self-employment *outflows* and unemployment is mixed, although in Germany and Ireland there does appear to be a positive relationship between the two variables throughout the period in line with the predictions of the pull hypothesis, with the outflow from self-employment increasing as unemployment increases, and vice versa. In the other countries the pattern is less clear, with the variables moving together for only part of the period examined.

It must also be recognized, however, that the two sets of flows are unlikely to be independent of each other, and outflows from self-employment may themselves be a lagged function of earlier inflows. That is, of a cohort of new entrants, a proportion can be expected to "fail" and leave self-employment within a fairly short period, largely irrespective of market conditions. This might be because the initial business idea was poorly thought out, or because the self-employed person possessed inadequate business management skills, or because the self-employed life-style did not match initial expectations. As shown in Meager 1992a and confirmed with more recent data (Campbell and Daly 1992), this effect is visible in U.K. data with an apparent lag of about two years. We do not, unfortunately, have a long enough data series from the ELFS to examine this more widely (although there does appear to be some evidence of such an effect in the French and Belgian data, with a lag of one to two years).

So far we have discussed the absolute size of the self-employment flows and trends in those flows over time. In order to compare the relative size of inflows and outflows between countries, however, we need to express them as *rates*, in proportion to self-employment stocks. Figures 6.4 and 6.5, therefore, show patterns of inflows and outflows in our four countries, as a percentage of total self-employment at the start of the year to which the flow refers.

Figure 6.4 shows that the ranking of inflow rates is very similar to the ranking of self-employment growth rates shown earlier. The United Kingdom has by far the highest inflow rate (around 18 percent per annum for most of the period), and, as we have seen above, the United Kingdom has experienced the fastest growth of any country over the same period. Then come France and Germany, with inflow rates of about 10 percent (and we saw above that they had very similar growth rates of self-employment—i.e., a slight increase during the 1980s). Finally, Denmark has much lower inflow rates than the other three countries (averaging 2–3 percent).

The rankings change somewhat when outflows are examined (Figure 6.5).

Figure 6.4 Self-Employment Inflows Over Year As Percent of Start of Year's Stock

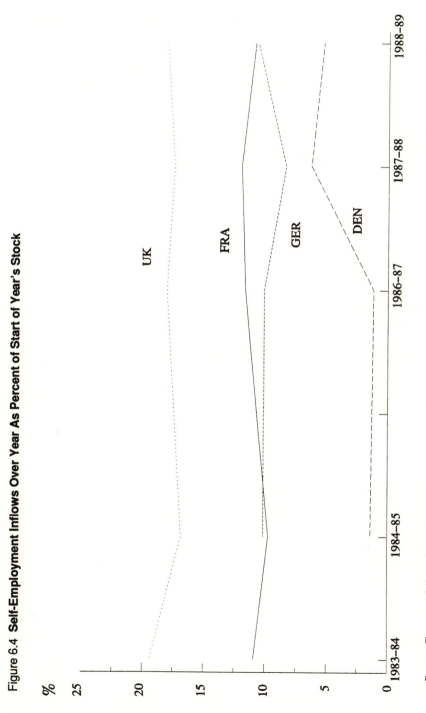

Source: European Labour Force Surveys.

200

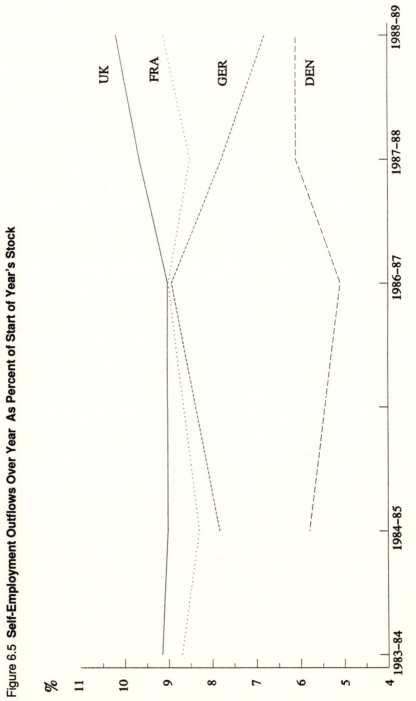

Figure 6.5 Self-Employment Outflows Over Year As Percent of Start of Year's Stock

Source: European Labour Force Surveys.

Denmark still records the lowest rate (averaging around 6 percent), and it is clear that Danish self-employment is unambiguously "less dynamic" than that in the other three countries. The low exit rate is likely to be a consequence of the low entry rate. That is, the stock of Danish self-employment is "older" and more stable than in the other countries. Danish self-employment is in decline not because of an unusually high exit rate or failure rate, but because the number of new entrants is insufficient to match even the relatively small outflow rate.

The outflow rates of the other three countries are more similar than the inflow rates, with France and the United Kingdom recording the highest rates (around 9 percent), and the German rate lying slightly below these two. The fast growth in U.K. self-employment results from this difference between inflow rates and outflow rates, with the former nearly twice the rate of the latter. The greater "dynamism" of U.K. self-employment compared with France and Germany is predominantly associated with this very high inflow. The United Kingdom's outflow rate has remained relatively low in comparison (although it is still higher than in nearly all other EC countries).

Figures 6.4 and 6.5 are notable for the fact that in most of the countries the flows (in both directions), when expressed relative to self-employment stocks, are remarkably stable throughout the period.[4] The differential trends in self-employment stocks observed above, therefore, arise from differences between relatively stable inflow and outflow rates in individual countries, rather than from increases or decreases in those rates of flow themselves. We must be careful, however, not to attribute permanence to these stable patterns. The U.K. pattern, for example, appears (Campbell and Daly 1992) to have changed drastically since 1989, with the onset of recession and a sharp increase in outflow rates, and an even sharper fall in inflow rates (consistent, incidentally, with the pull hypothesis, and counter to the push hypothesis, discussed above). More recent evidence from other countries is not available at the time of writing, but it is possible that this stability in flow rates, and the general tendency for self-employment growth, was a phenomenon of the mid to late 1980s, which was in most EC countries a period of relative economic growth, following the sharp recession of the early 1980s.

So far we have looked at the aggregate volume of flows to and from self-employment. In order to obtain a fuller picture of the complex dynamics of self-employment, however, we need to examine the composition of those flows in terms of their *sources* and *destinations* of outflows. Table 6.1 summarizes this information for nine EC countries. Of the four labor market states identified (wage employment, economic inactivity, unpaid family labor, and unemployment), *wage employment* is the largest source of entrants to self-employment in all countries, although its relative importance varies considerably between the countries, from 31 percent of inflows (Spain 1987–88) to 75 percent (Germany 1988–89).

As far as outflows are concerned, the picture is more mixed. In all countries (with the occasional exception of Ireland and Spain), wage employment is gener-

Table 6.1
Composition of Inflows to and Outflows from Self-Employment

Source/destination of flow	Inflows: status previous year (%)						Outflows: status subsequent year (%)					
	1982–83	1983–84	1984–85	1986–87	1987–88	1988–89	1982–83	1983–84	1984–85	1986–87	1987–88	1988–89
Germany												
out of labor force	22.4		10.5	12.4	13.1	12.9	37.6		15.9	19.4	24.8	24.2
employee	62.1		74.4	73.7	74.0	74.5	39.7		63.9	62.8	59.5	56.8
family worker	6.1		10.3	8.8	6.7	7.1	7.0		12.8	11.3	7.2	13.9
unemployed	9.3		4.8	5.1	6.2	5.5	15.6		7.4	6.5	8.5	5.1
France												
out of labor force	25.4	25.1	27.6	21.1	20.6	23.7	42.5	45.3	41.5	44.6	45.6	46.2
employee	46.4	44.8	42.4	41.6	44.4	41.5	34.0	31.0	29.6	27.4	28.0	27.9
family worker	19.0	19.0	17.3	20.6	18.9	19.0	13.0	13.0	17.4	16.6	16.1	14.6
unemployed	9.3	11.1	12.7	16.6	16.1	15.7	10.5	10.7	11.6	11.4	10.3	11.3
		Average 1982/3–1984/5			Average 1986/7–1988/9			Average 1982/3–1984/5			Average 1986/7–1988/9	
Denmark												
out of labor force		19.3			11.7			44.2			34.5	
employee		50.7			71.4			28.5			43.9	
family worker		1.3			0.0			2.5			0.5	
unemployed		28.7			16.9			24.8			21.2	
U.K.												
out of labor force	27.2	33.1	25.1	24.4	21.6	22.8	25.6	28.3	25.7	24.1	26.7	26.2
employee	55.8	46.9	53.0	52.2	56.0	58.6	46.6	39.0	43.2	45.6	50.5	53.2
family worker												
unemployed	17.0	20.0	21.9	23.3	22.4	18.6	27.8	32.7	31.1	30.4	22.8	20.5
Belgium												
out of labor force	30.4		29.0	29.5	33.0	31.0	38.7		44.6	47.8	45.8	42.6
employee	43.7		42.2	43.3	44.7	47.2	32.2		28.1	28.4	35.5	32.1
family worker	7.5		6.6	4.5	3.8	2.2	19.2		14.1	10.3	9.5	15.3
unemployed	18.4		22.2	22.7	18.4	19.6	9.9		13.3	13.6	9.3	10.0

	1982–83	1983–84	1984–85	Average 1982/3–1984/5	1986–87	1987–88	1988–89	Average 1986/7–1988/9	1982–83	1983–84	1984–85	Average 1982/3–1984/5	1986–87	1987–88	1988–89	Average 1986/7–1988/9
Greece																
out of labor force	35.1	31.4	32.2		29.2	31.4	35.3		34.6	36.8	38.2		45.3	42.6	49.6	
employee	44.2	44.8	45.5		42.8	41.9	40.2		28.9	30.4	29.7		29.9	33.2	30.9	
family worker	14.2	13.1	11.1		14.6	12.5	15.4		18.1	13.3	20.0		14.9	13.3	10.9	
unemployed	6.4	10.7	11.2		13.4	14.2	9.1		18.4	19.4	12.1		9.9	10.9	8.6	
Ireland																
out of labor force				26.6				27.4				22.3				32.9
employee				39.8				39.1				49.3				36.4
family worker				5.4				1.8				3.2				3.1
unemployed				28.2				31.7				25.3				27.6
Spain																
out of labor force					26.8	28.5	25.7						30.1	32.1	32.8	
employee					32.7	31.3	37.0						35.7	32.3	30.3	
family worker					18.2	10.2	9.3						22.3	24.9	24.1	
unemployed					22.4	30.0	28.1						11.9	10.7	12.8	
Portugal																
out of labor force						16.0	14.3							56.3	52.3	
employee						67.0	72.2							30.2	31.4	
family worker						4.7	4.2							7.3	10.0	
unemployed						12.2	9.2							6.2	6.3	

Source: Own calculations from European Labour Force Surveys.

Note: Small cell sizes for Denmark and Ireland necessitate aggregation of data from several years. 1982–83 data for Germany may be unreliable due to relatively large numbers of respondents whose previous employment status is "not known."

ally less important as a destination of outflows from self-employment than it is as a source of inflows. In most countries, this underrepresentation of wage employment in outflows (compared with inflows) appears to go along with a corresponding overrepresentation of *economic inactivity* in outflows. More detailed analysis of the data suggests that a high proportion of the flow from self-employment to inactivity occurs in the older age groups, and these patterns are consistent with the notion that self-employment may be an important step in a career path that goes from wage employment through self-employment to retirement.

Turning briefly to flows between unemployment and self-employment, these are of particular interest for two reasons: first, because of the role that growing unemployment is often hypothesized to play in contributing to self-employment growth; and, second, because of the emergence during the 1980s of policies aimed at facilitating the transition from unemployment to self-employment. Such policies are a central focus of the present study, discussed in depth in the following sections, and it is therefore worthwhile here to examine unemployment–self-employment flows as background to this subsequent policy discussion.

The largest proportions of the inflow to self-employment originating in unemployment are found in Ireland (28–32 percent), Spain (22–30 percent), Denmark (17–27 percent), the United Kingdom (17–23 percent), and Belgium (18–23 percent). The corresponding proportions are somewhat lower in Greece, Portugal, and France. Germany is again an extreme case, having by far the largest proportion of new entrants to self-employment coming from wage employment, and the smallest from unemployment. We have outlined above some possible reasons for these differences, notably the greater extent and complexity of regulation facing entrants to self-employment in Germany, which is likely to favor potential entrants with relevant recent employment experience over groups such as the unemployed.

Returning to the question of unemployment–self-employment flows, it seems from Table 6.1 that unemployment generally accounts for a fairly similar share of the destinations of outflows as it does of the sources of inflows. There are, nevertheless, differences between these two sets of flows, and in a majority of countries (Belgium, France, Ireland, Portugal, and Spain) unemployment is a more important source of inflows than it is a destination of outflows. In three other countries (Denmark, Germany, and Greece) the pattern is mixed, but the United Kingdom stands out as the only country in which the proportion of those leaving self-employment for unemployment is consistently higher than the (already comparatively high) proportion of those entering self-employment from unemployment. In this context, OECD 1992 notes:

> France and the United Kingdom, the two countries where there was a marked rise in inflows from unemployment, also had the largest programmes designed to help unemployed people set up in business on their own. . . . In the United

Kingdom, this was not accompanied by any increase in the outflow from self-employment to unemployment. In France, where there was such an increase, it was nevertheless slight. The bulk of the extra inflow from unemployment does not appear to have simply entered a revolving door back into unemployment. For the most part, the extra inflow from unemployment appears to have remained within employment, either self-employment or wage and salary employment, or to have left the labour force altogether. (OECD 1992, 166).

While this argument is generally consistent with the evidence presented here, the authors do not note the important difference between the United Kingdom and France—namely, that in France unemployment accounts for a lower share of outflows than inflows, while in the United Kingdom it accounts for a higher rate. We would, therefore, urge some caution in drawing the kind of optimistic policy conclusions suggested by the OECD. It is clear that there may be important differences between the United Kingdom and those other countries in which the inflow to self-employment from unemployment has increased, the increase coinciding with the introduction of policies apparently targeted at increasing that inflow. The most recent U.K. evidence (see Campbell and Daly 1992, 275) confirms a sharp increase in the share of self-employment outflows entering unemployment since 1989, at a time, moreover, when the share of unemployed in the inflow to self-employment had fallen off markedly.

We have looked at the sources of self-employment inflows as a proportion of the overall inflow to self-employment. This does not take any account, however, of the *relative size* of the stock from which the inflows come. Thus, for example, given that the unemployed stock in EC countries has always been considerably smaller than the employed stock, even if the probabilities of entering self-employment were identical for the unemployed and for employees, the former would form a smaller proportion of the inflows.

In Meager 1993, therefore, we look at rates of inflow to self-employment from the other labor market statuses, expressing the inflows from each status during the year as a percentage of the stock of people with that status at the start of the year. This shows the relative probabilities of unemployed people, employees, family workers, and the economically inactive becoming self-employed during the year. We will not present these findings in detail here (the interested reader is referred to Meager 1993). A key point of interest for the present discussion, however, is that with the occasional exception of Germany, the average probability of an *unemployed* person entering self-employment is in all countries and in all years greater (often much greater) than the probability of an employed or an economically inactive person doing so. Germany is again unusual in having both a relatively low rate of inflow from unemployment and a relatively high rate of inflow from employment, such that in some years the probability of entry to self-employment from employment is as high as or even slightly higher than the probability of entry from unemployment.

Figure 6.6 charts trends in the rate of entry from unemployment to self-em-

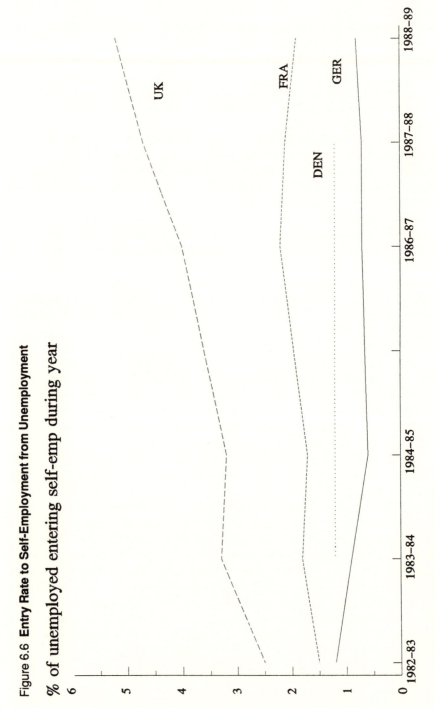

Figure 6.6 **Entry Rate to Self-Employment from Unemployment**

% of unemployed entering self-emp during year

Source: European Labour Force Surveys.

ployment during the 1980s. The highest rate is observed in the United Kingdom, where the rate grew strongly, more than doubling between 1982–83 and 1988–89 (Greece also records a relatively high rate—Meager 1993—but not an upward trend). Trends are generally less marked in other countries—with some increase over time in France, and some decline in Germany, where the rate of entry to self-employment from unemployment is less than 1 percent through most of the 1980s.

How can we explain these trends? In particular, does the unemployment push hypothesis discussed above provide any explanation? We argued above that the hypothesis was most likely to hold in relation to the subflow from unemployment to self-employment. A key problem in attempting to test the notion of unemployment push is that it is unclear from the earlier literature on the subject whether the hypothesis is about absolute flows or flow rates. A positive relationship between the inflow to self-employment, on the one hand, and the level (or rate) of unemployment, on the other, may not in fact indicate unemployment push. To see this, if the *rate* at which unemployed people enter self-employment (as shown in Figure 6.6) remains constant over time, implying no real behavioral change among the unemployed with regard to becoming self-employed, we would nevertheless still observe a positive relationship between the absolute inflow and the level (or rate) of unemployment. In its strongest form, however (e.g., as in Bögenhold and Staber 1991), the hypothesis implies rather more than this; namely, that as unemployment increases, the unemployed perceive a worsening in their chances of securing wage employment, and thus feel under greater pressure to consider self-employment. From this perspective, we would expect that the probability of an unemployed person's entering self-employment would increase, and as a result, rather than simply remaining constant, the flow rate into self-employment from unemployment will increase accordingly.

Meager 1993 relates for five EC countries (for which there exist five or more observations) trends in the flow rates from unemployment to self-employment to trends in the unemployment rate itself. The pattern is mixed—in Belgium and France is a relationship (albeit not a perfect one) in the predicted direction. In Germany and the United Kingdom, by contrast, any relationship is in the opposite direction, with falling unemployment associated with increases in the inflow rate from unemployment to self-employment, and vice versa. In these latter two countries, then, the probability of an unemployed person entering self-employment falls with increasing unemployment, which is more indicative of discouragement, associated with a worsening economic climate, than of unemployment push. Unemployment push is, therefore, on the evidence available, inadequate as a universal explanation of inflows to self-employment. A fuller explanation, across the range of EC countries, clearly needs to consider other major influences on the flow, and obvious candidates are those labor market policies introduced in all EC countries in the 1980s, aimed at encouraging the unemployed to become self-employed. We consider these policies in the next section.

Labor Market Policies for Self-Employment in EC Countries

During the 1980s, EC countries introduced a wide range of publicly funded schemes to stimulate or support the expansion of self-employment. In both analytical and practical terms, it is extremely difficult to separate those policies that are primarily labor market based, attempting directly to influence the level and nature of self-employment, from those that form part of a wider range of policy initiatives aimed at the small business sector, but that may also have some labor market impact. Johnson 1990 makes a useful distinction between those small firms policies, on the one hand, that can be seen as having primarily an industrial policy rationale, and those policies, on the other hand, that fall within the sphere of labor market policy. Some policies are relatively easy to assign to one or other of these categories. Thus, for example, policies to stimulate or support the export performance of small firms, or to encourage the adoption of new technologies in small firms, are clearly aimed at fostering growth and competitiveness, often in particular sectors. Even where such policies have important employment and labor market effects (job growth, for example), they are not *primarily* aimed at labor market performance in any sense, and as such they form part of an industrial policy toward small firms. An example at the other extreme would be those policies that aim to subsidize or support the entry of certain members of the labor force (such as the unemployed) into self-employment or small business proprietorship. Such policies (which are our main subject here) clearly form part of a labor market policy program.

For a mixture of analytical and practical reasons, we have concentrated our research effort in this internationally comparative study on those policies that both have a clear labor market emphasis and are national in their coverage and scope. This is partly to give the study some clear comparative focus, reflecting our interest in national differences in labor market performance (given that such policies exist in some comparable form in nearly all the EC countries), and our interest in self-employment as a labor market phenomenon. It is partly also for reasons associated with time and resources—our primary concern is with labor market policy and national differences, and the inclusion of all those industrial policies that have some labor market impact, or all those policies that operate at a local, regional, or sectoral level, would have vastly extended the scope of the study.

The most important type of policy initiative that meets both of these criteria (a primary focus in the labor market, and national coverage) consists of those schemes aimed at promoting self-employment among the unemployed, which exist in all the member states (although we exclude the main Italian scheme, which is confined to unemployed youth resident in the Mezzogiorno region).

Table 6.2 illustrates the extent and growing importance of such schemes in the overall labor market policy portfolios of EC countries, showing that they

Table 6.2

Self-Employment Schemes for the Unemployed As Share of Labor Market Policy Expenditure

Country	Share of total labor market expenditure (%)				
	1985	1986	1987	1988	1989
Spain	1.67	5.61	6.02	6.84	—
Greece	0.00	0.00	0.00	5.05	—
U.K.	1.03	1.31	1.88	2.19	2.27
Portugal	—	0.97	1.89	1.95	1.80
France	1.43	1.49	1.24	1.10	—
Ireland	1.49	1.48	1.02	0.74	—
Denmark	—	0.21	0.36	0.41	0.55
Germany	0.00	0.06	0.11	0.35	0.15
Belgium	0.00	0.00	0.38	0.29	—
EC9[a]	0.88	1.31	1.41	1.61	—

Source: OECD 1990a.

Note: Dash indicates data not available. 1985 data exclude Denmark and Portugal.

[a]9-country total calculated by aggregating individual country expenditures converted to US$ at average annual prevailing exchange rates.

constitute a small but clearly growing component of overall labor market policy expenditure (in 1988, they accounted for only some 1.6 percent of total expenditure on labor market schemes, but a proportion that had doubled over the 1985–88 period alone). The table also reveals some diversity between the different countries. At one extreme is Spain, where the scheme accounted for close to 7 percent of overall labor market policy expenditure by the late 1980s, and at the other is a group of countries—Denmark, Germany, and Belgium, where for most of the period in question, spending on self-employment schemes was below half a percent of overall labor market policy expenditure. The majority of countries exhibited a growth (absolute and relative) of expenditure on such policies during the second part of the 1980s.

The ranking of countries shown in Table 6.2 is somewhat sensitive to the overall size of each country's labor market policy program. In Table 6.3, therefore, we attempt to standardize in a common currency, the level of each country's expenditure on self-employment schemes, but this time relative to the overall size of the main target group for such schemes in that country (viz. the unemployed). The main difference between the two tables is that Greece and Portugal, by virtue of the relatively small scale of their overall labor market policy expenditure, drop from being "high" and "moderate" relative spenders respectively on self-employment schemes, to being "low" absolute spenders on such schemes per head of unemployment. Otherwise, the ranking of countries is largely unchanged. Spain retains its position with the largest scheme, spending

Table 6.3

Expenditure on Self-Employment Schemes for the Unemployed, per Head of Unemployment

Country	Per capita expenditure in US$[a]			
	1985	1986	1987	1988
Spain	30.2	142.0	192.8	256.1
U.K.	42.0	64.9	110.2	150.5
France	93.8	130.8	129.9	123.2
Denmark	—	54.6	91.4	114.3
Greece	0.0	0.0	0.0	81.6
Ireland	63.6	85.1	66.7	51.4
Germany	0.0	5.2	12.7	45.7
Belgium	0.0	0.0	51.2	44.3
Portugal	—	6.2	18.3	26.1

Source: OECD 1990c.

Note: Dash indicates data not available.

[a] Scheme expenditure data are derived from OECD 1990a; unemployment data from OECD 1990b; and expenditure data have been converted into US$ at the prevailing annual average of national exchange rates against the dollar for each year.

more than $250 per unemployed person, while the United Kingdom, France, and Denmark spend between $100 and $150 per head, and the other countries all spend less than $100. Table 6.3 also confirms the general upward trend in such expenditures.

These self-employment schemes generally consist of payments to those unemployed who become self-employed or set up a business, and these payments are (wholly or in part) in lieu of the benefits or insurance payments they would have received had they remained unemployed. This implies, incidentally, that the schemes are in principle extremely "cheap" in exchequer cost terms compared with some other labor market policies (Barker 1989). Thus, even if the final effect of such policies in terms of the reduction in unemployment or the creation of self-employment is small, after allowing for deadweight and displacement,[5] the net exchequer cost per job created is also likely to be small, given the negligible gross cost of the measures.[6]

The expenditure on such schemes can, therefore, be regarded as a direct substitution of part of the overall labor market budget, from "passive" to "active" labor market policies. While other active labor market policies (e.g., those "make-work" or training schemes that involve a payment or allowance to the participants in lieu of benefit) also involve such a substitution, the self-employment policies are unusual in design in that they often approach a one-to-one relationship between the outlay on the active measure and the associated reduction in the passive expenditure on income maintenance for the unemployed.

Comparative Evaluation: Some Research Questions

Identifying Scheme Objectives

A key difficulty in defining evaluation criteria is identifying the underlying objectives of the scheme in question. Is success to be measured in terms of the reduction of unemployment (and if so, is this a short-term "register effect" or a longer-term indirect job-creation impact)? Is the creation of small businesses itself also a specific aim of the scheme in its own right? Are there other less measurable impacts that are seen as objectives of the scheme (e.g., impacts on the quality of the labor supply, impacts on aggregate wages levels)?

An important initial decision is whether to concentrate on the *unemployment* impact of such schemes, or on their impact on *self-employment*. In most national evaluation studies, these two questions have not been clearly distinguished, or have been treated as equivalent. Clearly, in the short term, there is such an equivalence. Over time, however, more complex dynamic effects may also need to be considered. Do, for example, scheme participants whose businesses fail return to unemployment, or do they move into employment, perhaps because the experience of self-employment has added to their human capital and improved their labor market position? Or, are the businesses displaced by the subsidized self-employed, businesses that would otherwise have had better survival chances than those displacing them?

In this study, greater emphasis was given to the effects of such schemes on self-employment levels than to their effects on unemployment, but in explaining differences between schemes in their impact on self-employment, we take account, where possible, of differences in the underlying objectives of the policy-makers in those countries. These differences may be subtle ones, not obvious from the design of the scheme, that become clear only on a detailed reading of official texts. A good example emerges when we compare the United Kingdom's Enterprise Allowance Scheme (EAS) with its German counterpart, Überbrückungsgeld, ostensibly quite similar in design and objectives. They both involve the payment of a regular allowance to unemployed people entering self-employment, and in both cases the eligibility net is cast quite wide. In both cases the most obvious objective is the reduction of unemployment, although the official literature describing the German scheme is cast in a more traditional labor market policy framework, while the U.K. scheme includes significant objectives associated with the promotion of the "enterprise culture." More interesting, however, the German scheme has an explicit objective, which is the *Vermeidung von unterwertiger Beschäftigung* (the avoidance of undervalued or underpaid employment). To this end, it is an eligibility requirement that participants must show that the proposed self-employed activity can generate a reasonable minimum level of income (in 1988 this was 3,400 DM per calendar month). The position taken by U.K. policymakers was very different: many studies of EAS recipients note the low earnings generated by the subsidized self-employed activities. This is, however, seen as a supply-side "benefit" of the EAS; namely, that it contributes to reduced wage pressure in the economy.[7] In 1988, 80 percent of EAS recipients earned less than the 3,400 DM per month (£260 per week), and half of the EAS participants earned less than £100 per week. The EAS has often been criticized for encouraging the unemployed to enter low-margin, highly competitive activities in which they have poor survival chances, or tend to displace existing self-employed. It should be recognized, however, that such effects can, under some interpretations, be seen as consistent with one of the stated objectives of the scheme.

Controlling for Differences in the Environment

This is the most serious difficulty faced in a comparative study such as this one. In evaluating policies across countries, we must allow for differences between what would have happened anyway in those countries, in the absence of policy. Comparative evaluation must allow for the different economic and institutional environments into which the various schemes have been introduced, since these may well constrain or support self-employment and the flow from unemployment to self-employment. Some attempt has been made to set out the issues involved here in the earlier part of this chapter, which looked at the nature and composition of self-employment, together with recent self-employment trends in EC countries.

Deadweight and Displacement Effects

These effects (i.e., the extent to which the scheme participants would have entered self-employment anyway, and the extent to which the subsidized businesses displace unsubsidized ones) are the traditional meat and drink of labor market policy evaluation and are clearly important in any analysis of self-employment schemes for the unemployed.

Differences in Scheme Design and Implementation

Differences in the performance of individual schemes (e.g., with regard to deadweight, displacement, and survival rates) depend not just on the external environment into which the scheme is introduced, but also on differences in scheme design and implementation. The most important of these are:

- Eligibility
    There are two aspects to this: first, the extent to which the scheme is open or targeted to specific groups; and, second, if it is targeted, the question of who is targeted. In a general sense, all the schemes are designed to

increase the flow from unemployment to self-employment. As such, eligibility is normally confined to the unemployed.[8] In most countries, eligibility is widely defined to cover all those in receipt of unemployment compensation (or entitled to it). Some countries (notably Germany, the United Kingdom, and Ireland) qualify this to exclude the very short-term unemployed, while two countries—Portugal and Denmark[9]—confine eligibility to the long-term unemployed (the latter country also imposing an age criterion).

In evaluation terms, therefore, a contrast needs to be made between schemes with limited eligibility (concentrating on particular disadvantaged groups, for example), against those with wide eligibility. Within the latter, there is also a need to examine the extent to which those who do in fact benefit from the scheme are representative of the eligible group. Much previous evidence from several countries suggests that they tend not to be—that is, even where all unemployed are eligible, those entering the scheme are concentrated among the more advantaged unemployed (better qualified, male, with shorter durations of unemployment, etc.). A priori, it is not clear which kind of scheme design is likely to be more effective. On the one hand, a scheme with wide eligibility and self-selected participants runs the risk of high deadweight, while, on the other hand, a scheme targeted at disadvantaged groups may have lower deadweight but a poorer survival rate.

• Mode of financing

Although the schemes share broad similarities in their ultimate source of funding, there are notable differences between them with regard to the disbursement of those funds to participants in the schemes. The most important difference is between those countries (e.g., France and Spain) that provide the funds in advance, either in the form of a grant (which can be, as in Spain, a simple capitalization of the benefits that would have been received while unemployed) or, more rarely, in the form of a "soft" loan; and those countries (e.g., United Kingdom and Germany) that provide an allowance over time, in a similar way to the corresponding payment of unemployment compensation.

While there is little difference between these modes of financing from an exchequer viewpoint, they may have rather different outcomes in terms of labor market dynamics, and an important evaluative element should therefore be a comparison of the relative performance of the two types.[10] Simple economic theory suggests that the impacts of two schemes identical in their total budgets, one of which reduces the capital constraint on entry to self-employment, and the other of which increases the stream of income during the initial period of self-employment, may in practice be very different. Under perfect capital markets, of course, the two approaches would be equivalent;[11] but as is commonly argued in the literature, capital markets faced by new and would-be entrepreneurs are rarely perfect in this sense.

In particular, therefore, we need to consider how the funding mode influences the numbers entering the scheme, the type of people entering (is a grant better at attracting disadvantaged groups, or those who would not otherwise enter self-employment?), and the types of activity they enter. The latter may be particularly important in influencing survival rates in self-employment. We noted above that a common criticism of the U.K. scheme, for example, (an allowance) is that it encourages entry to markets with low entry-barriers, low value-added, and low returns. In these crowded, largely service-sector markets, survival rates are low and displacement rates high. A key question, therefore, centers on the extent to which a grant-based subsidy helps to achieve a "better" sectoral distribution of scheme participants.

• Support and training

Is any ongoing support and training provided for scheme participants, and if so, what kind? Are such mechanisms voluntary or compulsory; how are they administered; and how do they link in with other small business support and advisory networks that exist in the countries concerned? The existence of appropriate support may weaken the trade-off between deadweight and survival identified above.

• Scale and duration of payments

Here one needs to consider the interrelated questions of the size of the payments to scheme participants, the duration of payments, and the number of participants. To take the extreme cases, is it more effective to spend a given budget for such schemes on a small number of participants receiving a relatively large payment for a long time, or to "spread the money more thinly," with more participants, smaller payments, and shorter durations of payment? How do intermediate configurations perform?

Space precludes discussion of all these features in the present chapter, where we concentrate in our empirical work on the first two aspects above. Meager 1993, however, considers the other design features of such schemes in more detail.

Methodologies for Evaluation

Ideally, scheme evaluation would involve the kinds of control-group experimental approaches being adopted in the United States. Typically, however, such approaches have been ruled out in most EC countries on grounds of cost, ethical objections to experimental evaluations, or simply because political expediency required a rapid implementation of the scheme. Insofar as such evaluation has to be conducted *ex post*, then, at a very broad level there would seem to be three strategies for evaluating these types of schemes empirically:

• Scheme administrative data and follow-up surveys

This strategy is the most common and involves the use of administrative data to identify the characteristics of scheme participants, and surveys to identify their perceptions, experiences, survival rates, etc. Its main drawback is that without external comparisons of nonscheme participant entrants to self-employment, it is difficult to draw strong conclusions. Equally, reliance on participants' perceptions to identify deadweight or displacement is fraught with difficulties (although these can be eased through seeking collaborative perceptions from competitors and customers of scheme participants—see Elias and Whitfield 1987).

For internationally comparative evaluation, the usefulness of such data on their own is limited, since they are inevitably collected according to different research designs and tend not to be comparable between countries. We have, however, reviewed the findings from such studies in the present research (see Meager 1993) and argue that there is some scope for using such data in conjunction with base data from the ELFS (see below).

• Aggregate impact studies

Essentially these attempt to pick up the effects of the schemes in aggregate data, controlling for the effects of other economic and environmental factors. We discuss such approaches below and present some preliminary evaluations of our own at an aggregate level, but these methods are hindered by the lack both of a robust theoretical model explaining self-employment flows and, in most countries, of adequate time-series flows data with which to estimate such a model statistically.

• Inference through comparisons with representative microlevel data

Such approaches as these involve the use of flows data that enable us to look at the characteristics of the newly self-employed, and at the characteristics of those entering self-employment from unemployment. Similarly, one can examine outflows and their characteristics. Selected comparisons of these patterns with the characteristics of individual scheme participants (as collected through administrative and survey data) can then provide some insights on scheme performance.

To give a more concrete illustration of this approach, some working hypotheses might be:

1. The more the policies in question are targeted (at disadvantaged groups and people with characteristics not normally found among the self-employed), the less will be initial deadweight, but also the less will be the long-term survival rates in self-employment (unless the policies are accompanied by extensive support and training measures). Targeting is likely, therefore, to involve a trade-off between deadweight and survival, and it is unclear a priori where the optimal balance lies. Using ELFS flows data on entrants to self-employment in individual countries, we can build up a profile of the main personal characteristics of

people who tend to become self-employed in each country. By comparing this profile with data on the characteristics of scheme participants, we can make a preliminary assessment of whether deadweight is likely to be high or low. Similarly, insofar as it is possible to assess the survival chances of people with "atypical" characteristics for self-employment, we can provide some indications of the likely increased failure rates associated with policies that target such people.

2. Grant-based schemes are more likely to encourage people to set up businesses in markets with higher initial barriers to entry but with better long-term income and survival prospects, while (under imperfect capital markets) schemes providing an allowance are more likely to encourage entry to crowded markets with low entry barriers and low initial capital requirements. It is likely that displacement effects will be smaller in the first type of market as new entrants reduce the (protected) profits of existing businesses rather than drive them out of business. Again, the ELFS data can give us a picture of the kinds of business activities the newly self-employed typically enter. This picture can then be compared with the profile of the activities of scheme participants to assess whether these policies are indeed shifting the profile, and whether grant-based schemes appear to shift it in a different way from allowance-based schemes.

In conclusion, all three of these approaches have pros and cons for internationally comparative evaluation, and our research strategy has been to use elements of all three, in an attempt through "triangulation" to arrive at a better knowledge of the relative performance of different types of schemes. Inevitably, given the scale of the study and the number of countries involved, we can, in this chapter, only scratch the surface. It is hoped, nevertheless, that we can shed light both on the schemes themselves and on the possibilities of comparative evaluation offered through the availability of flows data from the ELFS.

Aggregate Evaluation of Scheme Impact: Is It Possible?

Perhaps the simplest question that can be posed in evaluating labor market policies for self-employment is whether the level of self-employment is higher than it would otherwise have been in the absence of the policy, and by how much. Despite the considerable sums that have been spent on such schemes, and despite the considerable effort expended in "evaluating" the schemes (typically through follow-up surveys of scheme participants),[12] this question is still far from being answered in all of these countries. As an OECD report concluded following a review of the evaluative material then available on such schemes in OECD countries:

> The self-employment schemes for the unemployed are in many countries still in their infancy. The schemes have received continuing support and many have progressed from the pilot stage to national implementation. However, the

dearth of longer-term evaluative material has, in many instances, limited the meaningful conclusions that can be drawn about their efficacy other than to underscore their potential to create new enterprises and employment. (Barker 1989, 48–49).

The review of national evaluation studies undertaken for the present research suggests that these conclusions still stand—while most countries now have good data on the composition and characteristics of participants, the duration of participation, and subsequent experiences, none of them have been able to undertake any rigorous assessment of deadweight and displacement effects, necessary for any overall impact evaluation of the schemes.

In part this results from the reliance on monitoring and following up scheme participants. In principle, surveys can obtain some estimate of deadweight effects—simply by asking participants whether they would have entered self-employment in the absence of the scheme, and under what circumstances (this approach has, for example, been adopted in U.K. evaluation studies of the EAS—see PA Cambridge Economic Consultants 1990). By definition, however, this can give no estimate of displacement (it is difficult to attach much credence to the approach of U.K. evaluation studies of simply asking scheme participants to estimate how much business they have taken from existing firms). Elias and Whitfield 1987 provide a comprehensive account of the methodological difficulties in the empirical measurement of displacement effects and conclude, having identified five possible strategies for assessing the displacement effects of the EAS, that in-depth, sectorally structured studies of impact in local labor markets offer the greatest potential.

To date, only one such detailed study appears to have been undertaken—a pilot study based on surveys of EAS participants, their competitors, and their customers in a local economy (Hasluck 1990). The study considered the impact of EAS in two specific sectors ("hairdressing" and "other business services") in a local labor market. In hairdressing, EAS displacement was found to approach 100 percent, while in business services it was much lower. These results, however, while interesting, reinforce the difficulties in generalizing from particular localities and sectors to deduce a displacement effect for the scheme as a whole.

Are there, then, alternative approaches to assessing overall scheme impact that might lead us to be able to draw conclusions at a national level, and to compare scheme effectiveness between countries? Few examples exist of macroeconometric studies of self-employment with scheme variables as explanatory variables. A notable exception is Johnson, Lindley, and Bourlakis 1988, which estimates a time-series aggregate model for the United Kingdom with self-employment levels (or rates) as the dependent variable and a policy variable for the EAS as an independent variable, alongside variables picking up unemployment, structural change, and other factors. The results are, however, inconclusive; the key problem with such analyses is their reliance on a dependent variable based on self-employment *stocks*. As noted above, the immediate objective of such schemes is to increase the inflow from unemployment to self-employment, and thus only aggregate modeling of self-employment *inflows* can indicate the extent to which there is such an effect (net of deadweight). Similarly, the combined effects of nonsurvival of scheme participants and displacement of nonparticipants can be picked up only by modeling the outflows.

In principle, then, the use of flows data offers a way forward. In practice, however, the flows data that we have constructed from the ELFS are inadequate for time-series modeling of policy impacts, as we have too few observations. Nevertheless, we explore below the possibilities of using these data in *cross-sectional* comparisons of scheme impact across countries, before going on to illustrate a methodology for time-series impact analysis using a unique German flows dataset.

Aggregate Scheme Impact: Cross-Sectional Analysis

In this section we ask whether there is any relationship across EC countries between the number of people entering self-employment from unemployment and the size of the self-employment scheme for the unemployed in the country concerned. If scheme deadweight is generally high, we would not expect to observe any such relationship, since the existence of the scheme would make little difference to the flow from unemployment to self-employment.

To examine this, we make use of comparable data compiled by OECD, which identify, for each country, numbers of scheme participants starting under the scheme in 1988. Clearly, these absolute figures do not indicate the relative scale of the scheme in each country, and we have therefore expressed them as percentages of the unemployed stock at the start of the period (i.e., in 1987). Figure 6.7 then plots the rates of entry from unemployment to self-employment over 1987–88, as calculated from the ELFS (see above), against these rates of scheme participation.[13]

The figure suggests a positive relationship between the two variables across EC countries (with a correlation of 0.7). There is, however, no reason to assume that self-employment schemes are the only, or the most important, variables influencing entry from unemployment to self-employment. As discussed, there is a considerable literature arguing that the scale of unemployment itself influences self-employment inflows, and the inflow from unemployment in particular. This is the unemployment-push hypothesis, which in its most plausible version posits a positive relationship between the flow rate into self-employment from unemployment, and the unemployment rate itself.

As a crude test of this, therefore, Table 6.4 presents a simple cross-sectional regression analysis for the nine countries, with the rate of inflow to self-employment from unemployment (1987–88) as the dependent variable and the rate of participation of the unemployed in the labor market scheme (as defined above),

Figure 6.7 **Self-Employment Schemes and Inflows from Unemployment, 1987–88**

% inflow rate to self-employment from unemployment

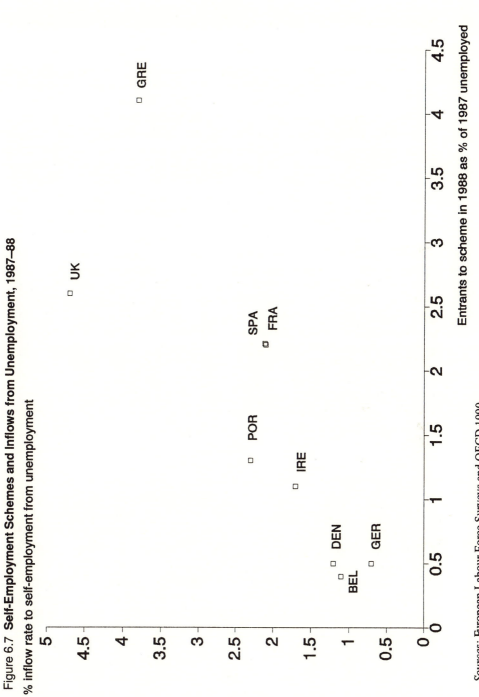

Entrants to scheme in 1988 as % of 1987 unemployed

Sources: European Labour Force Surveys and OECD 1990.

Table 6.4

Regression Results

	coefficient	t-statistic
Constant	0.89	
% of 1987 unemployed participating in scheme in 1988	0.88	3.71
1987 unemployment rate	-0.01	0.25
R^2	0.69	

Note: Dependent variable = % of unemployed entering self-employment over 1987–88.

together with the (1987) unemployment rate, as independent variables. The strong positive relationship between the scheme variable and the inflow to self-employment from unemployment persists when the unemployment rate is included as an explanatory variable.[14] The unemployment variable itself, however, has no significant impact. It is not surprising that we cannot observe any clear unemployment push relationship in a cross section, given that there are major differences between the composition of self-employment in the different countries and between their institutional environments, and given moreover that the time-series evidence within individual countries for such a relationship was somewhat mixed (see "The Dynamics of Self-Employment" above).

The strong relationship between the scheme variable and the inflow to self-employment from unemployment is nevertheless striking. It is clear that countries whose schemes have higher penetration rates among the unemployed also have higher overall rates of entry from unemployment to self-employment. Indeed, taking the regression results at face value suggests that such schemes might generally have very low deadweight elements—of the order of 12 percent[15]—and that in the absence of such schemes inflow rates from unemployment to self-employment would be around 0.9 percent (i.e., just under 1 in every 100 unemployed people would enter self-employment in the course of a year). We cannot, of course, interpret the results in such a strong form, if only because of the inadequacies of the flow variables constructed from the ELFS. In particular, they do not record all inflows from unemployment to self-employment during a year, and the proportion of scheme participants who will be recorded as part of the ELFS inflow will depend both on the average duration of the scheme and on the distribution of new starts on the scheme during the course of the year.

It is, therefore, not possible to attach much meaning to the precise slope of the relationship between the scheme variable and the inflow variable. It is nevertheless notable that variations in scheme intensity seem to explain a considerable proportion of the intercountry variation in the inflow to self-employment from unemployment. The fact that the relationship is both clearly positive and significant suggests at the very least that the schemes have some effect; the existence of the schemes tends to increase the inflow from unemployment to self-employment by a non-negligible amount (i.e., deadweight is less than 100 percent).

Aggregate Scheme Impact: Time-Series Analysis— A German Illustration

Reliable time-series data on aggregate self-employment flows are unfortunately scarce in most countries. Further, as we have seen, the flows data constructed from the retrospective questions in the ELFS are currently unsuitable for aggregate time-series analysis. Germany is, however, unusual in having available, since 1970, a consistent set of labor market accounts, based on gross annual flows data, the *Arbeitskräfte-Gesamtrechnung* (AGR). The construction of such a data set from a variety of sources inevitably involves a number of assumptions, and a certain amount of estimation, and it should therefore be used with some caution (see Reyher and Bach 1988). This is particularly the case with variables such as self-employment stocks and flows that are constructed as residuals and are therefore more "noisy" than variables like unemployment, where stocks and flows are measured more frequently and reliably for administrative reasons such as benefit payment. A further deficiency is that the self-employment data in the AGR include unpaid family workers (*mithelfende Familienangehörige*), who, from an analytical point of view, constitute a category distinct from the self-employed.

Nevertheless, we make use of the AGR flows data in our analysis as an illustration of the potential such data sets offer for the modeling of the determinants of self-employment flows, and the evaluation of the aggregate time-series impact of labor market policies designed to influence these flows. In particular, we use the data to examine a time-series equivalent of the cross-sectional relationship examined in the previous section, with inflows from unemployment to self-employment as the dependent variable and some measure of the scale of unemployment as an independent variable (to test the unemployment-push hypothesis), along with a measure of the intensity of the self-employment scheme for the unemployed.

The time-series approach raises a further difficulty, however, since in order to test whether there is in fact any relationship between unemployment and the inflow into self-employment, we need to allow for the possibility that any statistical significance apparently exhibited by unemployment as an explanatory variable derives simply from its acting as a proxy for a time trend. To allow for this empirically, and in the absence of any clear theoretical basis for our model, we include a time-trend variable.

Before setting out the model itself, however, it is worth briefly describing the main features of the German scheme to be included in the model (see Meager

1993 for further details). The scheme (instituted under paragraph 55a of the *Arbeitsförderungsgesetz*—AFG) involved the payment of a bridging allowance *(Überbrückungsgeld)* to eligible unemployed people who set up in self-employment. The allowance, introduced in 1986, was payable for up to three months (and following a revision in 1988 for up to six months), its value equivalent to the unemployment benefit or allowance previously received, subject to a ceiling (see Kaiser and Otto 1990).

Given its relative newness, a full evaluation of Überbrückungsgeld has yet to be conducted, although several surveys of participants have been undertaken, and preliminary results from these (showing, for example, the demographic characteristics of participants) have been published (see Kaiser and Otto 1990). As we have noted, the evaluation of such a scheme is a relatively complex process, particularly in light of the multiplicity of objectives typically inherent in such schemes. As with many such schemes in EC countries, Überbrückungsgeld embodies several of these objectives, but it is clearly intended to increase the inflow to self-employment from unemployment. In any empirical examination of the relationship between unemployment and this flow, and any testing of the unemployment-push hypothesis for Germany, we need to allow, therefore, for the possible impact of Überbrückungsgeld.

In addition to completing our explanatory model of self-employment inflows, however, the incorporation of a variable for Überbrückungsgeld into our analysis allows for a crude test of the short-term impact of the scheme itself. In other words, it can give some indication of whether there is a deadweight effect, and an approximation of how large that effect might be.

In practice, however, there may be difficulties in discerning the precise effect of the scheme statistically with aggregate data, since at the time of writing data are available only for the first four years of the scheme (1986–89). On the other hand, although the scheme itself is small compared with those in some other countries (it peaked in 1988 with 18,000 participants), and although it accounts for only a small proportion of the overall flow into self-employment, it is by no means negligible as a proportion of the flow into self-employment from unemployment. Thus, according to the AGR data, the total flow to self-employment from unemployment in 1988 was 89,000,16 implying that about a fifth of all those entering self-employment from unemployment were Überbrückungsgeld recipients, and it should be remembered that the data include family workers, so the percentage of the flow into self-employment per se accounted for by scheme participants may actually be somewhat higher than this. Despite its short life, then, the scheme is sufficiently large in the German context such that any influence it may have on the inflow ought to be detectable in statistical terms.

Turning now to the empirical examination, our earlier discussion suggests that we should attempt to estimate a model of the form:

$$I_t = f(U_t, t, \ddot{U}_t)$$
$$+ \quad ? \quad +$$

where:

I_t = the inflow from unemployment to self-employment in year t;
U_t = the unemployment level at the beginning of year t;
$\ddot{U}_t$ = some measure of the existence/intensity of Überbrückungsgeld in year t;
t = a time-trend variable;

and where, in line with our previous discussion, the expected signs on the independent variables would be as shown above.

We do not have any theoretical underpinning for a particular functional form for the basic relationship between I_t and U_t, but a preliminary plot of the data suggested nonlinearity and that some kind of log-linear or semilog function might be appropriate for estimation. Annual observations for I_t and U_t are obtainable from the AGR data set for 1970–89 (with I_t being calculated as a residual from these data). As far $\ddot{U}_t$ is concerned, one option is simply to include a dummy variable in the model for the four-year period 1986–89 when the policy was in operation. Data on the number of Überbrückungsgeld recipients are, however, available for each of these four years, and given that this number fluctuated considerably during the period (from a low of less than 6,000 in 1986 to a peak of nearly 18,000 in 1988), the assumption of a constant policy intensity, implicit in the use of a dummy variable, is clearly not valid, and it is preferable to set $\ddot{U}_t$ equal to the total number of scheme participants in each year.

Table 6.5 shows the results of an ordinary least-squares estimation of a model with a semilogarithmic relationship between It and ln(Ut). Four versions of this model are estimated. In version 1, It is simply regressed against ln(Ut). While this yields a clear positive and statistically significant coefficient on ln(Ut), the Durbin-Watson statistic lies below the lower bound of acceptance (at both 5 percent and 1 percent), indicating a strong possibility of (first-order) autocorrelation. This suggests that important variables may have been omitted from the model, or indeed that the observed correlation between It and ln(Ut) may be a spurious one.

In version 2, which includes a time trend, the overall fit of the equation is improved slightly, and $\ln(U_t)$ retains its significance. Interestingly, the time trend itself has a significant coefficient, but with a negative sign. This suggests not that the initial bivariate relationship between I_t and $\ln(U_t)$ was a spurious one, due to both variables being subject to similar time trends, but rather that I_t is subject to an underlying downward trend, which has been modified by the strong upward influence of growing unemployment during the period. Again, however, the Durbin-Watson statistic, although somewhat larger, is suggestive of autocorrelation and possible omitted variables. Versions 3 and 4 of the model, therefore, explore the possibility that the key omitted variable is the labor market policy variable $\ddot{U}_t$.

Table 6.5

Regression Estimates

Model Dependent variable	1 (1970–89) I_t	2 (1970–89) I_t	3 (1970–85) I_t	4 (1970–89) I_t
Constant	-42.662	-83.516	-121.936	-108.796,
	(4.034)[a]	(4.660)[a]	(8.538)[a]	(6.605)[a]
$\ln(U_t)$	17.112	24.981	32.890	30.214
	(11.254)[a]	(7.695)[a]	(12.193)[a]	(9.786)[a]
t		-1.282	-3.104	-2.513
		(2.652)[b]	(6.292)[a]	(4.583)[a]
$\ddot{U}_t$				0.927
				(3.191)[a]
R^2	0.88	0.91	0.96	0.95
D-W	0.55	0.60	1.70	1.64
F-stat	126.66[a]	88.06[a]	166.14[a]	93.81[a]

Note: Units of measurement are thousands; absolute values of t-statistics are given in parentheses.

[a] Indicates significance at 1 percent.

[b] Indicates significance at 5 percent (2-tailed tests for t-stats).

Version 3 is identical to version 2 but estimated over the shorter period 1970–85; i.e., it excludes the period in which Überbrückungsgeld operated. If Überbrückungsgeld is indeed the key omitted variable from the model, we would expect version 3 of the model to perform better than version 2, since we have excluded the period when the omitted variable would have been relevant. The results tend to confirm this expectation, with the model fitting slightly better than before, but more important, it now shows no evidence of autocorrelation, with the Durbin-Watson statistic lying above the upper bound of acceptance. The estimated coefficients retain their significance and signs. Finally, version 4 covers the whole estimation period 1970–89 and includes the Überbrückungsgeld variable $\ddot{U}_t$. This equation performs rather well. The overall fit is good, there is no evidence of autocorrelation, and the coefficients on all three independent variables are highly significant, with the coefficient on $\ddot{U}_t$ having the expected positive sign and the other two coefficients retaining their signs from previous versions of the model.

How are we to interpret these findings, which apparently confirm that all three of our independent variables have an important role to play in explaining the development of inflows into self-employment over time?

As far as the unemployment-push hypothesis is concerned, the evidence supports it only in its weak form, that is to say, in the form that concerns only the subflow from unemployment to self-employment, and that says simply that this flow increases in response to an increase in unemployment. The stronger version of the hypothesis, however, which argues that the rate of flow from unemployment to self-employment (or the probability of an unemployed person becoming self-employed) increases as the unemployment level increases, is not supported by the evidence. Indeed, the estimated equations given in Tables 6.4 and 6.5 confirm that the flow rate (I_t/U_t) tends to decrease with increasing unemployment.

Turning to the time trend, our results appear to suggest that but for the influence of unemployment and labor market policy, the flow from unemployment to self-employment is on a long-term downward trend in Germany, falling at a rate of 2–3,000 per year. This result is interesting, but some caution should be exercised, given our reservations about the construction of the self-employment data in the AGR and the fact that these data include unpaid family workers. This group, in Germany as elsewhere, is concentrated in certain sectors (such as agriculture), and is subject to a long-term historical decline (OECD statistics suggest, for example, that the total number of such workers fell from just under two million to some 850 thousand over the twenty-year period 1966–86). It is possible, therefore, that the observed negative time trend simply reflects the inclusion of this group.

Nevertheless, the significant results for the policy variable are of particular interest. If the coefficient on $\ddot{U}_t$ in version 4 is taken at face value, it seems not only that Überbrückungsgeld has a significant positive effect on the inflow into self-employment, but that in line with the earlier cross-sectional analysis, the deadweight effect associated with the scheme is extremely small. That is, for every 100 Überbrückungsgeld recipients in the 1986–89 period, the inflow from unemployment to self-employment apparently increased by 93 (a deadweight of 7 percent).

It is clearly sensible also to exercise some caution in interpreting this finding, which comes from only four annual observations, and it is, moreover, again possible that the inclusion of unpaid family workers in the data has affected this result. Thus, if, for example, every eighth Überbrückungsgeld recipient "employs" an unpaid family worker in the first years of self-employment, and the actual deadweight effect were 20 percent, we would observe an *apparent* deadweight effect of only 10 percent from the AGR data.[17] Further caution is suggested by the fact that these data indicate that the scheme performs rather better in deadweight terms than, for example, its U.K. equivalent, where survey evidence suggests that short-term deadweight may be as high as 30–40 percent.[18] A priori we might expect the German scheme to have a higher deadweight than the U.K. one, since the subsidy, although larger than the U.K. equivalent, is payable for a shorter period (six months compared with a year in the United Kingdom), while the eligibility criteria for the German scheme are stricter (requiring evidence of business viability, for example). Against this, it is arguable that the threshold arrangements introduced into the German scheme, whereby duration of the allowance increases with previous unemployment duration, tip the balance of the scheme in favor of more "disadvantaged" unemployed people who would have been unlikely to become self-employed without the subsidy.

It is unfortunate that official surveys of Überbrückungsgeld recipients have not included a direct question on whether the recipients would have become self-employed without the subsidy. There was, however, a question that asked participants to indicate the extent to which the financial support provided by the scheme was crucial in providing for the upkeep of the self-employed person and his or her family during the start-up phase. The results from this question (which are presented in more detail in Meager 1993) show that the subsidy played an important support role for more than two-thirds of the scheme participants (and possibly for more than 85 percent of them), which is consistent with relatively low deadweight.

Even if the AGR data are unreliable, this analysis at least demonstrates the potential for using such flows data sets to track labor market dynamics and thereby get a better empirical handle on the impact of labor market schemes such as Überbrückungsgeld.

Examination of Scheme Impact through Comparison with Representative Micro-Data

In this final section we consider the possibilities of using the flows data constructed from the ELFS to compare the performance of self-employment schemes for the unemployed across our four selected countries. The principles involved here were discussed in "Methodologies for Evaluation" above, and we examine the personal characteristics of scheme participants (for reasons of space, we confine ourselves in this chapter to analyzing gender),[19] and the characteristics of the businesses subsidized under the scheme (indicated by industrial sector).

Previous evaluations have compared the characteristics of the scheme participants with those of the self-employed as a whole. The important advantages offered by the ELFS data are, however, twofold. First, they enable us to compare the characteristics of scheme participants with those of other new entrants to self-employment from unemployment. Without such a comparison, it is impossible to conclude that the schemes are influencing the types of unemployed people who become self-employed.

Second, they enable us to compare scheme performance across countries, taking account of the different underlying structure of self-employment flows in those countries. Thus, if we find, for example, that the proportion of scheme participants in manufacturing is higher in Germany than in France, this does not necessarily imply that the German scheme is more successful than the French in encouraging or supporting the self-employed to set up in manufacturing, since we also need to take account of the different proportions of the overall flow from unemployment to self-employment in manufacturing in the two countries.

Before setting out the results of these comparisons, however, it is worth briefly describing the schemes themselves. These are summarized in Table 6.6 (more details are given in Meager 1993; see also Barker 1989 and OECD 1990d). The key differences are the relatively large scale of the U.K. and French schemes; the fact that the French scheme is a capital grant, while the others are allowance based; the initial targeting of the Danish scheme on the long-term unemployed (subsequently widened); the wide eligibility of the U.K. scheme and (until 1987) the French scheme, as against the German scheme, which requires greater scrutiny of the businesses in question. Of the three allowance-based schemes, the U.K. allowance is the smallest in financial terms (the maximum an individual could receive under the scheme was a total of 3,016 ECU in 1988) and the Danish the largest (the maximum receipt was 23,800 ECU in 1988); while the German scheme, although involving a larger monthly payment than the U.K. scheme, had considerably shorter duration (maximum six months). The maximum grant available under the French scheme was 5,800 ECU.

Table 6.7 compares the gender distribution of participants in the scheme with those of the self-employment stock and the inflows to self-employment in the countries in question. The most pertinent comparison is between the overall inflow to self-employment from unemployment (from the ELFS), and the characteristics of scheme participants. The British scheme shows the most remarkable growth in the proportion of female participants over the period (from 15 percent in the first full year of the scheme's operation to 36 percent in 1989). This would appear to be in part the result of a deliberate policy emphasis to encourage unemployed women to participate in the scheme, following a perception that they were initially "underrepresented" (although, in practice, when the comparison is made with the aggregate inflow from unemployment, rather than with the self-employment stock, this perception was probably wrong—Meager 1993). This increasing share of women, while apparently successful in targeting a group disadvantaged in terms of access to the means of setting up a business, and therefore reducing likely deadweight under the scheme, does not seem to have been at the expense of survival rates (although EAS evaluation studies show that survival rates of women were considerably lower than those of men— partly because they set up different types of business than their male counterparts—overall survival rates rose slightly over the period as a result of the generally improving U.K. economic situation in the late 1980s).

The Danish scheme also exhibits a considerable overrepresentation of women in comparison with the aggregate inflow to self-employment. This results from the overrepresentation of women in the scheme's target group of long-term unemployed, and it is notable that the proportion of women in the scheme fell following the widening of the eligibility criteria in 1989. Women are underrepresented among the self-employed to a greater extent in Denmark than in the other countries (only around 15 percent of Danish self-employed are women), and it seems, therefore, that this initial targeting of the Danish scheme on disadvantaged groups involved relatively low deadweight. This is confirmed by

Table 6.6

Summary of Self-Employment Schemes for the Unemployed in Four EC Member States

	Germany	France	U.K.	Denmark
Name of scheme Date introduced	Überbrückungsgeld 1986	Aide aux chômeurs créateurs d'entreprises 1979–80	Enterprise Allowance Scheme 1983	Ivoerksoetterydelsen 1985
Eligibility	Registered unemployed (after 11 weeks; reduced to 4 weeks in 1988). No legal entitlement (Bundesanstalt für Arbeit can operate budgetary ceiling for program).	All receiving or entitled to unemployment benefits (recently extended to include recipients of other welfare benefits).	Unemployed for at least 8 weeks and receiving unemployment or supplementary benefit (family credit). From 1991 limit reduced to 6 weeks, and local Training and Enterprise Councils (TECs) have discretion to waive 6-week rule for certain categories of unemployed.	Long-term unemployed over 25 (unemployed for at least 21 months and had at least one statutory "job offer"). Revised 1989 to include LTU under 25 (with 12 months unemployment and one job offer), and other "interested" unemployed with at least 5 months unemployment.
Form of support	Monthly allowance.	Capital grant.	Weekly allowance.	Monthly allowance.
Rate of payment	Equivalent to previous benefit entitlement (ceilings introduced and progressively reduced after revision of scheme in 1988), and contributions to some social security costs.	Between FF.10,750 & 43,000, (diminishes with length of previous unemployment); plus exemptions from some social security payments. (Extra grant if new enterprise creates jobs).	Flat rate of £40 per week. From 1991, individual TECs have discretion to vary payments (from £20–£90 per week).	50% of maximum unemployment benefit (up to a ceiling of DKr.54,000 p.a.).

Duration of payments	Up to 3 months. Increased to 6 months in 1988, and thresholds introduced, whereby duration of payments increase with duration of previous unemployment.	One-off payment.	Up to 52 weeks. From 1991 TECs have discretion to vary payment period (from 26 to 66 weeks).
Conditions for receipt of payment	Must have proposal approved by competent authority (bank, chamber of commerce, professional assoc., etc.); business must guarantee likely minimum income of DM3,400 p.m.	No restrictions initially. Since 1987, applicants must fill in detailed questionnaire, and are vetted on the likely viability of their proposed business.	Must have £1,000 initial own capital. Must work in new business for at least 36 hours per week. New business must be the whole investment. Certain types of "unsuitable" business activities excluded. From 1991 TECs have discretion to vary requirements—many now require business plans to be vetted prior to entry. No specific restrictions on applicants, or type of business. No own capital requirements.
Maximum value (1988)	5,800 ECU.	3,016 ECU.	23,800 ECU.
Support mechanisms	None tied to program, but participants eligible for wide range of advice/support through chambers of commerce, etc.	None tied to program, but participants eligible for normal state-funded business advice, etc.	Must attend initial "awareness day" prior to entry. Participants visited at least once by officials during year. Option of 3 free business counseling sessions during year. Recipients have option of participating in special courses for new entrepreneurs at technical or commercial schools.

(continued)

Table 6.6 continued

	Germany	France	U.K.	Denmark
Name of scheme Date introduced	Überbrückungsgeld 1986	Aide aux chômeurs créateurs d'entreprises 1979–80	Enterprise Allowance Scheme 1983	Iværksætterydelsen 1985
Number of participants	1986: 5,728 1987: 9,996 1988: 17,985 1989: 11,242	1979: 9,200 1986: 71,577 (peak) 1990: 49,316	1983–84: 27,600 1987–88: 106,300 (peak) 1990–91: 60,300	1985: 409 1987: 1,008 1989: 5,508 1990: 5,641
Survival rates	Not available, but of scheme participants in calendar year 1987, some 8% were again unemployed by May 1988. The corresponding figure for 1988 participants was 6%.	Aggregate figures are: after 1 year about 85% are still trading. After 2 years about 75%. Highest survival rates in construction and manufacturing, lowest in commercial services.	Of those who complete 12 months on the scheme, about ¾ survive a further 6 months, and about ⅔ survive a further 2 years.	About 76% of starters in 1989 were in business 2 years later. Earlier studies show that about 29% of participants do not survive the 3.5 years of eligibility.

evaluation data from surveys of early participants in the Danish scheme (Rosdahl and Mærkedahl 1987), which show that only 17 percent of participants would definitely have set up in self-employment without the scheme. A further 39 percent said that they might perhaps have done so without the scheme, but this nevertheless leaves 44 percent who clearly would not have done so, a much higher proportion than is typically recorded, for example, by surveys of EAS participants in the United Kingdom (between 14 and 34 percent—see PA Cambridge Economic Consultants 1990).

Of the other two schemes, the proportion of French scheme participants who are women is generally rather similar to the overall female share of new entrants to self-employment. The German scheme, on the other hand, stands out as containing a considerable underrepresentation of women, compared with the aggregate flow from unemployment. This is likely to reflect the rather more stringent entry criteria of the German scheme: business viability must be assessed by a "competent authority" and must be shown to generate a specified income. This latter criterion, in particular, is likely to discriminate against women; the U.K. data show that female EAS participants are much more likely than male participants to enter low-margin, highly competitive service sector activities such as hairdressing and other personal services. Many such activities are likely to be ruled out in the German case by the income requirements. A priori, we would anticipate that these restrictions would result in the German scheme having relatively high levels of deadweight but also high survival rates. In practice, however, as discussed above, the available evidence does not suggest that the German scheme has higher deadweight than its counterparts in other countries (it seems to be lower than in the U.K. case and closer to the Danish levels), although the data on postscheme reentry to unemployment (about 6–8 percent) *are* consistent with the prediction of high survival rates.

It is unclear why the German scheme might exhibit such low levels of deadweight, but one possible explanation may lie in the tapering of the payment eligibility according to duration of unemployment—thus in 1988 to obtain the full duration of twenty-six weeks' Überbrückungsgeld payments, the applicant had to have been unemployed for at least six months (in 1989 this was extended to twelve months and subsequently to eighteen months—see Kaiser and Otto 1990). If one assumes that the unemployed most likely to set up in business on their own without a subsidy are more likely to do so in the early months of unemployment, tapering the scheme in this way may help reduce the deadweight element. Thus it would seem that the design of the German scheme, giving greater weight to longer-term unemployed, while imposing relatively strict criteria for the viability and income potential of the proposed business, may increase survival rates (and possibly also reduce displacement—see below) without increasing deadweight unduly, albeit at the expense of discouraging female participation in the scheme.

Table 6.7

Gender Composition of Self-Employment, Self-Employment Flows, and Scheme Participants

	% Female share of:			Participants in self-employment scheme for the unemployed[a]
	Self-employed stock	Inflow to self-employment	Inflow to self-employment from unemployment	
U.K.				Enterprise Allowance Scheme
1982–83	23.6	32.7	11.8	7.0
1983–84	24.0	34.0	17.7	14.6
1984–85	25.0	35.8	19.2	19.1
1985–86				22.5
1986–87	25.1	34.8	20.8	24.7
1987–88	24.8	32.8	18.5	30.3
1988–89	26.7	33.1	21.3	35.8
Germany				Überbrückungsgeld
1982–83	22.5	31.6	Average (1982–85): 39.5	
1983–84	23.2			
1984–85	22.6	34.7		19.2
1986–87	23.5	36.2	Average (1986–89): 29.1	21.0
1987–88	23.9	34.6		22.4
1988–89	24.1	37.0		22.3

					L'aide aux chômeurs créateurs d'entreprises
France					
1982–83	21.1	39.1			
1983–84	21.0	34.4	Average (1982–84): 19.3		
1984–85	21.2	39.1	30.1		19.1
1985–86					21.0
1986–87	22.3	37.1	21.2		21.7
1987–88	22.8	34.6	16.5		23.0
1988–89	24.0	40.8	22.0		24.0

					Ivœrksætterydelsen
Denmark					
1982–83	12.4				
1983–84	15.9	Average (1982–85): 35.4	Average (1982–89): 33.8		
1984–85	14.9				50
1985–86					55
1986–87	14.8	Average (1986–89): 29.2			58
1987–88	12.9				63
1988–89	14.8				46

Sources: ELFS for aggregate stock and flows data. For scheme participants: national evaluation studies and administrative sources — see Meager 1993 for details.

[a] Data on the composition of scheme participants are derived from administrative records, and in some cases follow-up surveys of participants (in the United Kingdom's case they are average estimates from several data sources for each year).

Finally, in Table 6.8 we examine the kinds of businesses set up by scheme participants in the four countries and compare these with the activities of the newly self-employed in general and the newly self-employed who were previously unemployed in particular. Looking first at the United Kingdom, the features of the businesses set up by EAS participants that stand out are the relative overrepresentation of certain service sector activities, especially the "other services" category, which includes a wide range of small-scale personal service activities, and to a lesser extent the distribution, hotels, and catering category. This is broadly consistent with the expectation that the EAS, being an *allowance* rather than a grant, involving a relatively small weekly payment and having few eligibility conditions, would have a relatively high proportion of participants entering small-scale service sector activities, with few entry barriers and requiring little in the way of initial financial or human capital. It is interesting to note that service sector activities where such barriers/requirements may have been higher (including business services and transport and communications) were not overrepresented among EAS participants.

The sector that is most underrepresented among EAS participants is construction, which accounts for around 15 percent of EAS participants as against 25–30 percent of the overall inflow to self-employment from unemployment. Self-employment grew strongly in the U.K. construction sector in the 1980s, and the present finding is consistent with the argument put forward in previous work (see Meager 1991) that much of the newly self-employed construction work force was a form of "disguised employment" reflecting the growth of "labor only" subcontracting in the industry and the convenience of the self-employed label for tax and employment law purposes. If much of the inflow from unemployment to self-employment in construction was of this type, it is to be expected that this will not be reflected among EAS participants, since it would not meet the eligibility conditions of the scheme (see Evans and Lewis 1989 for an account of developments in the U.K. construction industry in the 1980s).

Turning to the German scheme, which, as we have argued, is similar in conception to the EAS but with more stringent entry requirements (in terms of proving business viability and income generation potential), we find a very different picture. Service sector and agricultural activities are considerably underrepresented among Überbrückungsgeld recipients, and manufacturing activities are overrepresented, in comparison with the aggregate inflow to self-employment from unemployment. Table 6.8 shows that manufacturing activities account for a much higher proportion of self-employment stocks and of inflows to self-employment in Germany than in most other EC countries. The table also shows that the unemployed may be disadvantaged in entering such activities, since the representation of manufacturing in the flow from unemployment is rather lower (this is broadly consistent with the institutional features of the German situation discussed in Meager, Kaiser, and Dietrich 1992 and in "Some Theoretical Con-

Table 6.8

Sectoral Composition of Self-Employment, Self-Employment Flows, and Scheme Participants (%)

Sector (NACE)	Self-employed stock		Inflow to self-employment		Inflow to self-employment from unemployment		Participants in self-employment scheme for the unemployed			
	1983	1989	1983–85	1987–89	1983–85	1987–89	1986	1987	1988	1989
Germany										
Agriculture (00)	22.2	15.4	11.2	10.4	8.5	7.6	2.3	2.4	2.6	2.4
Production (10–40)	13.0	13.6	20.9	21.8	12.7	8.9	15.9	15.9	14.0	14.1
Construction (50)	7.6	7.7	8.4	7.0	5.7	8.3	10.0	9.0	8.5	8.3
Distribution, hotels, catering (60)	31.1	28.5	30.3	25.8	32.8	31.2	35.3	36.2	35.6	34.0
Transport, comm. (70)	3.4	4.1	3.8	4.3	4.7	5.1	4.0	4.1	4.1	4.3
Finance, business services (80)	10.1	15.1	11.9	14.5	19.7	17.2	32.5	32.4	35.2	36.9
Other services (90)	12.7	15.4	13.4	16.1	15.7	21.7				
	1983	1989	1983–85	1987–89	1983–85	1987–89	1987	1988	1989	
France										
Agriculture (00)	35.3	32.3	29.8	26.6	8.6	9.7	(1.8)			
Production (10–40)	8.0	7.9	8.9	8.3	12.2	9.1	18.0	23	21	
Transport, comm. (70)	1.9	2.3	2.3	2.5	2.1	2.3	4.1			
Construction (50)	11.2	11.4	9.0	9.7	16.1	17.3	18.5	18	19	
Commerce & services (60,80,90)	43.5	46.0	50.0	52.9	61.0	61.6	57.8	59	60	

(continued)

236

Table 6.8 (continued)

Sector (NACE)	Self-employed stock		Inflow to self-employment		Inflow to self-employment from unemployment		Participants in self-employment scheme for the unemployed	
	1983	1989	1983–85	1987–89	1983–85	1987–89	1983–85[a]	1987–89[a]
U.K.								
Agriculture (00)	11.8	8.6	4.3	3.2	3.2	4.9	4.7	3.2
Energy, water (10)	0.1	0.2	1.7	1.2	(1.3)	1.3	0.1	0.0
Minerals, chemicals (20)	0.7	0.7					0.8	0.8
Metals, engineering (30)	2.6	3.1	2.7	3.5	3.7	3.1	4.4	1.6
Other manuf. (40)	4.7	6.0	6.7	6.8	5.7	8.0	10.4	9.0
Construction (50)	20.3	24.1	19.3	22.2	29.1	25.6	14.9	15.7
Distribution, hotels, catering (60)	31.1	24.6	28.1	23.5	29.6	21.9	30.1	25.9
Transport, comm. (70)	4.3	5.0	4.2	5.5	5.1	8.5	4.6	4.3
Finance, business services (80)	89.7	11.4	10.7	12.8	6.2	8.8	8.2	10.8
Other services (90)	14.6	16.3	22.4	21.3	15.9	17.8	22.0	27.4
Denmark	1983	1989	1983–85	1987–89	1983–89		1989	
Agric. production, construction (00–50)	52.5	49.6	18.0	30.3	12.7		23	
Distrib. hotels, catering (60)	23.7	22.5	49.3	31.3	49.0		35	
Other services (70–90)	23.8	27.9	32.6	38.4	38.3		41	

Sources: As for table 6.7.

[a]Note: that the U.K. data are averages of the sectoral structure of participants over the period in question, derived from several data sources.

siderations" above). It seems, therefore, that the payment of Überbrückungsgeld may go some way to redress that imbalance, with its (in comparison with the United Kingdom) relatively generous support, coupled with stricter scrutiny of eligible businesses. It is likely, for example, that manufacturing and Handwerk activities are more likely to satisfy the income-earning conditions of Überbrückungsgeld than their counterparts in the service sectors (German evidence presented in Gout and Büchtemann 1987 confirms that the service sectors contain a much higher proportion of self-employed with very low incomes than do the production sectors).

Our earlier hypothesis, however, was that among self-employment schemes, those that are grant-based, providing the funds to recipients in an initial lump sum, might be most effective in shifting the sectoral composition of supported businesses away from more marginal, low-earning, service sector activities in crowded markets, since relaxation of the capital constraint may be important in overcoming initial barriers to entry to more capital-intensive activities in higher-margin, more protected markets. The data from the French (*chômeurs créateurs*) scheme are consistent with this hypothesis, since participants in the French scheme exhibit the greatest overrepresentation of production activities among the schemes examined (the proportion of chômeurs créateurs in the production sectors is around twice as high as the proportion of the aggregate inflow from unemployment to self-employment in these sectors).

None of these findings are conclusive, and confirmation requires more detailed examination of the characteristics and performance of individual schemes and a consideration of a wider range of participants' characteristics than is possible here. They do, nevertheless, illustrate the considerable potential offered by the use of flows data as one element in the evaluation of the impact of different scheme designs, within an internationally comparative framework.

Concluding Remarks

This chapter has ranged quite widely over recent trends in self-employment in EC countries, their nature and causes, and the role of the new institution of labor market schemes for self-employment in contributing to these trends. Given this range, the treatment has of necessity been somewhat superficial. We have nevertheless managed to illustrate a strategy for comparing such developments across countries and evaluating such policy schemes, which relies heavily on the use of comparative labor force survey data, and flows data in particular.

We have discussed some major definitional and theoretical issues in describing and explaining recent self-employment trends, and stressed the importance of taking account of variations in the institutional environment when comparing different countries' experience, exemplifying this through an Anglo-German comparison. We have considered the difficult issue of separating out cyclical fluctuations in self-employment from underlying trends and shifts, and have developed a critique of previous research on cyclical influences on self-employment, arguing that much of this research is inconclusive or misleading because of its reliance on stock rather than flow measures of self-employment. The common argument that much of the recent growth in self-employment in advanced economies is the result of unemployment push is particularly vulnerable to such a critique, and we present empirical evidence for this using newly constructed flows data from the European Labour Force Surveys (ELFS).

The ELFS data reinforce some of the evidence on the role of institutional and policy differences (generating a much more "dynamic" picture of self-employment in the United Kingdom than in Germany, for example) and provide a new dimension to comparative evaluation of the self-employment schemes for the unemployed, introduced in all EC countries in recent years. We have, more generally, identified the main methodological issues to be tackled in such evaluations and have begun to tackle them. We conclude that the existence of the schemes does seem to make a difference: they are not purely "deadweight"— both the cross-country comparisons and the time-series example for Germany suggest that more unemployed people enter self-employment as a result of the schemes than would otherwise be the case. This does not, of course, imply that all scheme designs are equally effective, and that the self-employment generated is necessarily sustainable (the rapid fall in U.K. self-employment in the post-1989 recession is stark evidence of this). Scheme design also makes a difference, and our preliminary evidence presented here, for example, is consistent with the notion that more selective eligibility criteria and/or a grant- rather than an allowance-based scheme may help to shift such schemes toward the development of sustainable self-employment with significant earnings potential (and perhaps subsequent employment generation potential).

Many questions remain unanswered and require further research—we have, for example, been unable to develop a convincing explanation for why Denmark, uniquely in the EC, has not shared in the recent reversal of the historical decline in self-employment. Promising avenues of explanation, however, in line with our Anglo-German comparisons ("Some Theoretical Considerations" above), would involve a mixture of cyclical, structural, and institutional factors. Danish self-employment shares many of the features of German self-employment that distinguish the latter from the U.K. case—including a policy emphasis on existing small businesses rather than start-ups, and a relatively small-scale and selective self-employment scheme for the unemployed. In addition, Danish self-employment contains a large agricultural component, and it is further possible that the relatively high level of unemployment and welfare benefits in Denmark in relation to average earnings act as a dampening factor on any unemployment push element that might otherwise have contributed to self-employment growth in recent decades.[20] A further factor is that the Danish labor market is relatively unregulated (Denmark ranks lowest of our four case study countries on the "job security" index calculated by Bertola 1990). An argument can be developed (see

OECD 1992) that a high degree of employment protection may generate high levels of self-employment and add to the impetus for self-employment to increase during times of economic downswing, since it provides an incentive for employers to subcontract as much as possible to small enterprises and the self-employed. An economy in which dependent employment is less protected in this sense, it is argued, would lack this pressure for self-employment. Such a hypothesis is, of course, difficult to square with the U.K. experience of rapid self-employment growth occurring despite deregulation of the labor market and a reduction of employment protection legislation from already relatively low levels.

Such institutionally based international comparisons do, however, appear to offer the most scope for improving our understanding of the causes and implications of the historically unprecedented recent developments in self-employment in many European countries, as well as for evaluating the new range of labor market schemes aimed at stimulating self-employment, and drawing conclusions about scheme design and impact that can be transferred across countries.

Notes

1. In practice, however, attitude surveys (Blanchflower and Oswald 1990a) and case studies (Blackburn, Curran, and Woods 1991) have found little evidence of pervasive attitudinal change to self-employment and the enterprise culture in the United Kingdom during the 1980s.

2. Namely: Belgium, Denmark, France, West Germany, Ireland, Italy, Luxembourg, the Netherlands, and the United Kingdom.

3. Another would be that there is in fact no causal relationship between unemployment and self-employment, but that they are both subject to underlying secular trends (of increasing unemployment and decreasing self-employment).

4. Meager 1993 confirms that this is also the case for the other EC countries not considered here.

5. The concepts of "deadweight" and "displacement" are explored further below.

6. One can, of course, envisage circumstances where this argument would not hold, e.g., if those unemployed becoming self-employed were typically the "best" unemployed, who, but for being diverted into self-employment by the scheme would otherwise have quickly obtained (long-duration) dependent employment, but as a result of having been on the scheme, return rapidly to unemployment as their financial support runs out and their businesses fail.

7. "In addition to the directly measurable effects of EAS there are also important indirect—or supply side effects . . . . The latest survey of EAS participants . . . shows that survivors' median pre-tax net takings are £105 per week in 1987. This compares with the estimated median weekly earnings of all adults of £175 per week. Such figures might suggest that EAS is also helping to reduce wage pressure. The impact on wages will be even greater in the early stages of EAS businesses." (Owens 1989, 6).

8. Occasionally, eligibility also extends to some other groups of people disadvantaged in the labor market, e.g., young people, certain categories of labor market entrants, and people at risk of job loss.

9. In Denmark, eligibility was widened to include short-term unemployed in 1989.

10. It is interesting to note that an experimental evaluation of such schemes is taking place in the United States. This involves the implementation of two pilot self-employment

schemes for the unemployed (one in Washington state and one in Massachusetts), both funded through unemployment insurance, but one of which involves the payment of a regular allowance, and the other pays an initial capital sum to scheme participants. It is unfortunate that no such experimental evaluation exists in Europe, and that the U.S. results are not available at the time of writing (see Wandner and Messenger 1991).

11. Except that under the allowance approach, even if the capital market allowed the scheme participant to borrow against the guaranteed income stream, he or she would nevertheless pay interest, while under most versions of the grant approach, the subsidy is effectively interest free.

12. Such surveys have been particularly widespread in the United Kingdom, but all three of our other case study countries (Denmark, Germany, and France) have undertaken similar survey evaluations.

13. Note that in practice the denominators of both variables (unemployment in 1987) are not identical, since the x-axis denominator is based on ELFS respondents who said in 1987 that they were currently unemployed, while the y-axis denominator is based (for consistency with the numerator) on those who said in 1988 that they were unemployed a year earlier.

14. Although unemployment enters into both explanatory variables (as the numerator of one and the denominator of the other), they are not multicollinear—the intercorrelation coefficient is 0.01.

15. The coefficient on the scheme variable is 0.88, suggesting that for every 100 scheme participants the inflow from unemployment to self-employment increases by 88.

16. This figure is larger than the corresponding inflow figure for 1987–88 calculated for Germany from the ELFS. We have already argued that ELFS flows data understate the true volume of flows, due to their one-year retrospective nature and nonrecording of multiple flows. The inclusion of unpaid family workers in the AGR data further adds to the difference between the two flow estimates.

17. I.e., for every 100 Überbrückungsgeld recipients, 80 would be net additions to the flow to self-employment, and 10 of these would employ an extra family worker, so the observed increase in the combined flow to self-employment and family work would be 90.

18. See, for example, PA Cambridge Economic Consultants 1990.

19. Meager 1993 also considers their age profile.

20. Denmark has by far the most generous unemployment compensation system in this sense in the EC (see, for example, Commission of the European Communities 1992, chapter 7).

References

Acs, Z.; Audretsch, D.; and Evans, D. 1992. *The Determinants of Variations in Self-Employment Rates across Countries and over Time.* Wissenschaftszentrum Berlin für Sozialforschung. Discussion paper FS IV 92–3.

Allen, S.; Truman, C.; and Wolkowitz, C. 1992. "Home-Based Work: Self-Employment and Small Business." In *The New Entrepreneurs: Self-Employment and Small Business in Europe*, eds., P. Leighton and A. Felstead. London: Kogan Page.

Aronson, R. 1991. *Self-Employment: A Labor Market Perspective.* Ithaca, N.Y.: ILR Press.

Bannock, G., and Albach, H. 1991. *Small Business Policy in Europe: Britain, Germany and the European Commission.* London: Anglo-German Foundation for the Study of Industrial Society.

Barker, P. 1989. *Self-Employment Schemes for the Unemployed.* Local Initiatives for Employment Creation, Cahier No. 10, Paris, OECD.

Bertola, B. 1990. "Job Security, Employment and Wages." *European Economic Review* 34: 851–86.

Blackburn, R.; Curran, J.; and Woods, A. 1991. *Exploring Enterprise Cultures: Small Service Sector Enterprise Owners and Their Views*. Kingston Business School, Kingston upon Thames (mimeo).

Blanchflower, D., and Oswald, A. 1990a. "Self-Employment and Mrs Thatcher's Enterprise Culture." In *British Social Attitudes: the 1990 Report*. Aldershot: Gower.

———. 1990b. *What Makes a Young Entrepreneur?* Working Paper, 3252, Cambridge, Mass., National Bureau of Economic Research.

Blau, D. 1987. "A Time-Series Analysis of Self-Employment in the United States." *Journal of Political Economy* 95:445–67.

Bögenhold, D., and Staber, U. 1990. "Selbständigkeit als ein Reflex aus Arbeitslosigkeit." *Kölner Zeitschrift für Soziologie und Psychologie* 42, no. 2.

———. 1991. "The Decline and Rise of Self-Employment." *Work, Employment and Society* 5:223–39.

Burrows, R. 1991. "Who Are the Contemporary British Petit Bourgeoisie?" *International Small Business Journal* 9, no. 2: 223–29.

Campbell, M., and Daly, M. "Self-Employment: Into the 1990s." *Employment Gazette* (June): 269–92.

Commission of the European Communities. 1992. *Employment in Europe 1992*. Directorate-General for Employment, Industrial Relations and Social Affairs, Brussels/Luxembourg.

Danish Technological Institute. 1991. *Survey of Initiatives in Sweden, Great Britain, Schleswig-Holstein and within the EEC Which Aim at Reducing the Problems and Financing of SMEs and New Companies*. Taastrup, Dansk Teknologisk Institut.

Doran, A. 1984. *Craft Enterprises in Britain and Germany: A Sectoral Study*. London: Anglo-German Foundation for the Study of Industrial Society.

Elias, P., and Whitfield, K. 1987. *The Economic Impact of the Enterprise Allowance Scheme: Theory and Measurement of Displacement Effects*. Report to MSC, Institute for Employment Research, University of Warwick, Coventry.

Evans, D., and Jovanovic, B. 1989. "Estimates of a Model of Entrepreneurial Choice under Liquidity Constraints." *Journal of Political Economy* 97, no.4:808–27.

Evans, S., and Lewis, R. 1989. "Destructuring and Deregulation in the Construction Industry." In *Manufacturing Change: Industrial Relations and Restructuring*, eds., S. Tailby and C. Whitson. Oxford: Basil Blackwell.

Felstead, A. 1991. "The Social Organisation of the Franchise: A Case of 'Controlled Self-employment.'" *Work, Employment and Society* 5, no. 1:37–57.

Gout, M., and Büchtemann, C. 1987. *Développement et structure du travail "indépendant" en R.F.A.* Wissenschaftszentrum Berlin (mimeo).

Hakim, C. 1987. "Trends in the Flexible Workforce." *Employment Gazette* (November).

———. 1988. "Self-Employment in Britain: A Review of Recent Trends and Current Issues." *Work, Employment and Society* 2, no. 4 (December).

Hasluck, C. 1990. *The Displacement Effects of the Enterprise Allowance Scheme: A Local Labour Market Study*. DE Programme 1989/90: Project Report, Institute of Employment Research, University of Warwick.

International Labour Office. 1990. *The Promotion of Self-Employment*. International Labour Conference, 77th Session, Report VII. Geneva: International Labour Office.

Johnson, S. 1990. *Small Firms Policy—An Agenda for the 1990s*. Policy Research Unit, Leeds Polytechnic (mimeo).

Johnson, S.; Lindley, R.; and Bourlakis, C. 1988. *Modelling Aggregate Self-Employment: A Preliminary Analysis*. Department of Employment Programme 1988/89 Project Report, University of Warwick, Institute for Employment Research, December.

Kaiser, M., and Otto, M. 1990. "Übergang von Arbeitslosigkeit in berufliche Selbständigkeit." *Mitteilungen aus der Arbeitsmarkt—und Berufsforschung*, 22, no. 2.

Kneppers-Heynert, E. 1992. " 'Hard' and 'Soft' Franchising—Legal Classification: Some Dutch Evidence." In *The New Entrepreneurs: Self-Employment and Small Business in Europe*, eds., P. Leighton and A. Felstead. London: Kogan Page.

Meager, N. 1991. *Self-Employment in the United Kingdom*. IMS Report no. 205. Brighton: Institute of Manpower Studies.

————. 1992a. "Does Unemployment Lead to Self-Employment?" *Small Business Economics* 4: 87–103.

————. 1992b. "The Fall and Rise of Self-Employment (Again): A Comment on Bögenhold and Staber." *Work, Employment and Society* 6, no. 1:127–34.

————. 1993. *Self-Employment and Labour Market Policy in the EC*. Report to the European Commission (DGV) under the MISEP Program. Berlin: Wissenschaftszentrum.

Meager, N.; Kaiser, M.; and Dietrich, H. 1992. *Self-Employment in the United Kingdom and Germany*. London/Bonn: Anglo-German Foundation for the Study of Industrial Society.

OECD. 1986. *Employment Outlook: September 1986*. Paris: Organisation for Economic Cooperation and Development.

————. 1990a. *Labour Market Policies for the 1990s*. Paris: Organisation for Economic Cooperation and Development.

————. 1990b. *Labour Force Statistics 1968–88*. Paris: Organisation for Economic Cooperation and Development.

————. 1990c. *Economic Outlook, No. 48*. December. Paris: Organisation for Economic Cooperation and Development.

————. 1990d. *Report by OECD Evaluation Panel No. 11*. Paris: Organisation for Economic Cooperation and Development (mimeo).

————. 1992. *Employment Outlook: July 1992*. Paris: Organisation for Economic Cooperation and Development.

Owens, A. 1989. *Enterprise Allowance Scheme Evaluation: Sixth 6-Month National Survey*. Sheffield: Employment Service, Research and Evaluation Branch, August.

PA Cambridge Economic Consultants. 1990. *Evaluation of Jobclubs and the Enterprise Allowance Scheme in Great Britain*. Cambridge.

Rainbird, H. 1991. "The Self-Employed: Small Entrepreneurs or Disguised Wage Labourers?" In *Farewell to Flexibility?*, ed., A. Pollert. Oxford: Basil Blackwell.

Rees, H., and Shah, A. 1986. "An Empirical Analysis of Self-Employment in the UK." *Journal of Applied Econometrics* 1.

Reyher, L., and Bach, H-U. 1988. "Arbeitskräfte-Gesamtrechnung: Bestände und Bewegung am Arbeitsmarkt." *Beiträge zur Arbeitsmarkt— und Berufsforschung*, no. 70.

Rosdahl, A., and Mærkedahl, I. 1987. *Uddannelses og iværksætterydelsen til langtidsledige*. Copenhagen: Socialforskningsinstituttet.

Rubery, J., and Burchell, B. 1992. "Categorising Self-Employment: Some Evidence from the Social Change and Economic Life Initiative in the UK." In *The New Entrepreneurs: Self-Employment and Small Business in Europe*, eds., P. Leighton and A. Felstead. London: Kogan Page.

Sengenberger, W.; Loveman, G.; and Piore, M. 1990. *The Re-emergence of Small Enterprises: Industrial Restructuring in Industrialised Countries*. Geneva: International Institute for Labor Studies.

Steinmetz, G., and Wright, E. 1989. "The Fall and Rise of the Petty Bourgeoisie: Changing Patterns of Self-Employment in the Postwar United States." *American Journal of Sociology* 94, no. 5 (March): 973–1018.

Wandner, S., and Messenger, J. 1991. *From Unemployed to Self-Employed: Self-Employment as a Re-employment Option in the United States*. U.S. Department of Labor, Employment and Training Administration, Washington, D.C. (mimeo).

Equality and Efficiency in the Labor Market

Toward a Socioeconomic Theory of Cooperation

Günther Schmid

Introduction

It has become common to justify increasing inequalities in market income with reference to the economic disaster in Eastern Europe. The so-called socialist economies seem to remind us of an old economic wisdom: "You can't have your cake of market efficiency and share it equally." Apart from the counterfactual evidence of a nomenclature that made a small political elite more "equal" than ordinary people, however, the egalitarian approach of "real socialism" was far from conforming to widely accepted principles of justice in liberal democracies. The allocation and evaluation of jobs according to political loyalty and alleged proletarian origin or status—to mention only two examples—contradict even the most rudimentary values of justice in any type of market economy: equal access to jobs for all, and at least some performance-oriented remuneration of jobs.

Thus, the failure of bureaucratic socialism teaches us no lesson with regard to the real challenges in front of us. The current widespread crossing of political, technological, and social frontiers is a necessary but still not a sufficient condition for synchronizing economic and social progress. The extended field of play-

The author wishes to thank Richard Hattwick (editor of the *Journal of Socio-Economics*) for allowing him to reprint this article (see Schmid 1993) in a slightly revised version. Thanks for valuable comments to an earlier version go also to Gernot Grabher and Nigel Meager. I am especially indebted to Inga Persson (University of Lund, Sweden) and Jan van Wezel (University of Tilburg, Netherlands) whose perceptive and critical suggestions went sometimes beyond my capacity to do them justice.

ers in the market game as well as the increased range of games requires new "civilized boundaries" by institutions that must be seen as both constraints and supports, as limiting but also as guiding norms of cooperation. Here the term *cooperation* refers to development of accepted procedures for engaging in competition, command work, teamwork, or care. Accepted institutions of distributive justice are essential to bring about effective cooperation. Only with their help can the expanded possibilities of voluntary cooperation be used economically without infringing on social objectives.

In this chapter, I will show that institutional innovations supporting high standards of social as well as economic equality are in fact the precondition for effective cooperation and, hence, for the efficiency of spatially or socially expanded labor markets. The socioeconomics of cooperation deals with strategies that bring about the effective interaction of the main coordinating institutions of society—markets, hierarchies, social networks, and civil rights. Whereas markets and hierarchies have received due attention during recent decades, it is still not well known how they are effectively to be combined. In addition, social networks and civil rights have been neglected or not properly dealt with. Institutionalizing values of justice beyond the economic principle of equity (fairness and proportionality) through the principles of equal treatment and solidarity that underlie social networks and civil rights is crucial, however, if socially as well as economically effective cooperation in enlarged societies is to be established.

The sections of this chapter sketch the challenges caused by the external (spatial) as well as internal (social) extension of the cooperative framework; recall strategies of effective cooperation from an evolutionary point of view; evaluate the alleged "big trade-off" of equality and efficiency, explain the employment relationship in terms of transaction costs, and extend the model by a third dimension; and demonstrate actual and potential equality with efficiency measures in the areas of wage determination, equal opportunity policy, and income protection for the unemployed.

Challenges in the 1990s: The New Cooperative Context

The challenges to social cooperation come from three main sources in a world of increasing uncertainty and conflict: (1) asymmetric migration caused by the opening of national borders or by the struggle for sheer survival; (2) preference changes accompanied by the rise of unrealistic expectations as paradoxical consequences of the increasing speed and the overall access of information; (3) rising contingencies of labor supply especially through the breakdown of traditional family ties, their conversion into looser social networks, and the irresistible (from a normative as well as an empirical point of view) demand of women to become equal partners in the market game. I consider briefly the impact of these changes on the cooperative context of the labor market.

The Spatial Extension of the Cooperative Game

The completion of German unification is a good illustration of the challenges of new migration movements. For the West German labor market, the few months before and after the fall of the Berlin Wall on November 9, 1989, brought about an additional labor supply of approximately half a million Germans (*Übersiedler*) resettling from the eastern to the western part of the country. Both these and the subsequent migration streams after unification were extremely asymmetrical, with the younger and more highly skilled workers emigrating or commuting to work in West Germany and the older and less qualified staying at home. With conditions rapidly becoming critical on the labor markets of the five new federal states (*Länder*) since 1991,[1] some 500,000 commuters to the western German states are counted (as opposed to a small number of commuters out of the western states), along with almost 800,000 Übersiedler settling in West Germany. Is it possible to arrest this process and avoid an osmotic emaciation of the regions in the former German Democratic Republic?

Perestroika has opened the borders for another population group. In 1987, 78,200 ethnic German immigrants were admitted to the Federal Republic, with 202,800, 377,100, and 397,000 in the next three years, respectively. How long will this stream of additional labor from Eastern European countries continue to be absorbed with relatively few problems, and what are the alternatives to migration? Beyond this, the flow of people seeking political asylum is growing. Official statistics reveal that 57,000 such people registered in West Germany in 1987, and the figures have climbed from 193,063 in 1990 to 438,191 in 1992. Although many of these refugees are denied asylum and few are ultimately permitted to enter the German labor market, they represent, as it were, the advance delegation of a vast global majority who would like to participate in the prospering labor market of a small global minority.[2] There is also the pressure that the non-German population of Eastern Europe will exert in the east, the pressure to cross the remaining national frontiers. Is perestroika opening those borders as well? Will the River Oder become the Rio Grande of Europe?

Other sovereign territorial boundaries fell at the end of 1992 with the completion of the Single European Market. All inhabitants are now able to choose freely their place of work and residence. The only exceptions are foreigners not belonging to the EC; they remain temporarily subject to the various national regulations. Will the various established national standards for wages and salaries, wage compensation during short-term disability, unemployment benefits, protection against unfair dismissal, and the right to further training and to parental or nursing leave be adjusted to conform to the lowest standards in each sphere? Or will the rich countries impose their higher social standards, thus reducing the cost competitiveness of the poorer countries?

The Value Extension of the Cooperative Game

Brutal borderlines (walls and barbed wire), sovereign borders (customs barriers and national currencies), and political boundaries (dictatorial regimes) are not the only ones that are falling. Technological change is sweeping away barriers that used to limit the scope and speed of information and, hence, changing the character of communication. Ever greater amounts of, and access to, information and the acceleration of its dissemination is likely to be the prime driving force behind further breathtaking "frontier crossing." This will have the effect of reducing mental and cognitive constraints, with the result that more and more values, needs, and ways of interpreting reality will be competing with each other. Are we able to institutionalize an even greater diversity of working and living styles, or are valuable cultures succumbing to the increased competition only because they do not prove to be efficient here and now?

By breaking down the barriers created by nature, science and technology have shown us not only more freedom but new limits as well—the finiteness of energy sources and the limited capacity of the environment. The revolutionary wave in Eastern Europe and elsewhere could, paradoxically, demonstrate just as impressively the limits of social growth or even reverse the social progress achieved by the welfare state. We have been used to congested traffic for a long time; will we have to become accustomed to "congestion" on the labor market as well? In other words, will we have to get used to long lines for "good jobs" (and respective idle capacities) and lack of labor for "bad jobs"? Or will the problem be "solved" by increasing income inequalities that enable the rich to buy cheap services by forcing the poor into low-paid service jobs?

The Social Extension of the Cooperative Game

Last but not least, we are facing a basic social change toward the gender-neutral family.[3] The family seems to be the last resort of status-related inequalities by allocating family tasks according to sexual differences, i.e., in accordance with innate, unchangeable characteristics. From the labor market point of view, the traditional labor division in social reproduction creates unequal opportunities in the competitive game for market income. There is overwhelming empirical evidence that gender-specific wage differentials, occupational segregation by gender, the compression of women in low-skilled, dead-end, or precarious jobs is mainly caused by the unequal distribution of family tasks and not, for instance, by open discriminatory behavior. At the same time, the opening of cultural boundaries through, for example, the liberalization of sexual behavior and divorce laws, plus the "second renaissance" of (increasing) individualism will also lead to new uncertainties and conflicts. Will we be able to avoid the already visible trend of the feminization of poverty and the often traumatic as well as economically disastrous consequences of family breakdowns for children through better coordinating institutions that support both justice and economic well-being in families?

Toward a New Balance of Equality and Efficiency

Without institutional innovation, the increased uncertainties and conflicts through the enlarged context of cooperation will intensify old and create new economic and social inequalities—including high, persistent, and unequally distributed unemployment. The increasing importance of internal labor markets and the concentration of investment in firm-specific human capital is another trend that can be interpreted as a rational reaction by strong market actors to increasing uncertainty and conflict. Here, as in many other cases, the danger is that the "cooperative rent" goes only to the "insiders" at the cost of the "outsiders" under the existing institutional regimes. What is called for is a new balance between the main coordinating institutions of society—markets, hierarchies, networks, and civil rights—to secure a complementary relationship between equality and efficiency, i.e., effective social cooperation.

A labor market with nearly complete freedom of movement within Europe's borders poses the question of what the institutional conditions are for the establishment of enduring and socially advantageous cooperation among a widened circle of "players" whose economic and social contexts are very unequal. The same question can be asked related to the expansion of the labor market's sociopolitical space. A primary condition for effective cooperation is that people engaged in cooperation feel treated in a "just" way. Certainly, principles of justice are primarily ethical, humanitarian norms requiring no further justification. But social action oriented on such principles depends upon appropriate institutions.

In the search for suggestions as to how such institutions can be structured, I commence by looking at some insights of evolutionary theory to the problem of cooperation. Subsequently, I turn to the equality-efficiency conundrum, suggesting a solution based on an extended version of transactions cost theory.

Effective Cooperation in Evolutionary Perspective

The consequences of opening the field for more players is a central topic of evolutionary theory. One alternative common in biology—that the existing players in the game kill the newcomer or vice versa—is certainly not a model for a civilized society (although, unfortunately, it happens daily). What we are interested in is how cooperation to the benefit of all can arise in an extended competitive context. Three approaches seem to provide more than just stimulating thoughts: the sociological theory of civilization, the game theory of cooperation, and the theory of competitive advantage. I shall look briefly at each approach and summarize their basic ideas.

The Evolutionary Theory of Civilization

Attaining external freedoms by transcending physical and material limits is, according to Norbert Elias (1982), possible only through a growth of internal constraints, like the taming of instincts by social norms and new centers of social integration and coordination. Border openings reduce the dependencies within the former borders and, by broadening "exit options," provide for a more equal distribution of opportunities to acquire and exercise power. In return, however, people are woven into spatially and temporally longer chains of interdependencies, which for the individual constitute functional contexts that are less and less controllable. The larger playing field and greater number of possible partners in the game thus mean that people who are functionally interdependent in this way become more dependent at many levels on the efficiency of coordinating institutions.

Seen very abstractly and in terms of the labor market, this means that the freedom of movement and choice gained through border openings must be flanked by new, broader regulatory mechanisms of wage formation, social security, and vocational education or training in order to convert the acquired potential for cooperation into higher real income as well as more equitable income structures.

Evolution of Cooperation in Game Theory

An example of game theory is Robert Axelrod's (1984) fascinating book about the evolution of cooperation. It teaches us that whenever territorial borders or social borderlines open, the danger of ruinous competition increases for as long as there are no common rules or equal chances for cooperation within the widened circle of players. Furthermore, effective cooperation requires the "shadow of the future," that is, an awareness by the cooperating partners that they will be dealing with each other in the future as well. If traditional ties like kinship or neighborly relations do not suffice to cast this shadow, then it is necessary to take institutional precautions such as the obligation to pay into a universal system of unemployment insurance or to announce mass dismissals in advance, to mention just two examples.

Cooperative competition under an evolutionary perspective is, therefore, not characterized by the survival of individual successful persons but by the rapid mutual learning and imitation among rivals, and by potential or actually cooperating partners. It is not competition with the objective of permanently driving out or even destroying the opponent but competition with the objective of repeatedly measuring one's strength. Playing with strong and changing partners is stimulating and keeps one alert; playing with weak partners is frustrating and lulls one to sleep. In the socioeconomic game, of course, strong partners will tend to exploit the weak by wielding their power.[4] The message, however, is clear for both cases: If the partners are weak, their playing strength must be increased by improving their educational, technical, and social skills; in the case of the long-term unemployed, for example, the main remedy is simply to provide opportunities to participate in the market game.

The Economic Theory of Competitive Advantage

The institutionally oriented business economics of recent years empirically substantiates the strategic rules of game theory. In a widely noted book on the competitive advantages of nations, Michael E. Porter (1990) states that the only plants, regions, and countries to prevail in international competition in the long run are those surrounded in their immediate vicinity by strong partners that are simultaneously rival and cooperating. Regional comparative studies, both intra- and international, show also that prosperous regions or the successful restructuring of traditional industrial regions depend on a "dense" network of autonomous plants that are embedded in a well-developed social and public infrastructure (Grabher 1990).

To sum up, evolution needs time. To integrate and reorganize societies is a complicated process of interlinking that cannot be effected in a "heave-ho" approach like a political revolution. To be sure, there is no blueprint for the transformation of societies. Nevertheless, strategies are discernible, principles of action by which the evolutionary process admittedly cannot be controlled—while it can be influenced in its direction and speed. We must create the conditions for a dynamic socioeconomic balance analogous to nature's dynamic ecological balance.

A fundamental prerequisite for that is social cooperation governed by principles of justice. New coordinating centers in organizational as well as in normative terms, the "shadow of the future," and a wide variety of competent players have to be institutionalized. Another important condition for effective social cooperation is the governance of exchange relationships by civil rights (and their corresponding civil obligations). This means, in the first place, the endorsement of egalitarian standards in situations that require teamwork, mutual trust, and respect. Second, the provision of social security and/or public services to complement equity standards in competitive situations: if the players change partners for reasons of higher returns of exchange and if the capacity of reciprocal exchange is diminished for various reasons outside the domain of individual responsibility, solidarity must be available to compensate for the willingness to assume risks. Such cooperation with "weak ties" (Granovetter 1973) will be stable the more it generates both equality and efficiency. Thus, I turn now to the institutional conditions of equality with efficiency.

The Remarriage of Equality and Efficiency

A good starting point is the seminal work *Equality and Efficiency. The Big Trade-off* by Arthur Okun (1975). The reading of this famous essay is not only illuminating but also gives great pleasure. It is obviously an elaboration of an earlier article by James Tobin, who criticized the common attitude of mainstream economists to separate allocation from distribution, concentrating on questions of allocative efficiency while distastefully and arrogantly leaving equality to politics. One example is Henry Simons of the Chicago School: "It is urgently necessary for us to quit confusing measures for regulating relative prices and wages with devices for diminishing inequality. One difference between competent economists and charlatans is that . . . the former sometimes discipline their sentimentality with a little reflection on the mechanics of an exchange economy" (Simons 1948, 83–84).

Tobin, after a little more reflection, came to the conclusion that instruments of redistribution are not neutral in their allocative effects. He even saw the case—which I will emphasize later—for policies to reduce unequal income distribution before taxes and transfers. These policies "include removal of those barriers to competition . . . which protect some positions of high wealth and income. They include efforts to diminish inequalities of endowment of human capital and of opportunity to accumulate it" (Tobin 1970, 276). Tobin recommended also non-market egalitarian distributions of commodities essential to life and citizenship in case of inelastic supply. This argument is of special interest if one considers employment not only as instrumental for earning wages but also as instrumental for "psychic income" and as an essential means of developing self-respect and sociability.

As soon as one accepts the interdependence of allocative and distributive measures, the equality-efficiency relationship becomes much more intricate. It is largely owing to Okun that we have at least some guidelines for moving in this labyrinth. Before entering, some definitional considerations may be helpful as a sort of "Ariadne's Thread."

Equalities

Who is to be equal to whom with respect to what, according to which approach, to which values, and to what extent? Not less than five dimensions lurk behind the suggestively simple normative idea of equality. This is probably the reason most people restrict the treatment of this problem to mere confessions or to utterly simplified conceptions—e.g., equal opportunity versus equal results. The complexity of equality may also be one reason for the discrepancy of widespread egalitarian ideologies and persistent inequalities. It is the merit of Douglas Rae and his collaborators to have started to develop a "grammar of equality," which every serious discussion on equality now has to take into account (Rae 1981). It will probably take decades for this grammar to become natural practice. In addition, unfortunately, the grammar does not always intuitively appeal and—alas—is still underdeveloped. The main deficit is the missing link between equalities and social perceptions or valuations. Considerations of equity or justice, however, play a prominent role in labor markets, as will be explained later.

Equality splits—according to Rae—into five distinct notions, each an element in its grammar: Equality's subject (1) may be individual-regarding, bloc-regarding, or segmental; its domain (2) may be straightforward, marginal, or global; the approach (3) to the realization of equality may be direct (equal results), or may be a version of equal opportunity (which in turn may equate means or prospects); the underlying value (4) of equality may be based on uniform lots or on lots equally accommodating differences; and, finally, the distribution principle (5) may be absolute or relative (and if relative, based on at least four different criteria: maximin, ratio, least difference, and minimax). Without taking into account further possible differentiations, the five grammatical components yield three subject structures, three domain types, three treatments of opportunity and result, two value structures, and two main outcomes of the absoluteness-relativity distinction. In generating combined types, these terms multiply with one another, yielding $3\times3\times3\times2\times2 = 108$ structurally distinct interpretations of equality (Rae 1981, 132–33).

These distinctions must be combined with one another if equality is to be given flesh. The combinations may converge but may also be mutually exclusive. The illustrative example in Figure 7.1 may provide an impression of both the grammar's usefulness and its complexity:

Fine distinctions are certainly analytical assets, but for strategical reasoning and communication some simplification is necessary. The "equality grammar," however, enables us to select a set of relevant combinations without losing too much complexity. In the field of labor economics, we usually make reference to individuals as subjects of equality; and with respect to the domain of equality we tend to think of total disposable income and not only of the margins; due to the necessity of investment, a straightforward distribution shall be excluded, too; finally, concerning the value structure, I assume the "person regarding" criterion—i.e., taking account of individual differences—to be relevant. In other words, in selecting the relevant combinations of equality, I submit to concentrate on distributional rules (absolute versus relative equality) combined with two approaches to equal opportunities (equal means versus equal prospects); the direct approach to equality—examples would be the enforcement of employment quotas and the prohibition of wage increases—is generally incompatible with a social or free market economy and shall therefore be excluded. This procedure generates four relevant types as shown in Figure 7.2.[5]

Two main conclusions come out of this exercise, one conceptual and one speculative. First, it becomes clear that equity—often used synonymously with equality—covers only "one corner" of the equalities' dimensional space. Under the equity perspective, equality mirrors only the balance between input and output considered by cooperating partners as fair. Equality converts into proportionality between investment and return relative to others, thus pinching off the utopian touch of absolute equality (Lautmann 1990, 43). Although equity considers the results of cooperation, equity and (other dimensions of) equality may vary independently from each other

Figure 7.1 **An Illustration of the Dimensions of Equality**

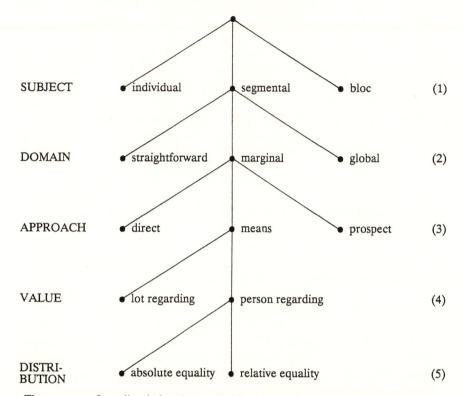

The sequence of equality choices (see vertical line) is the selection of a segmented subject (1); only a marginal domain shall be equally distributed (2), further restricted by equality of means (3); persons' value differences in the segment shall be regarded (4), and the distribution shall not end in absolute but only in relative equality (5).

A labor market example could read in the following way: Only male full-time workers (1) get profit shares (2) and the same amount of further training (3); their shares are related to their personal needs, e.g., family status (4), but shall respect the minimax/maximin criterion (5).

(Burgess and Nielsen 1974, 428). The equity principle, as William J. Goode remarks without illusion, establishes a rule of inequality although introduced as a principle of equality. It mixes egalitarian and differentiating principles in a strange way, and its persuasive power is largely due to rhetoric (Goode 1978, 350).

Second, the relevance of the four main types of equality seems to vary contextually. The guiding hypothesis may start with the following speculation: equity or distributive justice is relevant when both supply and demand on the labor market are elastic; redistributive justice is relevant when supply is elastic and demand inelastic; equal opportunity is relevant when demand is elastic but supply inelastic; finally, egalitarian relationships are relevant when both supply and

Figure 7.2. **Relevant Equalities in Labor Markets**

| | | Equalities of (Wage) Income | |
		Relative (b)	Absolute (d)
Equality of Opportunity	(a) Means	Distributive Justice	Redistributive Justice
	(c) Prospects	Equal Opportunity	Egality

1. Distributive Justice (Equity)

(a) Individuals are endowed with equal means of attaining labor market productivity (e.g., basic education) assuming no discrimination;

(b) the allocation of wages follows certain principles of distributive justice related to labor input or effort, in other words: equity.

2. Redistributive Justice

Equality of opportunity same as 1 (a);
(d) market income differentials are compensated by transfers according to standards of absolute equality assuming person-regarding value structures.

3. Equal Opportunity

(c) Individuals are endowed with unequal means, the differentials aimed at compensating for premarket disadvantages, earlier discrimination, or differences in natural endowments (e.g., compensatory education, means-tested student grants, day-care centers for dependent children); wage allocation same as 1 (b).

4. Egality
Equal opportunity same as 3 (c); wage allocation same as 2 (d).

demand are inelastic. The context-specific transformation of the equality typology thus looks like Figure 7.3.

The overall elasticity case, obviously, fits with perfect market conditions: Equity may be achieved if scarcity (i.e., the necessity of optimizing resource allocation), full information, mobility of resources, and competition are given. Group sociology and economic psychology seem to support this hypothesis: Equity principles are preferred to egalitarian principles when social groups are confronted with external and instrumental problems such as adjustment to changes and goal attainment, and also when efficiency considerations determine group organization and resource allocation. Thus, in cooperative relations in which economic productivity is a primary goal, equity rather than equality is the

Figure 7.3 **Relevance of Equalities in Context**

		Demand	
		Elastic	Inelastic
Supply	Elastic	Distr. Justice (Equity)	Redistr. Justice
	Inelastic	Equal Opportunity	Equality

dominant principle of distributive justice (Deutsch 1975, 143). The new socio-logical functionalism even sees outcome distribution according to performance (*Leistungsgerechtigkeit*) and corresponding inequalities as a necessary condition for attaining and maintaining the flexible and innovative capacities of social systems (Hondrich 1984, 290f). Egalitarian principles, on the other hand, are dominant in situations of internal and expressive problems (group cohesion, solidar-ity). Further contextual conditions of equality choices[6] have been found in time constraints, transaction or bargaining costs, and in one-time or repeated exchange relationships (Lautmann 1990, 62; Yuchtman 1972, 592f). Economic psychology even suggests gender-specific preferences of choices: equity being a typical "male" (absolute), equality a typical "female" choice (Kahn et al. 1980, 176–88).

In a context where supply is elastic and demand inelastic, redistributive jus-tice may be necessary to avoid or to compensate for monopoly rents related to "positional goods" such as hierarchical positions in the labor market. Although there are no strict limitations to such positions—there is probably more scope to reduce hierarchies as presently realized—the limited number of "good jobs" is a structural feature of real labor markets. To allow unrestricted competition or to invest more into equal opportunities would induce a rat race and be economically a waste of resources.

When labor demand is elastic and labor supply inelastic, however, then we have a clear case for equal-opportunity policies. Such policies could compensate for inelasticities such as family obligations (e.g., by providing day-care centers, paid parental leave), or they could do away with the determinants of elasticities (e.g., by improving the public transport system, raising skill levels).

Inelasticity on both sides of the labor market, finally, represents the out-standing—but not necessarily the only—case for egalitarian policies in terms of both allocation and distribution. Job guarantees via temporary public job creation at prevailing market wages or a means-tested basic income guarantee may be examples.

Efficiencies

No "efficiency grammar"—comparable to the one developed for equality—has yet been developed. Many terms, however, are flying around and are often used to suit a particular purpose: Pareto efficiency, static efficiency, dynamic efficiency, etc.; even concepts of social efficiency and political efficiency have been suggested (Schmitter 1990, 29), although waiting for "warming clothes"; and a number of terms are related to efficiency such as competitiveness, high performance, productivity, efficacy, effectiveness, and so on.

Time and space place limits on our discussion of this issue. Thus, we start immediately with a simplification, taking Okun's definition of economic efficiency as the maximum output (of goods and services) from a given input (of labor and capital). Note, however, that this definition leaves out, e.g., the domain of input utilization, i.e., whether only the most productive workers or the entire population of working age should be included in the definition of input. In place of a discussion of the implications of this definition, I will merely add a proposal, conceived in analogy to the "equality grammar," for distinguishing four types of labor market efficiency (Figure 7.4).

Contingencies of Equality and Efficiency

Why should (relative) economic equality, i.e., small disparities in families' disposable income affect economic efficiency? The underlying assumption in standard neoclassical economics is simply that markets generate differential income according to differential inputs by individuals and to the valuation of the output by the market. Differential inputs depend on acquired assets, natural abilities, and efforts that determine together the individual's level of productivity; the valuation of the output reflects the tastes of the consumers as well as the production decisions of others (law of supply and demand). Because the rules of the game are the same for all, the differences in outcome are viewed as fair as long as every loser has the chance to change his or her decisions according to the market signals so as to be a winner in the following rounds. On these assumptions, any intervention to redistribute market income must lead to a reduction of efficiency almost by definition. Efficiency losses arise mainly through reduced work efforts, disincentives to private saving, and administrative costs of redistribution or—in other words—through the famous "leaky bucket" (Okun 1975, 91ff).[7]

Okun, however, was well aware of the difference between economic equality and equality of opportunity. In fact, he devoted a whole chapter (out of four) to the ways in which civilized societies promote equality (and pay some costs in terms of efficiency) by establishing social and political rights that are distributed equally and universally and that are intended to be kept out of the marketplace. Contrary to extreme libertarian views, he recommended restricting the market clearly to its proper range of economic issues: "The imperialism of the market's valuation accounts for its contribution, and for its threat to other institutions. It can destroy every other value in sight. If votes were traded at the same price as toasters, they would be worth no more than toasters and would lose their social significance" (Okun 1975, 13). We will have to come back to this conclusion,

Figure 7.4 **Relevant Efficiencies for Labor Markets**

		Flexibility of Labor Capacities	
		Low	High
Utilization of labor capacities	Low	Static Efficiency	Intensive Efficiency
	High	Extensive Efficiency	Dynamic Efficiency

because people value jobs not only in economic terms (i.e., market income) but also in social terms (i.e., psychic income).

Okun was also conscious of complementary relationships between equality and efficiency and did not assume—as many mainstream economists persist in doing—the universal applicability of the trade-off: "Measures that might soak the rich so much as to destroy investment and hence impair the quality and quantity of jobs for the poor could worsen both efficiency and equality. On the other hand, techniques that improve the productivity and earnings potential of unskilled workers might benefit society with greater efficiency and greater equality" (Okun 1975, 4).

The latter possibility has been poignantly reformulated and extended in a more recent work as the "opportunity-based vision of a handup and not a handout" (Haveman 1988). In his informative and stimulating book *Starting Even*, Haveman criticizes the old-style welfare state that attempted to offset competitive handicaps primarily by redistributing market outcomes. The United States was particularly consistent in pursuing this maxim. Looking back on the last forty years, however, Haveman finds out disappointingly that progressive tax rates and, in particular, increasing transfer payments were only able to neutralize the growing economic disparity before taxation and transfer payments. He claims that nothing has changed with regard to the unequal distribution of disposable income. It has also been shown theoretically that increasing redistribution of disposable income does lead to more equality but at a lower average standard of living (Baumol 1986). Haveman shows that "equality cum efficiency" measures are possible, especially if the equalizing policy is focused on opportunities instead of on outcomes, e.g., by the improvement of technical and social skills of the working poor.[8]

> Okun also stressed the potential economic value of equality of opportunity: Whenever trading decisions in the marketplace are influenced by the personal characteristics of buyers and sellers as distinct from the quality and characteristics of the products they wish to deal in, that market generates an inequality of opportunity as well as an economic imperfection. Consider, for example, cases where job opportunities are influenced by race and sex. These may involve poorer pay for a given job—exploitation—or exclusion from the good jobs. When a women gets as good a job as a man with equal skills would obtain but

is paid less, the exploitation creates unjustified inequalities; but it may not have much effect on efficiency, at least in the short run. On the other hand, if women are excluded from responsible jobs, they are prevented from using their skills to the fullest extent; that is inefficiency—in effect, the worker's hand is tied behind her back. The empirical evidence identifies exclusion as the main form of discrimination in labor markets. It produces a triplet of evils: unequal opportunity, unequal income, and inefficiency. Moreover, unequal opportunity at one point in time generates unequal opportunity over time. Once people are excluded from good jobs, they are deprived of the incentives and opportunities to develop the skills that would otherwise qualify them for good jobs (Okun 1975, 77) [Another evident source of economic inefficiency is the unequal access to, in particular, the higher education system (Okun 1975, 81)].

Unequal treatment may also result in an inefficient allocation of resources. Where, for instance, equally productive men and women are hired for different jobs and women's jobs are lower paid due to occupational segregation, prices do not serve as accurate indicators of social costs. In comparison to the nondiscriminatory situation, society produces "too little" of the outputs that use "overpriced" male labor, given that equally productive female labor is available at a lower price to expand production. Society produces "too much" of the outputs that use "underpriced" female labor, given that the contribution of equally productive labor is valued more highly in the male sector. The public sector may be a candidate. Inefficiency caused by discrimination is even greater when taking into account feedback effects. If women are deterred from investing in their human capital because of discrimination, society loses a valuable resource. Thus, opening doors to women that were previously closed (or only slightly ajar) benefits society as well as individual women by bringing their talents and abilities to bear in new areas (Blau and Ferber 1986, 262–63).[9]

From a theoretical point of view, Schotter adds a further argument against wide differentials of rewards: Excessive differentials between market outcomes may be considered as unfairly affecting work incentives.

> An "efficiently organized" economy may define outcomes that a substantial portion of the population may consider unfair. Those people that do relatively well under the existing set of institutions may have an incentive to work hard, but those who do poorly may become discouraged and stop trying. Now, contrast this situation with an "inefficiently organized" economy that the overwhelming majority consider to be fair. If this sense of fairness increases the effort of the previously discouraged population to a point where the average effort of workers in the economy is increased, then this "inefficient" but equitable set of institutions may produce a greater output than the "efficient" economy. Hence, if people think they are playing a fair economic game and this belief causes them, on average, to try harder, equitable economic institutions may turn out to be efficient as well. (Schotter 1985, 30–31)

Figure 7.5 **Contingencies of Equality and Efficiency**

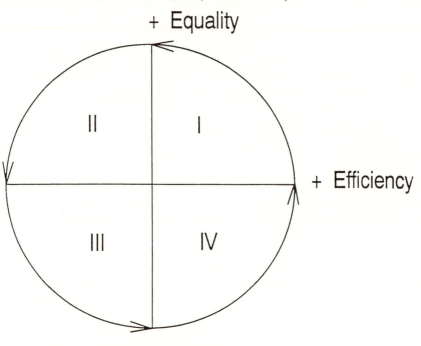

I   The "classical tradeoff"
II   The "vicious marriage"
III   The "neo-classical tradeoff"
IV The "virtuous marriage"

Finally, a remark on the analogy of games theory: a labor market game differs from sporting games in one essential element at least: most players on the labor market have to play, whereas sportsmen and women can choose the game with rules that best suit their talents. Thus, on the labor market the rules of the game have to be adjusted to (many) players, whereas in sport it is the players who have to adjust to the rules.

As the above considerations show, there is no necessary trade-off between equality and efficiency; the relationship is contingent, as shown in Figure 7.5. It depends on the problem and on the efficacy of coordinating institutions whether the "marriage" of equality with efficiency develops into a harmonious and mutually productive liaison or into a vicious circle that may end in disaster in a process reminiscent of marriage scenes by Virginia Woolf. The most promising candidates for a "virtuous" relationship seem to be measures enhancing earnings capacities, providing equality of employment opportunity, supporting a wage structure considered as fair, and providing income security to cover risks or uncertainties.

Two questions, however, remain to be answered: Which institutions and which institutional mixtures promise to support such a "virtuous marriage"? How far shall we go with (which) equality-promoting measures at the cost of (which) efficiency? An extended transaction cost perspective will be used to illuminate the first question, while the second question will be discussed using theories of justice or injustice.

Institutions in an Extended Transaction Cost Perspective

An excellent clarification of the comparative efficiency of institutions has been provided by William G. Ouchi. His article "Markets, Bureaucracies, and Clans" (Ouchi 1980) is especially helpful due to links it establishes between transaction costs and equity issues in the employment relationship. It takes explicit account of the fact that the exchange of labor against wages is often different from the exchange of marketable goods and services or capital.

Ouchi assumes that individuals evaluate transactions (or exchanges) according to socially accepted standards of reciprocity. It is this demand for equity that brings about transaction costs. "A transactions cost is any activity which is engaged in to satisfy each party to an exchange that the value given and received is in accord with his or her expectations" (Ouchi 1980, 130). Transaction costs arise principally when it is difficult to determine the value of the goods or services. Such difficulties can arise from the underlying nature of the good or service or from lack of trust between the parties.

According to this view, institutions developed for reducing transaction costs, or (in other words) for inducing cooperation by securing equitable exchanges. Markets are only efficient institutional devices if performance ambiguity between the trading partners is low, and if the content of exchanged goods or services reflects comparative advantages and different interests (goal incongruency); there is no market between equals in any respect. Clans developed as institutional solutions for the simultaneous occurrence of high performance ambivalence and high common interest (i.e., low goal incongruency); a typical example would be teamwork in research projects. Bureaucracies are established, according to Ouchi, when both performance ambiguity and goal incongruence are moderately high.[10] So far, so good. Something, however, is missing from a socioeconomic point of view. Let me start with an example from the service market:

If I go to the doctor, I rely on the reputation and professionalism of that person and not (at least only to a small extent) on the price charged for the service. In other words: I rely on the efficiency of the social "network" (Ouchi's "clan") called "the medical profession." I assume also that the price of the service is fair because it has been bargained between other social networks (say, the trade union and the doctors' association) or has been determined by another legitimized institution (a "hierarchy," or, in Ouchi's terms, a "bureaucracy") and is essentially equal for the "same" service provided by different doctors. Or—and this is the missing element in Ouchi's approach—I don't even bother about the price because I am entitled to the service by some standard of (absolute) equality without being charged personally. Nor will I search for the cheapest doctor, simply because my toothache is so bad or because wasting time could even cause death. Even if I had time for comparing prices, the outcome in terms of efficiency would probably be worse. Due to informational asymmetries, it might well be rational to choose the most expensive doctor because the high prices of medical services presumably will reflect high quality. Institutions that endow individuals with entitlements (often, but not necessarily, legally enforced) according to socially accepted standards of equality and independent of individuals' capacity to reciprocate shall be called "civil rights"; their exchange medium is solidarity, whereas the well-known exchange media of markets, hierarchies, and networks are money prices, power, and trust, respectively (see Figure 7.6).

Civil rights—in combination with markets, hierarchies, and networks—are also an important institution governing the employment relationship. If I work—say, as a skilled worker at the VW assembly line in Wolfsburg—I trust in the fairness of my wages due to the efficiency of the social network of which I am a member (trade union or works council); I accept also the authority (power) of the VW management (the "hierarchy") to relate my remuneration properly to the wage of my boss and to less experienced (less senior) colleagues, and to see that my wage is not significantly different from that of a comparable colleague at Daimler Benz in Stuttgart; I expect, finally, to be entitled by law to a fair (i.e., proportional to my salary and relatively equal to others) replacement of my wage in case of unemployment; in other words, I expect civil rights backed up by solidarity.

Ouchi's approach—which is similar to Williamson's (1985)—is summarized in Figure 7.6 but extended by a third structural category of the employment relationship to take into account an important (and widely neglected) precondition of efficient market transactions: a high capacity of reciprocity. A socioeconomic approach, however, has to include the type of transactions or exchanges that are not and cannot be governed by the rule of "reciprocity." Such situations arise when individuals are by nature, by accident, or by social status incapable of reciprocal responses or only able to provide such responses in the long run (and this usually under high uncertainty). Inability to reciprocate is quite different from situations of performance ambiguity, which assume the possibility of reciprocity in principle. Coordination by some socialized and legally enforced ethic of solidarity, named "civil rights," i.e., is the only institution that can efficiently deal with such situations.[11]

Figure 7.6   **Efficiency Conditions of Coordinating Institutions**

	Markets	*Hierarchies*	*Networks*	*Civil Rights*
Performance Ambiguity (Uncertainty)	Low	Moderately High	High	High
Goal Incongruency (Conflict)	High	Moderately High	Low	High
Reciprocity Capacity (Autonomy)	High	Moderately High	Moderately High	Low

[ ]   =   according to Ouchi
(hierarchies = bureaucracies; clans = networks)

Regulatory Media

Markets	--->	Prices
Hierarchies	--->	Power
Networks	--->	Trust
Civil Rights	--->	Solidarity

Trade-off Choices in Theories of Justice and Injustice

> Equality must be equal for equals.
>
> —Aristotle, *The Politics*

It seems self-evident that the "justice" of equality is based on a value judgment. It depends especially on the decision of whom we include in the evaluating balance sheet. The statement by Aristotle looks only at first glance plausible and innocent. However, as Armatya Sen, for instance, observed, the Athenian intellectuals discussing equality did not see any great problem in excluding the slaves from the orbit of discourse (Sen 1973, 1). The same sort of neglect in theories of justice also affects women (Moller Okin 1989; O'Neill 1990).

Less clear is that efficiency itself is a value among others (Etzioni 1988,

245–48). The evocation of a trade-off between equality and efficiency is already a concession that there may be a difficult choice of preferences, a concession that radical libertarians would not make. In addition, the seemingly neutral concept of Pareto efficiency is also highly dependent on whom one includes in the concept of the society or community whose welfare one studies: Who is considered as a full member of the active labor force (c.f., the concept of "full employment")? Are married women with children included? Adults with physical handicaps but full mental faculties? Are future generations encompassed? If so, how long into the future? What about illegal immigrants and starving or suffering people in other countries? In practice, societies answer these questions in the institutionalized form that solidarity takes in each case.

In the following I abstain, however, from these larger questions. I shall restrict the discussion to economic equality and efficiency on the labor market, i.e., to wages, employment, unemployment, and productivity. What then is the break-even point, given a trade-off between equality and efficiency, and how can this point be shifted upward?

Figure 7.7 displays intuitively several "break-even points" according to various theories of justice.[12] The strict libertarian position would stop any equality-inducing measure at point L, at which the trade-off is starting: Some efficiency would have to be given up in favor of equality by moving beyond this point to the left. This position—giving priority to efficiency—is clearly implied by Milton Friedman's discussion in *Capitalism and Freedom* (Friedman 1962, 161–66).

The moderate libertarian (or utilitarian) would maximize both equality and efficiency according to the marginality principle: Promote equality up to the point where the added benefits of more equality are just matched by the added costs of greater inefficiency. This concept of equity would lead to the break-even point at U.

Another variant follows from Rawls's theory of justice based on two fundamental principles—the principle of equal basic liberty and the "difference principle" combined with the requirement of fair equality of opportunity. The second principle is relevant here. It insists that "all social values . . . are to be distributed equally unless an unequal distribution of any . . . is to everyone's advantage"—in particular, to the advantage of the typical person in the least-advantaged group (Rawls 1971, 62). This view implies that no inequality is tolerable unless it raises the lowest income of the society. According to this "maximin criterion," society is worse off if the lowest-income family loses one dollar, no matter how much everybody else in the society gains. Following Rawls, we would end up at point C on the curve: Up to this point it would always be possible to increase someone's income without necessarily reducing someone else's income, because there is still some gain in efficiency; above this point, however, someone would lose, because efficiency becomes negative.[13]

A radical egalitarian, finally, would put absolute priority on equality and go up to the point E, when both equality and efficiency start to fall. This opinion

Figure 7.7 **Trade-off Choices Between Equality and Efficiency**

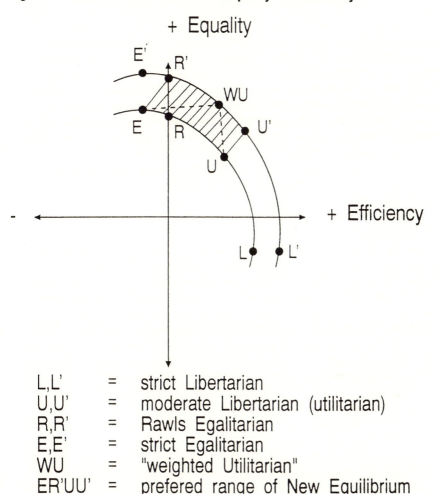

L,L'	=	strict Libertarian
U,U'	=	moderate Libertarian (utilitarian)
R,R'	=	Rawls Egalitarian
E,E'	=	strict Egalitarian
WU	=	"weighted Utilitarian"
ER'UU'	=	prefered range of New Equilibrium

probably fits with the majority of present-day economists who maintain that the welfare state has already reached something like the state at point E (or even further to the left). Their policy advice is to cut social transfers and to deregulate the labor market to come back to point L or at least to point U. Is that the only choice we have?

The discussion in the foregoing paragraph has already indicated possibilities to move the trade-off curve upward. Reducing high long-term unemployment alone would probably make it possible to move from the paretian suboptimal point U to U'. The consistent application of efficiency-enhancing equity standards suggested above would exploit the area ER'UU', possibly allowing society to reach the new equity equilibrium point WU. This point reflects a "weighted utilitarianism" as advocated by Arneson (1990) and Weirich (1983). It represents a combination of Rawlsian and utilitarian principles and gives more weight to securing gains and avoiding losses for the worse-off than for the better-off.

My justification for this choice, however, is not simply normative. It derives from the assumption that a relatively larger increase of reciprocity capacity—i.e., the capacity of independent transactions (see the extended transaction cost model on page 260)—for the least advantaged on the labor market helps to move the trade-off curve upward. Weighted utility, hence, is at least compatible with efficiency (i.e., increasing equality will not shift the efficiency point to the left) and may even be complementary (i.e., increasing equality shifts the efficiency point to the right). The strategies to move into the preferred range of a new equilibrium, if possible to WU, instead of the path currently being pursued (E →R →U →L) will be discussed in the next section.

Figure 7.8 summarizes the main arguments so far in graphical form. Two feedback-loops in this representation have not yet been discussed: the judgment of the "equity balance" by the voters, and both the distributional and allocational incidence of taxation in its widest sense (including also contributions or payroll taxes). The shifting (and culturally varying) preference of voters regarding the choice between transfers versus job creation as a measure to correct inequalities of wages and job opportunities is one aspect among others.[14] Arneson (1990, 1130) observes that even if cash grants worked more efficiently to boost the utility of disadvantaged persons than provision of employment, a program of state-guaranteed employment (through public works or wage subsidies for private job creation) might be more palatable to voters in modern democracies. Opinion surveys seem to show that the majority of citizens harbor grave qualms about the wisdom of a state policy of handing out unearned income to the able-bodied, while they support programs that offer employment opportunities to the able-bodied unemployed.

Strategies of Effective Social Cooperation

To sum up the reflections so far, effective social cooperation depends on several conditions: First, the existence of many autonomous persons with high capacities to reciprocate; in other words, a large number of competent agents is a precondition for the social engagement in competitive cooperation. The enhancement of this basic market condition is crucial if the playing field becomes larger and the players by origin more unequal. Second, social incentives to cooperate, the type of which depends on the nature of transactions—wage differentials (markets), transparent long-term career paths (hierarchies), professional reputation (networks), or a combination of all three. Third, civil rights and corresponding obligations for care are a necessary (and often forgotten) complement where individual autonomy of action is lacking or severely restricted. These "caring"

Figure 7.8 **Political Economics of Equality and Efficiency**

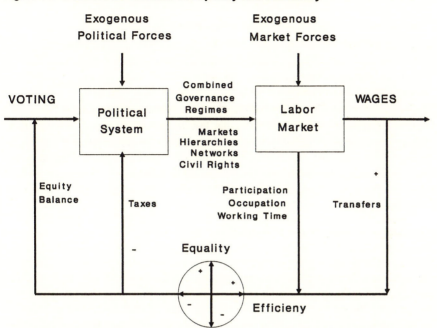

functions can take the form of basic income support, social security and employment protection, educational and social help for various kinds of risks during the life cycle (natural or social handicaps, unemployment, sickness, special family obligations, disability, family breakdown).

Our deliberations on the equality-efficiency puzzle, in addition, have brought another three conclusions: First, it may be worthwhile to consider more seriously equality-enhancing measures before redistribution due to "leaky buckets" in administering redistribution, but also due to adverse allocational effects of large-scale redistribution; on the other hand, basic income support, fair wages, and employment security may be positive incentives to work hard, to cooperate, and to shirk less. Second, equal employment-opportunity measures, especially for new players entering the game, are the most promising candidates for a "virtuous marriage" between equality and efficiency. In the following pages it will be shown, however, that universal or all-encompassing measures are more appropriate and consistent with "cooperative competition" than selective or targeted measures. Third, income security, employment protection, and active labor market policy—properly designed—still have an unexploited potential for creating equality cum efficiency.

In the following pages, I shall reflect on this pair of three conditions and possible strategies in more detail, although very much by way of a sketch.

More Equality before Redistribution

> I don't pay good wages because I have a lot of money; I have a lot
> of money because I pay good wages.   Robert Bosch

> Beggars do not envy millionaires, though of course they will envy
> other beggars who are more successful.   Bertrand Russell

The two main messages of this paragraph are represented by the above citations: first, low wages do not necessarily mean low labor costs; second, apart from a socially constructed (and therefore changing) consensus on a civilized minimum standard of wages and income, workers tend to evaluate economic equality by comparing themselves with their "social neighbors" and not with those at the top of the income scale. In the following deliberation of policy strategies, I elaborate on the two arguments separately.

A Moderate but Not Modest Wage Policy

High wages can stimulate work effort as well as willingness to learn, to stay with the firm, and to cooperate in teams (among others Akerloff and Yellen 1986, 1990; Raff and Summers 1987). Evidence in the member states of the European Community shows that low wages tend to go hand in hand with low productivity, meaning that unit labor costs are often higher in low-wage areas or industries than in high-wage areas. Moreover, there is little evidence of close relationship between relative labor costs and competitiveness, as manifested, for instance, in the trade performance of the EC member states. Those countries experiencing the lowest rates of increase in unit labor cost have not necessarily expanded their share of intra-Community trade the most (Commission 1990, 69). It appears also that the regions with the lowest wage levels tend to be those with the greatest employment difficulties (Commission 1991, 122).The reason for this has been made clear: wages and other costs of production are only one element in the competitive process. Qualitative factors—like the design of a product, its reliability and performance, related customer services—can be equally if not more important and are likely to become increasingly relevant as real income grows and people can afford to become more selective and discriminating in what they buy.

Enhancing equality before redistribution thus means, among other things, that wage and income differentials that have become conspicuous in the extended European single market, especially those in the united Germany, are to be eliminated primarily by equalizing the gap in technical and social skills rather than by equalizing outcomes by transfers. Wherever possible, this specifically means avoiding, e.g., the temporarily easy route of structural adjustment by extending the duration of unemployment benefits or by imposing early retirement. The more promising policy strategy is to enhance transaction capacities, such as improving the workers' skills through retraining and further training, and offsetting irremediable shortcomings in the skills of older employees or persons with impaired performance through shorter working hours or wage subsidies.[15]

Fair, but Not Egalitarian Wages

Competitive labor markets are characterized by flexibility, that is, by high mobility or elasticity of labor supply. In principle, labor supply can acquire this property in two ways, by the spatial and temporal mobility of individual workers ("numerical flexibility") or by their versatility in terms of skill or intellect—i.e., qualifications—at one and the same place of work ("functional flexibility"). Textbook wisdom attaches great importance to wages and their variation or variability to bring about both sorts of flexibility. As far as cooperative competition is concerned, however, wage variation is a necessary but not a sufficient condition for competitiveness.

An everyday example will illustrate this point. Responding to the proposal of a high-ranking East Berlin city council member for economic affairs that the low wage level be used to enable East Germany to become as West Germany's "extended workbench," a small businessman from Potsdam pointed to the almost completely outmoded technology of GDR plants and the fact that the GDR's market had been taken over by western products. Moreover, he continued, many plants near the border area had already lost their best workers to firms in West Berlin or West Germany because of the wage differential. This businessman therefore maintained that it was an illusion to think that low wages were an advantage for Brandenburg plants.

From both the evolutionary and the equity perspective of cooperative competition, the strategy of maintaining low wages and large wage differentials must be criticized. It is not price competition that plays the decisive role in models based on evolutionary theory; it is competition based on both process and product innovation. In process-oriented innovation competition, firms use more cost-effective production procedures in an attempt to gain a cost advantage on their competitors. In product-oriented innovation competition, firms create new products and achieve better quality in order to gain a temporary monopoly, increase their sales at the expense of their competitors, or recoup sales losses they themselves might have suffered. Most research on the impacts of new technologies on the labor market has shown impressively that the availability of a work force whose qualifications allow for flexible deployment is a key prerequisite for gaining a foothold in innovation competition (Matzner, Schettkat, and Wagner 1990; OECD 1988; Schettkat and Wagner 1990). It is particularly noteworthy that the most innovative sectors managed to develop this necessary flexibility not primarily by exchanging parts of the labor force with the external labor market but mostly by reassigning workers internally. The willingness of the workers to accept structural change, allow themselves to be assigned new jobs, or acquire additional skills increases with job security—which admittedly has to be made contingent on this willingness—and with remuneration that is felt to be good and equitable. Wages, too, have to be guided more by functional than by numerical principles, that is, more by actual performance centered on skill and cooperation than by age, seniority, or rank. The most innovative sectors have both the greatest expansion of employment and the least risk of unemployment.

Other reasons also favor the strategy of taking the moderate high-wage policy's function of promoting structural changes and combining it with elements that retard the emergence of large wage differentials. The greater the range of wages, the less likely it is that members of high-wage sectors will allow themselves to be forced into a low-wage sector or into a function that is usually paid less. Even the productivity growth of manufacturing and service industries, which is unequal for technological and organizational reasons, speaks against the existence of a close tie between wages and numerical productivity growth. Otherwise, we would have long since been lacking teachers, hairdressers, nurses, and other providers of personal services, for whom there is little or no chance of productivity growth, at least not at the rate possible for the capital-intensive production of goods.

If productivity ultimately depends not only on individual performance but on cooperation as well, then considerations of incentive and justice speak against excessive wage differentials. Information theory and learning theory have long recognized the significance that "tacit knowledge" has for high productivity and competitiveness. That is the knowledge that comes from experience, knowledge that, in a sense, is contained in people's hands and minds, not in reference manuals or textbooks. Working people will avoid passing this knowledge on if doing so would jeopardize their jobs or living standards because of competition. Furthermore and from an evolutionary point of view, the larger the playing field and the cognitive divergence of players cooperating, the less likely it is that "tacit knowledge" associated with acquired and habitual skills can be known or appreciated by any center, e.g., the top of a management hierarchy (Hodgson 1988, 259). If it is acknowledged that the (cooperative) exchange of such knowledge is crucial for productivity or innovation, then incentives for voluntary exchange will be important; a fair wage structure—and that means in this case wages that are not widely dispersed—is a necessary element for cooperation between very divergent players with complementary tacit knowledge.

Wage structures that are felt to be inequitable also eventually manifest themselves in a lack of motivation and of willingness to adapt and cooperate. Very little innovation would occur in a purely competitive context. The reason has been set clearly in our extended transactions cost framework: employment relationships related to research and development are characterized by high performance ambivalence, strong interest congruence and teamwork necessities, and by extremely high investment risks.

More Equality of Employment Opportunities

In real life, labor markets are horizontally and vertically segmented. Formal and informal institutional rules set borders between occupational, sectoral, and internal labor markets, and there are barriers to be overcome when moving into higher positions. This segmentation of the labor market is evident in all European countries, albeit to greatly varying degrees.

This labor market segmentation may have economic as well as social reasons. One example for efficient segmentation rules is occupational quality standards for practicing certain vocational activities. The universalization of such standards by means of a craft certificate, master craftsman's certificate, or diploma promotes cooperative competition in several respects. It increases mobility and, hence, the range of options for cooperation. Universalization of standards reduces transaction costs and thus also obstacles to cooperation. It contributes to professional ethos, thereby reducing deceptive offers of cooperation. It controls supply in the corresponding segment and thus reduces the danger of cutthroat competition.

Following evolutionary lines of thought, such as the ideas propounded by Norbert Elias (1982), one of the major future tasks of the labor market in a Europe without internal borders will be to revitalize and harmonize labor market segments for skilled workers and professionals. It will be necessary to set the professional quality standards at a high level but also to generalize them to facilitate diversity on the regional level and in the plant. Whether this will succeed is another question. Skepticism is warranted by the growing significance of what are already partly multinational labor markets tailored to specific plants and by the still only rudimentary development of transnational institutions in the realm of industrial relations—institutions like European professional associations, European unions, and European employers' associations.

Other institutional barriers to horizontal and vertical mobility of labor markets, however, are outmoded, discriminatory, and inefficient. This is especially true of sex discrimination, which is unjustifiable on any premise of cooperative competition. In the framework developed above, discrimination means nothing else than, first, excluding people from taking part in the game; second, excluding people from learning the rules of the game; and, third—to close the vicious circle—generating inequality (e.g., lower skills or work experience), which then is used as a reason for further discrimination. Because women have at least as good an education as men, their underrepresentation in senior status positions represents a partially untapped potential for cooperation (see, among others, Blau and Ferber 1986, 262–70; Moller Okin 1989; Fuchs 1988). Moreover, the concentration of women in just a few occupations and sectors reduces the options for cooperation and raises the risk and the duration of their unemployment if economic restructuring becomes necessary.

The differences in sex segregation within Germany illustrate mistakes of past equal opportunity policies. True, the labor market participation rate of women in the former GDR—unlike that of women in the former FRG—was almost as high as that of men. The average level of occupational qualification among East German women also was higher, and their representation in at least middle management positions was greater than that of their West German "sisters." These achievements, however, were tied partly to economic exigencies (low living standards) and partly to regulations that target women specifically instead of aiming at the total possible labor supply regardless of sex. The regulations applying solely to women included the monthly "household day," the right to take leave in order to care for their children when they fall ill,[16] and the one-year, guaranteed parental leave (normally granted only to mothers or grandmothers) at between 60 percent and 90 percent of the beneficiary's net income.

Such special regulations handicap women in cooperative competition, for they make women into a special group on the labor market, burden them with the tie between family and job, while releasing men from this responsibility. If the benefits derived from family policy or educational policy are to be neutral for the competition between the genders, then they must apply to both genders. By the same token, the direct and indirect costs related to benefits of social policy and legal claims related to parenthood must on principle be borne by society at large or imposed equally upon everyone, just as with the costs of other public or merit goods, such as primary and secondary schooling. In this sense, the extensive public facilities for child care in the former GDR are to be seen positively.

Whereas the standards in East Germany were generous but deficient in terms of the principle of universality, the standards in West Germany were lower but (formally at least) universal. In the process of unification, the lower standards— and thus Grasham's law—got their way. As of 1 July 1991, the regions of the former GDR are subject to the regulation that leave to care for a sick child can be granted to men, too—however, only if the child is under eight years of age and only up to five days under relatively unfavorable financial conditions. The functionality of lower standards appears to be questionable not only from the stance of equal opportunity but also from the economic perspective. The Europe of tomorrow cannot afford to continue investing in education and science and then have a large share of her highly qualified people, usually women, sitting at home against their will in their most creative phase of life because their children are not cared for adequately outside the home or because young parents are not able to combine flexibly caring and producing functions.[17]

Efficiencies and Inefficiencies of Unemployment Benefits

> Equality does make very good sense as a form of group insurance. Any hunter knows that hunting is chancy, that an empty-handed return is only too likely, in which case it is good to know there might be another source of supply.   Barrington Moore

The occurrence of involuntary unemployment is a case for "solidarity." But how is this modern form of insurance to be organized without negative (and maybe even with positive) effects on the efficiency of the chancy labor market? The crucial parameters of unemployment insurance are the benefit level and the benefit duration. A cross-matrix reveals, then, four possible strategies[18]:

		Benefit Level	
		high	low
Benefit	long	1	2
Duration	short	3	4

I shall argue that strategy 3, with a number of caveats, is best suited to an equality with efficiency strategy.

Strategy 1 creates equality at the cost of efficiency due to its emphasis on redistribution without improving, *ceteris paribus*, employment opportunities in the long run. Strategy 2 is suboptimal both in terms of equality and efficiency: the redistributive effect will by definition be small and may not even compensate for nonpecuniary losses, whereas the incentive to work and the political pressure to fight unemployment remain low due to the provision of a permanent—although meager—social safety net.

Strategy 4 reflects the libertarian standpoint, according to which generous unemployment benefits create negative incentives to take up work in the first round, and distort market wages in the second round, thus inducing a vicious circle of increasing unemployment. On the demand side as well, generous unemployment insurance induces the adoption of production methods with higher layoff risks and lowers employers' willingness to hire due to increased labor costs. This is at first glance a plausible model, although it puts the main burden of adjustment to structural change on those individuals who happen to be hit by unemployment. Thus, any income loss in favor of—from the point of view of the individual—doubtful allocational gains for the whole economy may be considered as unfair, but not necessarily if the labor market is viewed as a casino. In any case, equality loses in favor of efficiency, at least in the short term.[19]

However, doubts can also be raised with regard to the efficiency impacts of this model. As chapter 3 (Reissert and Schmid) in this volume has shown, neither the theoretical nor the econometric literature actually confirms significant disincentive effects corresponding to benefit levels; of greater importance seem to be the disincentives of long-duration benefits. The model assumes immediately downwardly and upwardly flexible wages, which are neither socially—see "More Equality before Redistribution," pages 266–7—nor economically efficient, see below. It also neglects micro-macro interrelationships, such as the possibility of contagious unemployment in which low unemployment benefits would further reduce effective aggregate demand.

Strategy 3 seems to be both an equality- and efficiency-enhancing arrangement, at least given the following conditions. Social wages rather than market wages regulate the employment relationship according to the principle of "comparable worth."[20] The burden of adjustment to structural change thus lies in the first place with the firms: social wages increase the wage cost pressure on "lame ducks" and decrease it for innovative firms, in this way stimulating structural change. Unemployment insurance, in this model, has the function of supplementing social wages in order to push labor out of unprofitable skills by compensating the acceptance of workers' adjustment to structural change—in the form of either high short-term unemployment benefits or training and educational stipends. The benefit period, however, should remain short (up to about one year) to put pressure on both the individual and collective agencies to adjust actively to new circumstances. This pressure is both individually and institutionally relieved if unemployment benefits can be extended indefinitely or if they are replaced by disability or early retirement schemes (as largely practiced in the Netherlands) if no "suitable jobs" are available.

Germany is a good case of institutionalized disincentives for employment opportunity measures ("active labor market policy"). As shown by international comparison of the modes of financing labor market policies (Schmid and Reissert 1989 and Schmid, Reissert, and Bruche 1992), the institutionalized mode of fund-raising, spending, and employment opportunity measures affects the outcome of policymakers' decisions without them necessarily being aware of it. In other words, the "hidden hand" of institutional traditions—many of which, of course, reflect (old) power relationships or vested interests—is at work.

The present German financing system, however, has clearly revealed defects, particularly with regard to institutional incentives to pursue employment opportunity measures. There is a clear bias in favor of financing unemployment compensation rather than training or job creation. Germany's financing institutions contain, in evolutionary terms, no "stop rules" of relatively generous transfer payments that make sense in the short term. In addition, the institutionalized priority on unemployment benefits or assistance crowds out active measures (i.e., those able to improve individual competitiveness) in both fiscal and operative terms.

In contrast, for instance, to Sweden, the fiscal burdens of active labor market policy are institutionally largely incongruent with fiscal reliefs in Germany. In other words, agencies spending on active labor market policy (the employment offices, the municipalities) do not get all, or even most, of the fiscal returns in terms of taxes or contributions coming from newly created jobs. As a result, important decentral collective actors have no financial incentive to give a "hand up" instead of a "handout." The lack of financial incentives for decentralized adjustment activities is reinforced by organizational defects. With increasing numbers of unemployed, the employment offices are becoming increasingly preoccupied with the administration of unemployment benefits and have little time to provide and promote organizationally demanding employment services. Especially striking in Germany is the absence of a mechanism to terminate unemployment assistance (means tested, but still benefits related to former net income), which can be guaranteed until the employment offices are able to offer a reasonable job.

An example of a meaningful evolutionary "stop rule" would be the obligation of local authorities and employment offices to offer jobs or training places for all long-term unemployed, with the federal government providing grants for the necessary investment and infrastructure instead of simply providing unemployment assistance. Under the assumption of a reasonable limit on central public funding this would even create a competition for public funds, that is, a stimulus for innovative employment or job creation.[21]

A Metaphorical Summary

The equality and efficiency topic is an old puzzle. It goes back at least to the Book of Matthew:

> The kingdom of heaven is like a householder who went out early in the morning to hire laborers for his vineyard. After agreeing with the laborers for a denarius a day, he sent them into his vineyard. And going out about the third hour he saw others standing idle in the marketplace, and to them he said, "You go into the vineyard too, and whatever is right I will give you." So they went. Going out again about the sixth hour and the ninth hour, he did the same. And about the eleventh hour he went out and found others standing; and he said to them, "Why do you stand here idle all day?" They said to him, "Because no one hired us." He said to them, "You go into the vineyard too." And when evening came, the owner of the vineyard said to his steward, "Call the laborers and pay them their wages, beginning with the last, up to the first." And when those hired about the eleventh hour came, each of them received a denarius. Now when the first came, they thought they would receive more; but each of them also received a denarius. And on receiving it they grumbled at the householder, saying, "These last worked only one hour, and you have made them equal to us who have borne the burden of the day and the scorching heat." But he replied to one of them, "Friend, I am doing you no wrong; . . . Take what belongs to you, and go; I choose to give to this last as I give to you. Am I not allowed to do what I choose with what belongs to me?" (Matthew 20:1–16; quoted in Rae 1981, 24)

The affirmation of private property rights is certainly not the interesting point in the context of this paper. One could add, however, that the parable supports the view of the recent Encyclica by the Pope, "Centesimus Annus," that private ownership of the means of production is justified only if it is used for productive work, i.e., for creating employment opportunities (Johannes Paul II 1991, 43).

As I understand it, the parable is about the contingencies of equality and efficiency. It depends on both the standpoint and the context whether a given constellation is judged equal and efficient, and whether to go apart or together. It could be, for instance, that the decision of the vineyard householder was wise in saving the whole vine harvest (in the face of stormy weather) by hiring the last marginal worker and paying that person the same. In that case, the work of only one hour would have had more value than the total work of all the others. If, however, the vineyard householder—in case of replantation or daily chores on the vineyard—depends on continuous teamwork of his staff, she or he probably has to pay fairly equal wages to get good and reliable work done. Many other interpretations are possible, but not all would be compatible with the "equality cum efficiency" maxim.

The contingent valuation of work effort is nothing new. Overtime work, Sunday work, shift work, etc., are paid more than work at ordinary working times. Entitlements related to work are also increasingly becoming decoupled from numerical work input. An example is the equal counting of part-time work if related to parental obligations with respect to seniority or pension entitlements. More and more status-oriented large-wage differentials are being abolished. A closer look at the reasons behind such changes would very likely reveal the logic or rationale of effective social cooperation beyond cooperative competition. To put it rather provocatively: Why should the working hour of an economics professor be paid five to ten times more than the working hour of a (mostly female or foreign) laborer in the fish food industry? Would an hourly wage of two or three times more not be enough? Maybe these laborers would then pass some "tacit knowledge" to the economists.

To sum up: The willingness to engage in effective social cooperation depends on shared values of justice concerning the assessed "equality" of allocating people in the cooperative game and distributing the outcome from cooperation. These values operative in a "just" world will and should depend, however, upon circumstances. I have distinguished four contingent types of the employment relationship. First, in relationships of cooperative competition, that is in typical market situations in which static economic efficiency is the primary goal, allocation according to competence and distribution according to the proportional contribution (i.e., equity) rather than equality will and should be the dominant principle of justice. Second, in employment relationships characterized by hierarchies, some status-related principles of distributive justice (e.g., seniority, hierarchical position) will be functional, but the importance of this employment relationships seems to be diminishing. Detrimental for both social and economic efficiency, however, are employment relationships still governed by social or political hierarchies that allocate labor according to traditionally rather than functionally defined roles (such as the male breadwinner role). Third, allocation according to professionality and egalitarian rather than equity principles of distributive justice will be efficient in employment relationships under teamwork conditions; social networking on an equal basis is characterized by great difficulties of measuring individual productivity and by the need for innovative capacities in the face of highly uncertain environments. Fourth and finally, in employment relationships characterized by dependency, lack of competence, and immediate reciprocity capacity, solidarity principles of redistributive justice and entitlements (and respective care responsibilities) have to be implemented. The overall efficiency of an active and cooperative society depends on the flexible coordination of these principles. Trust and solidarity will be preconditions for reaping the fruits of enlarged cooperative competition and professional competence in our globalizing economy.

To sum it up metaphorically: Competition in the sense of a contest is good. However, the willingness to engage in such a contest in the first place declines with diminishing chances of winning or at least improving one's position somewhat. To that extent, a social market economy worthy of the name should be not only a contest but also a dance, at which cooperation among "equals" is the important thing.

Notes

1. The number of registered unemployed in the former GDR almost doubled within only half a year from 445,000 (September 1990) to 801,000 (March 1991); the figure rose to 1.3 million in February 1992, and has remained since then stable at 1.1 million. Women—whose labor force participation rate of about 90 percent had almost equaled that of men—are especially hit by unemployment. The number of employed decreased from 9.9 to 6 million. Without measures of active labor market policy (short-time work, training, temporary public job creation, early retirement) the unemployment rate (15.1 percent) would have been at a level of around 30 percent in the first half of 1993. Meanwhile, this source of immigration has been regulated downward to a level of 200,000 per year.

2. Meanwhile, the new act on asylum—much criticized among liberals—is effectively reducing this stream of immigration. However, nobody knows to what extent this reduction in officially reported figures will be compensated by illegal streams of immigrants.

3. "Gender" refers here to the deeply entrenched institutionalization of sexual differences, and a "gendered" family means the distribution of responsibilities, roles, and resources in the family not in accord with principles of justice or with any other commonly respected values, but in accordance with innate differences that are imbued with enormous social significance; see, e.g., Moller Okin 1989:6, 22.

4. Karl Deutsch's definition of power as the ability not to have to learn fits well into the game theoretical framework (Deutsch 1966, 111).

5. According to Burgess and Nielsen (1974), we would come up with a comparable typology based on the combination of effort (input) with outcome:

		OUTCOME	
		unequal	equal
INPUT	equal	equitable if proportional (in)justice	redistributive
	equal	disruptive (in)justice	equitable if egalitarian

6. This is a marker for further research. The following points are partially taken up later in the chapter, when I extend the transaction cost model.

7. For a systematic evaluation of efficiency losses and efficiency gains through redistributive measures, see Haveman (1988, 46–49).

8. Haveman, writing in the U.S. context, suggests five major provisions for an equality-cum-efficiency strategy: an income safety net, a minimum income in retirement, a national child-support program, an employment subsidy to increase jobs for low-skill workers, and a capital account for youth to equalize start-up opportunities (Haveman 1988, 24, 149–77).

9. These costs may be significant as, e.g., a Canadian task force reports: By increasing participation and eliminating misallocation of women's labor force, gross domestic product per person in Canada would be 20 percent higher by 2006 than it would be if present trends continue. Removing discrimination alone (without accelerating participation) would increase output by 10 percent (Canada 1990, vol. I:116).

10. Ouchi did not clearly distinguish the three constellations of goal incongruency, congruency, and indifference. Clans (or networks, as I call them) require in any case a high degree of common interest and not only low goal incongruency, whereas bureaucracies or hierarchies are usually characterized by goal indifference.

11. The lack of reciprocity capacity (or the capacity to act independently) as a source of unfair social and economic inequality has been tackled from a philosophical point of view by Onara O'Neill (1990).

12. Theories of "justice" are not, as one might assume, implicitly also theories of "injustice." The political scientist Judith N. Shklar made this point persuasively clear: "One misses a great deal by looking only at justice. The sense of injustice, the difficulties of identifying the victims of injustice, and the many ways in which we all learn to live with each other's injustices tend to be ignored, as is the relation of private injustice to the public order" (Shklar 1990, 15). How this suggestion affects trade-off choices will be considered in a later stage.

13. Rawls's position can easily be attacked by plausibility considerations. Assume an average yearly net income (full-time job) of 30,000 DM, and a range of 10,000 to 100,000 DM; an employment policy increasing the average to 40,000 and the range from 9,000 to 120,000 would not be acceptable under a Rawlsian justice regime. This would approximate to a move from R to U'. Intuitively, this doesn't appeal, because one could easily imagine a redistributional correction later on if the political majority wishes to make one.

14. The role of voting systems on "equality/efficiency choices" needs much more deliberation than the anecdotal observation that follows. In addition, I will touch only marginally on the role of the second feedback-loop, the revenue flow (or "taxes" in their broadest sense), on page 265. It does make a difference for the final outcome how equality or efficiency-enhancing policy measures are financed. With respect to the financing of unemployment insurance and active labor market policy see Schmid and Reissert 1989; Schmid, Reissert, and Bruche 1992.

15. This doesn't mean that any transfer policy is bad. Intermediate redistribution can make sense if the enhancement of transaction capacity needs some time. If monetary policy is not available to adjust for different productivity levels (as is the case in the unified Germany, where the common currency meant practically a huge revaluation for the East German regions), functional equivalents have to be implemented. In the absence of mobility barriers between rich and poor areas (i.e., high and low productivity areas), young and qualified workers will—at given huge wage differentials—move out of the poor regions and further deteriorate the attractiveness of the regions for investment capital. To prevent such a vicious circle, the moderate (but not modest) wage policy could be complemented by offering wage subsidies as a functional equivalent to the (now politically impossible) depreciation of the currency as proposed a long time ago by Nicholas Kaldor (1936). Such a policy, however, only makes sense if accompanied by massive investment incentives and the provision of public infrastructure.

16. The GDR law entitled mothers to several weeks of leave to care for sick children under fourteen years of age. Single working mothers with one child were entitled to four weeks of such leave; with two children, six weeks; with three children, eight weeks; and so on, up to thirteen weeks.

17. Although very important, I have not discussed here another strategy of enhancing equality cum efficiency: the increase of equality through worker participation. Hodgson cites plentiful evidence that worker participation can lead to substantial increases in motivation, work effort, and hence efficiency. In terms of evolutionary systems theory, worker participation can be interpreted as providing increasing internal variety as a solution to the increasing exposure of firms to external varieties, i.e., uncertainty (Hodgson 1988, 257f).

18. Some welfare states fit strategy 1 (e.g., France, Germany, the Netherlands, Belgium); Italy—apart from the Cassa Integrazione Guadagni—is a case for strategy 2; Sweden and the United States are clear cases for strategies 3 and 4, respectively.

19. The long-run effects would have to consider the incidence of unemployment on lifetime income, for which there are no comparative figures available.

20. Which I consider a modern form of a "solidaristic wage policy" for its account of professionality, performance, and responsibility-oriented criteria, on the one hand, and across-the-board application (sectoral/regional), on the other hand.

21. As expected, the German system for funding labor market policy came under renewed political pressure due to the huge deficits caused by the reunification process. The federal government has started to limit the expenditures for active labor market policy—especially in the booming public works industry (the so-called ABM-measures).

References

Akerloff, George A., and Yellen, Janet L., eds. 1986. *Efficiency Wage Models of the Labor Market*. Cambridge: Cambridge University Press.

———. 1990. "The Fair Wage–Effort Hypothesis and Unemployment." *Quarterly Journal of Economics* 105 (May): 255–83.

Arneson, Richard J. 1990. "Is Work Special? Justice and Distribution of Employment." *American Political Science Review* 84, no. 4:1127–47.

Axelrod, Robert. 1984. *The Evolution of Cooperation*. New York: Basic Books.

Baumol, William J. 1986. *Superfairness. Applications and Theory*. Cambridge, Mass.: MIT Press.

Björklund, Anders. 1990. "Unemployment, Labour Market Policy and Income Distribution." In *Generating Equality in the Welfare State. The Swedish Experience*, ed., Inga Persson, 201–21. London: Norwegian University Press.

Björklund, Anders; Haveman, Robert; Hollister, Robinson; and Holmlund, Bertil. 1991. *Labour Market Policy and Unemployment Insurance*. Oxford: Clarendon Press.

Blau, Francine D., and Ferber, Marianne A. 1986. *The Economics of Women, Men, and Work*. Englewood Cliffs, N.J.: Prentice-Hall.

Burgess, Robert L., and Nielsen, Joyce McCarl. 1974. "An Experimental Analysis of Some Structural Determinants of Equitable and Inequitable Exchange Relations." *American Sociological Review* 39:427–43.

Burtless, Garry. 1987. "Jobless Pay and High European Unemployment." In *Barriers to European Growth. A Transatlantic View*, eds., R.Z. Lawrence and Ch.L. Schultze, 105–62. Washington, D.C.: Brookings Institution.

Canada. 1990. *Beneath the Veneer*. 1990. *The Report of the Task Force on Barriers to Women in the Public Service*. Ottawa: Canadian Government Publishing Centre, vols. 1–4.

Clark, K.B., and Summers, Lawrence H. 1982. "Unemployment Insurance and Labor Market Transitions." In *Workers, Jobs, and Inflation*, ed., M.N. Bailey, 279–323. Washington, D.C.: Brookings Institution.

Commission of the European Communities. 1990. *Employment in Europa*. Luxembourg: Directorate-General V.

———. 1991. *Employment in Europe*. Luxembourg: Directorate-General V.

Deutsch, Karl. 1966 [1963]. *The Nerves of Government. Models of Political Communication and Control*. New York: The Free Press; and London: Collier-Macmillan.

Deutsch, Morton. 1975. "Equity, Equality, and Need: What Determines Which Values Will be Used As the Basis of Distributive Justice?" *Journal of Social Issues* 31, no. 3:137–49.

Elias, Norbert. 1982. *Power & Civility: The Civilizing Process*, vol. 2. Pantheon.

Etzioni, Amitai. 1988. *The Moral Dimension. Toward a New Economics*. New York: The Free Press; and London: Collier Macmillan.

Euzéby, Alain. 1988. "Leistungen bei Arbeitslosigkeit und Beschäftigungslage in den marktwirtschaftlichen Industriestaaten." *Internationale revue für Soziale Sicherheit* 12, no. 1:3–26.

Friedman, Milton. 1962. *Capitalism and Freedom*. Chicago: University of Chicago Press.

Fuchs, Victor R. 1988. *Women's Quest for Economic Equality*. Cambridge, Mass., and London: Harvard University Press.

Goode, William J. 1978. *The Celebration of Heroes*. Berkeley: University of California Press.

Grabher, Gernot. 1990. *On the Weakness of Strong Ties. The Ambivalent Role of Inter-Firm Relations in the Decline and Reorganization of the Ruhr*. Discussion Paper FSI 90–4, Wissenschaftszentrum Berlin für Sozialforschung.

Granovetter, Mark. 1973. "The Strength of Weak Ties." *American Journal of Sociology* 78, no. 6:1360–80.

Haveman, Robert H. 1988. *Starting Even. An Equal Opportunity Program to Combat the Nation's New Poverty*. New York: Simon and Schuster.

Hodgson, Geoffrey M. 1988. *Economics and Institutions. A Manifesto for a Modern Institutional Economics*. Oxford: Polity Press.

Hondrich, Karl Otto. 1984. "Der Wert der Gleichheit und der Bedeutungswandel der Ungleichheit." *Soziale Welt* 35:267–93.

Johannes Paul II. 1991. Encyclica CENTESIMUS ANNUS in Memory of 100th Anniversary of RERUM NOVARUM, 1 May.

Kahn, Arnold S., et al. 1980. "Equity and Equality: Male and Female Means to a Just End." *Basic and Applied Social Psychology* 1:173–97.

Kaldor, Nicholas. 1936. "Wage Subsidies as a Remedy for Unemployment." *Journal of Political Economy* 44, no. 6:721–42.

Lautmann, Rüdiger. 1990. *Die Gleichheit der Geschlechter und die Wirklichkeit des Rechts*. Opladen: Westdeutscher Verlag.

Matzner, Egon; Schettkat, Ronald; and Wagner, Michael. 1990. "Labour Market Effects of New Technology." *Futures* (September): 687–709.

Moller Okin, Susan. 1989. *Justice, Gender, and the Family*. New York: Basic Books.

Moore, Barrington. 1978. *Injustice: The Social Basis of Obedience and Revolt*. Armonk, N.Y.: M.E. Sharpe.

OECD. 1988. *New Technologies in the 1990s. A Socioeconomic Strategy*. Paris: Report of a Group of Experts on the Social Aspects of New Technologies.

Okun, Arthur M. 1975. *Equality and Efficiency. The Big Trade-off*. Washington, D.C.: Brookings Institution.

O'Neill, Onara. 1990. "Justice, Gender and International Boundaries." *British Journal of Political Science* 20, part 4: 439–59.

Ouchi, William G. 1980. "Markets, Bureaucracies, and Clans." *Administrative Science Quarterly* 25:129–41.

Porter, Michael E. 1990. *The Competitive Advantage of Nations.* New York: The Free Press.

Rae, Douglas. 1981. *Equalities.* Cambridge, Mass.: Harvard University Press.

Raff, D.G.M., and Summers, Lawrence H. 1987. "Did Henry Ford Pay Efficiency Wages?" *Journal of Economics* 5, no. 4:S57-S86.

Rawls, John. 1990 [1971]. *A Theory of Justice.* Oxford: Oxford University Press.

Schettkat, Ronald, and Wagner, Michael, eds. 1990. *New Technologies and Employment. Innovation in the German Economy.* Berlin and New York: De Gruyter.

Schmid, Günther, and Reissert, Bernd. 1989. "Do Institutions Make a Difference? Financing Systems of Labor Market Policy." *Journal of Public Policy* 8, no. 2:125–49.

Schmid, Günther; Reissert, Bernd; and Bruche, Gert. 1992. *Unemployment Insurance and Active Labour Market Policy. Financing Systems in International Comparison.* Detroit: Wayne State University Press.

Schmitter, Philippe C. 1990. "Sectors in Modern Capitalism: Modes of Governance and Variations in Performance." In *Labour Relations and Economic Performance*, eds., R. Brunetta and C. Dell'Aringa, 3–39. London: MacMillan.

Schotter, Andrew. 1985. *Free Market Economics. A Critical Appraisal.* New York: St. Martin's.

Sen, Amartya. 1973. *On Economic Inequality.* Oxford: Clarendon Press.

Shklar, Judith N. 1990. *The Faces of Justice.* New Haven and London: Yale University Press.

Simons, Henry C. 1948. *Economic Policy for a Free Society.* Chicago: University of Chicago Press.

Tobin, James. 1970. "On Limiting the Domain of Inequality." *Journal of Law and Economics* 13 (October): 263–77.

Van Parijs, Philippe. 1990. "The Second Marriage of Justice and Efficiency." *Journal of Social Policy* 19, no. 1:1–25.

Weirich, Paul. 1983. "Utility Tempered with Equality." *Nous* 17:423–39.

Whittington, Dale, and MacRae, Duncan, Jr. 1986. "The Issue of Standing in Cost-Benefit Analysis." *Journal of Policy Analysis and Management* 5, no. 4:665–82.

Williamson, Oliver E. 1985. *The Economic Institutions of Capitalism. Firms, Markets, Relational Contracting.* New York: The Free Press; London: Collier Macmillan.

Yuchtman, Ephraim. 1972. "Reflections on Equity Theory." *American Sociological Review* 37:581–95.

Index

Contributors

Peter Auer studied economics and political science in Paris, Vienna, and Bremen. Since 1981 he has held several research positions at the Social Science Center Berlin (WZB), where he is presently a project leader in the area Interfaces between Internal Labor Markets and Public Employment Policy. In addition, he is project director of MISEP (Mutual Information System on Employment Policy), an employment policy monitoring system of the European Community. He has published multiple articles on labor market policy, labor market research, and the links between work organization and labor market development. His address is: Wissenschaftszentrum Berlin für Sozialforschung, Reichpietschufer 50, D–10785 Berlin, Tel: +49–30–25491123, Fax: +49–30–25491100, e-mail: auer@medea.wz-berlin.de.

Friederike Maier is an economist, specializing in labor economics. She received her Ph.D. from the Free University of Berlin in 1987. From 1980 to 1992 she worked as a research fellow at the Social Science Center Berlin (WZB), mainly in the fields of implementation of labor market policy, labor market and social policy, and women and employment, doing international comparative studies. Since 1992 she has been a professor of macroeconomics and economic policy at the Fachhochschule für Wirtschaft in Berlin. She is in the Network of Experts on the Situation of Women in the Labor Market of the European Commission. Her main publications are: *Implementationsprobleme offensiver Arbeitsmarktpolitik* (Problems of Implementation of Active Labor Market Policy, with F.W. Scharpf, D. Garlichs, and H.E. Maier 1983), *Beschäftigungspolitik vor Ort* (Regional Employment Policies 1988), and numerous articles and reports on labor market issues, especially on women and employment, genderspecific labor market segregation, and women's wages. Her address is: Fachhochschule für Wirtschaft, Badensche Str. 50–51, D–10825 Berlin, Tel: +49–30–8678233, Fax: +49–30–8678270.

Nigel Meager studied at Wadham and Nuffield Colleges, Oxford, where he was trained as an economist. After holding research posts at the Universities of Bath and Glasgow, he joined the Institute of Manpower Studies (IMS) at the University of Sussex as a research fellow in 1984. In 1991, he spent a year as a senior guest fellow at the Social Science Center Berlin (WZB) undertaking comparative research on European labor market policy evaluation. He is currently an associate director of IMS, responsible for employment policy research. His research interests include public and corporate employment policy, the functioning of local labor markets, labor market disadvantage and equal opportunities, and the labor market impact of growing self-employment. He has published widely. His address is: IMS, Mantell Building, University of Sussex, Brighton BN1 9RF, UK Sussex BN1 9RF, Tel: +44–273–686751, Fax: +44–273–690430.

Hugh Mosley received his Ph.D. in political science from Duke University and is a research fellow in the labor market and employment research unit at the Social Science Center Berlin (WZB). His current research is on comparative labor market policies and on European integration. He is the author of *The Arms Race: Economic and Social Consequences* (1985). His address is: Wissenschaftszentrum Berlin für Sozialforschung, Reichpietschufer 50, D–10785 Berlin, Tel: +49–30–25491112, Fax: +49–30–25491100.

Bernd Reissert received his Ph.D. in political science from the Free University of Berlin. Until 1993, he was a senior research fellow at the Social Science Center Berlin (WZB) and a consultant to the Commission of the European Communities, Directorate for Employment. He is now a professor of political science at the Berlin Polytechnic University (FHTW). His publications include *Politikverpflechtung* (Intergovernmental Policy-Making, with F.W. Scharpf and F. Schnabel), *Die Finanzierung der Arbeitsmarktpolitik* (Financing Labor Market Policy, with G. Bruche), *Unemployment Insurance and Active Labor Market Policy* (with G. Schmid and G. Bruche), and numerous articles and reports on labor market policy and fiscal policy issues. His address is: Fachhochschule für Technik und Wirtschaft (FHTW), FB 5, Treskowallee 8, D–10313 Berlin, Tel: +49–30–5042614, Fax: +49–30–5042257.

Günther Schmid received his Ph.D. in political science from the Free University of Berlin. From 1978 to 1989, he was research coordinator and deputy director at the Social Science Center Berlin (WZB), where he is now director of the research unit on labor market policy and employment. He is also a professor of political economics at the Free University of Berlin and the author of *Bürokratie und Politik* (Bureaucracy and Politics, with Hubert Treiber), *Strukturierte Arbeitslosigkeit und Arbeitsmarktpolitik* (Structured Unemployment and Labor Market Policy), *Unemployment Insurance and Active Labor Market Policy* (with B. Reissert and G. Bruche), and numerous articles and reports on labor market policy issues. His address is: Wissenschaftszentrum Berlin für Sozialforschung, Reichpietschufer 50, D–10785 Berlin, Tel: +49–30–25491129/30, Fax: +49–30–25491222, e-mail: gues@medea.wz-berlin.de.

Klaus Schömann, a graduate of University College Cardiff, completed his Ph.D. in sociology at the Free University of Berlin in 1992. Between 1989 and spring 1992, he worked as an associated expert at the Office of Statistics of UNESCO in Paris. Since then he has joined the research unit on labor market policy and employment at the Social Science Center Berlin (WZB). Recently he published *Country, Sex and Sector Differences in the Dynamics of Education and Wage Growth—A Comparative Longitudinal Analysis Using Life History Data*. Current research priorities deal with fixed-term labor contracts, further education policy, and working time flexibility. His address is: Wissenschaftszentrum Berlin für Sozialforschung, Reichpietschufer 50, D–10785 Berlin, Tel: +49–30–25491128, Fax: +49–30–25491222.